TURKISH GUEST WORKERS IN GERMANY

Hidden Lives and Contested Borders, 1960s to 1980s

Turkish Guest Workers in Germany tells the story of the Turkish "guest workers" recruited by West German employers to fill their workforce's depleted ranks after the Second World War. Jennifer A. Miller's unique approach starts in the country of departure rather than the country of arrival and is heavily informed by Turkish-language sources and perspectives.

Miller argues that the guest worker program, far from creating a parallel society, involved constant interaction between foreign nationals and Germans. These categories were as fluid as the Cold War borders they crossed. Miller's extensive use of archival research in Germany, Turkey, and the Netherlands examines the recruitment of workers, their travel, initial housing and work engagements, social lives, and involvement in labour and religious movements. She reveals how contrary to popular misconceptions, the West German government attempted to maintain a humane foreign labour system while the workers themselves made crucial, often defiant, decisions. *Turkish Guest Workers in Germany* identifies the Turkish guest worker program as a post-war phenomenon that has much to tell us about the development of Muslim minorities in Europe and Turkey's ever-evolving relationship with the European Union.

(German and European Studies)

JENNIFER A. MILLER is an associate professor in the Department of Historical Studies at Southern Illinois University Edwardsville.

Turkish Guest Workers in Germany

Hidden Lives and Contested Borders, 1960s to 1980s

JENNIFER A. MILLER

UNIVERSITY OF TORONTO PRESS
Toronto Buffalo London

ISBN 978-1-4875-0232-4 (cloth)
ISBN 978-1-4875-2192-9 (paper)

(German and European Studies)

Library and Archives Canada Cataloguing in Publication

Miller, Jennifer A., 1976–, author
Turkish guest workers in Germany : hidden lives and contested
borders, 1960s to 1980s / Jennifer A. Miller.

(German and European studies ; 28)
Includes bibliographical references and index.
ISBN 978-1-4875-0232-4 (cloth)   ISBN 978-1-4875-2192-9 (paper)

1. Foreign workers, Turkish – Germany – History – 20th century.
2. Turks – Germany – Social conditions – 20th century. 3. Turks –
Germany – Economic conditions – 20th century. I. Title. II. Series:
German and European studies ; 28

HD8458.T9M55 2018   331.6′24961043   C2017-905739-1

University of Toronto Press acknowledges the financial assistance to its
publishing program of the Canada Council for the Arts and the Ontario
Arts Council, an agency of the Government of Ontario.

Canada Council   Conseil des Arts
for the Arts   du Canada

ONTARIO ARTS COUNCIL
CONSEIL DES ARTS DE L'ONTARIO
an Ontario government agency
un organisme du gouvernement de l'Ontario

Funded by the   Financé par le
Government   gouvernement
of Canada   du Canada

Canada

*In honour of my mother, Margaret Waldrep Miller,
and in loving memory of my father, Nathan Miller (1937–2015)*

Contents

List of Illustrations and Tables ix

Acknowledgments xi

Introduction 3

Part One

1 The Invitation 31
2 In Transit 57
3 Finding Homes 78

Part Two

4 Contested Borders 107
5 Imperfect Solidarities 135
Conclusion: Good Intentions and
Contested Histories 162

Notes 181

Bibliography 239

Index 265

Illustrations and Tables

Illustrations

1   "Don't be late!" 30
2   "Imagined riches." 35
3   "Confusion over contracts." 35
4   "How does one go to Germany to work?" 42
5   "The medical exam." 53
6   "At home." 87
7   "Lovers." 117
8   "People smugglers." 129

Tables

1   "Comparison of the average hourly wage of West German and Italian workers at the Volkswagen plant in Wolfsburg, Germany, in the years 1963–1973." 145
2   "Female foreign guest workers in West Germany, 1961–1973." 148

Acknowledgments

The debt of gratitude I owe to individuals and institutions, near and far, spanning the last dozen years, is immeasurable. Attempting to thank everyone will fail, but I ask for understanding.

I would like to thank the following institutions for their generous funding: the American Research Institute in Turkey, the German Academic Exchange Service, the Rutgers Graduate School–New Brunswick, the Institute of Turkish Studies, the New York University Kevorkian Center, the Princeton Office of Population Research, the Rutgers Center for Historical Analysis, and the Berlin Program for Advanced German and European Studies, with funds provided by the Free University of Berlin. The conclusions, opinions, and statements are my own and not necessarily those of the sponsoring institutions.

I am also indebted to multiple librarians, professors, and archivists across the globe. I am especially thankful for the archivists and scholars at the Documentation Center and Museum of Migration in Cologne, especially archivist Nina Matuszewski; the Archive of Social Movements in Bochum; the German National Archives in Koblenz; the Friedrichshain-Kreuzberg Museum; the History Foundation in Istanbul; the Institute of Migration and Intercultural Studies of Osnabrück University; and the German Federal Commissioner for the Stasi Records, especially archivist Christel Tinz.

For their helpful comments, queries, inspiration, and support, I would like to thank the many seminars that allowed me to workshop various parts of the book: the 2003 Rutgers Modern European Seminar, especially Marc Matera, Cynthia Kreisel, and Kris Alexanderson; the 2003 Transatlantic Summer Institute "Citizenship in Twentieth Century Germany," especially Winson Chu; the 2006–7 Berlin Program, especially Micheal

Meng, J. Griffith Rollefson, and Nicholas Schlosser; the 2007 German Historical Institute Transatlantic Doctoral Seminar, especially Quinn Slobodan and William Morris; the 2007–8 Rutgers Center for Historical Analysis Seminar, "The Question of the West"; and the 2011 Fulbright German Studies Summer Seminary, "Ethnic Diversity and National Identity," especially Gillian Glaes and Amy Foerster.

I am also indebted to the Rutgers Graduate School–New Brunswick for providing not only research support but also excellent cohorts of fellow thinkers, readers, and scholars across disciplines, who inspired and sustained me. For their advice on tricky translations, my gratitude goes to Özlem Serdaroğlu, Dilan Mete, Merve Doruk, Pinar Gibbon, Derrick Miller, Elisabeth Ernst, and Karolina May–Chu. For their wide-ranging and charitable support, I would like to express thanks to Teresa Delcorso, Jochen Hellbeck, Temma Kaplan, Laura Marhoefer, Peter Polak-Springer, and Horst and Regina Tacke. I am especially grateful for the support and scholarly council of Belinda Davis, whose encouragement, patience, and insightful advice, spanning years, has never wavered. Thank you.

My colleagues at Southern Illinois University Edwardsville have welcomed me, and my students make my job a joy. In addition, internal grants and a sabbatical provided the time and support to complete the book. I am also grateful to the many colleagues who thoughtfully listened to, read, and commented on drafts. I am very fortunate.

I am especially indebted to the external readers whose careful reading, thoughtful comments, and constructive criticism greatly improved the manuscript. For excellent editorial support I would like to thank Amy Benson Brown, Andrea Mongler, and Richard Ratzlaff. Of course, any errors are completely my own.

This book is dedicated to my parents, Margaret Waldrep Miller and Nathan Miller, whose brilliant minds and generous hearts inspired me to love learning and stay curious. My parents shaped who I have become with their lifelong support of my education and their encouragement to research, travel, and write. Though my father died as I was completing the book's final editing, I know he would be proud.

TURKISH GUEST WORKERS IN GERMANY

Hidden Lives and Contested
Borders, 1960s to 1980s

Introduction

Twenty-year-old Elif departed Istanbul for West Berlin on 10 November 1964.[1] A photo snapped moments before departure shows her as a smiling woman hanging on to an exterior train step, lock armed with the young man standing next to her.[2] Just behind her, two more smiling young women peer out from the interior of the train through an open window. In the picture, Elif is a petite brunette, sporting a trendy bob hairstyle with bangs and wearing a knee-length plaid skirt with flats. Her excitement is palpable. Before departure, Elif had worked as a seamstress in a Greek Cypriot's Istanbul shop. Elif's life changed, however, when a civil war between Greek and Turkish Cypriots raged on the eastern Mediterranean island of Cyprus from 1963 to 1964. The hostilities were brutal. During the "Bloody Christmas" of 1963, 109 Turkish Cypriot villages were damaged, making some 25,000 Turkish Cypriots refugees, and, most viciously, a Turkish Cypriot officer's family, including the young children, was found violently murdered in their bathtub.[3] Not surprisingly, the conflict carried over to Istanbul, where tensions between ethnic Greeks and Turks had long simmered. Elif's boss was just one of many harassed in 1964. Feeling threatened, he closed his shop and departed Istanbul, leaving Elif unemployed and unsure of her future. Indirectly, the civil war in Cyprus prompted her to make a choice that was popular at the time – she moved to West Berlin with a contract as a *Gastarbeiter*, or "guest worker," just one of many who would forever change the course of German history, culture, and society.

Elif departed for Berlin from the Vinegar Seller's Station in Istanbul. The station is famous not only as the last stop on the illustrious Orient Express but also as a point of departure for thousands of guest workers leaving Turkey for Western Europe, travelling the route in reverse of the direction suggested by the well-known name, from the "Orient" to Europe. It is adjacent to a bustling market area on the edge of the Golden Horn with a panoramic view of the Bosporus Strait – the geographic boundary between Europe and Asia. This oft-photographed vista includes gorgeous views of sixteenth-century imperial mosques, the old town that was once the heart of Byzantium – the Greek-speaking Eastern Roman Empire – and the 1348 Genoese Galata Tower, known in Latin as the "Tower of Christ." Elif was caught up in her city's and people's histories. Though her people's eight thousand-year history constrained her in some ways, I argue she was also a protagonist and shaper of future conditions. These juxtapositions of East and West, Christian and Muslim, and new and old set the stage for Elif's new adventure, one in which she would become a central actor in new and timeless debates, but in a novel context: Cold War Europe.

In 2003, Elif and I met in Berlin's Kreuzberg Museum. Through open windows, the clamour of cars pumping bass beats; children playing and shouting "*anne!*" or "mom" in Turkish; and aggressive bicycle bells provided the background noise. We sat among an exhibition on Turkish guest worker migration to Berlin's Kreuzberg neighbourhood, the westernmost sector of West Berlin that abutted the Berlin Wall and is known as "Little Istanbul." Elif is nothing like the picture of a typical ethnic Turkish woman in Berlin: she has short, uncovered hair and a sleeveless sweater; she once spoke Greek in addition to Turkish and German; and she is independent, divorced, and owns her own business. Her smile and hearty laugh preceded almost everything she said. She admitted that, at just twenty years old, she had been a bit naive when she arrived in West Germany. "It was an adventure," Elif told me. She recounted thinking, "If I make it, it is OK, and if I don't, that is OK, too. I was single; no one was expecting me. I had no children. I was not yet married. I was very, very self-confident and often very independent. I had no limitations – not from my extended family or from my parents."[4] In an archived interview from 1995, Elif started with a brazen, almost defensive comment: "I want first to emphasize that I have no regrets. I made the right decision."[5] Likewise, when we met, she began by stating that she was most often asked not just why she had come but why she had stayed in West Germany. A Japanese journalist had recently asked her why she stayed past her contract period of one year. "Why should I leave? I like it here," she apparently replied. Her frustration ran deep.

Elif, like thousands of others, did not overstay her contract; West German employers extended it. And yet journalists have not sought out

former employers to ask them the same questions. Elif is representative of the crossroads between Turkey and post-war Germany but not
necessarily of the standard images, reports, and histories of the guest
worker program of the last fifty years – stories that have reported on
honour killings, failed multiculturalism, headscarf debates, and continuities with Germany's dark past. Elif and many of the other people
who agreed to be interviewed were eager to share and recast their personal histories, and these stories of success and adventure are significant because they complicate narratives of solely miserable, confused,
and exploited guest workers.[6] This book emphasizes individuals, interactions, and everyday experiences in order to contribute to the growing scholarship on guest worker social and cultural experience in order
to help rethink less complex political narratives.[7] Inherent in merging
sources ranging from government files to film to oral history is a shift in
perspective. It is important to recognize individual actors, including the
limits of their agency, and to nuance ideas of post-war Europe, divided
Berlin, labour migration, and intercultural integration.

Guest Workers in the Long Post-war

Despite her arrival in the mid-1960s, long after the rubble had been
cleared, Elif believed she lived in "post-war" West Germany. She
noted that her German colleagues were of the generation who had
been young women and girls during the war and its aftermath. "They
were *Trümmerfrauen* [or "rubble women"]," Elif noted. "They cleaned
all those bricks … They barely slept and had no roof over their heads.
They were eyewitnesses to so much," she said before trailing off.[8]
She looked back fondly on these colleagues who had helped her at
work, taught her German, and stayed in touch with her for years after
their retirement. Women who had borne witness to the Nazi state and
its aftermath were now colleagues and friends with a foreign guest
worker, someone who represented another aspect of their post-war
constellation.

Elif arrived in a divided Berlin that was still mired in post-war reconstruction. Indeed, when guest workers arrived in the late 1950s through
the early 1970s, Germany was still suffering from extreme housing
shortages due to extensive aerial bombing and in-street fighting during the war and was still debating political and social "normalcy."[9]
Earlier descriptions of the "zero hour" – the moment after the Second
World War when Germany started from scratch to rebuild not

just its buildings and economy but also society, families, culture, and nationalism – included transient populations and displaced persons.[10] However, the complexities and experiences of guest workers, the first arriving in 1955, have largely remained a separate narrative, disconnected from this pivotal era in German history. Foreign workers also played complex roles in the "long post-war."[11] Historian Tony Judt sees the Cold War itself as an aspect of the post-war, making the case that the Second World War had an "epilogue that lasted another half century."[12] Within this recent turn towards the long post-war – one that see the effects of the war impacting all aspects of society for decades – foregrounding immigration and demographic shifts can help measure the success of opposing post-war ideals.

Within the context of the long post-war, the guest worker program was, in fact, central to the split between East and West as Cold War alliances developed and as the Western industrial and capitalist model of production influenced West Germany's new national identity. The building of the Berlin Wall, a Cold War manoeuvre, spurred the expansion of the guest worker program. Furthermore, Western European countries continuously relied on extra-European labour to shore up their industry against the Eastern Bloc. Ideas of "East" and of "Asia" continuously changed throughout the twentieth century, in part because of the Cold War. However, guest workers also defied Cold War boundaries. Some who were considered non-European came from former Western European colonies in Africa, NATO ally Turkey sent its workers through the Eastern Bloc en route to West Germany, and, likewise, Yugoslavian guest workers crossed from east to west of the Iron Curtain. After 1989, some of former "Soviet Central Asia" became prospectively "European." Alliances and migrations helped construct and challenge Europe's borders in the post-war era.

It is fitting that Elif worked alongside former "rubble women," as both sets of women were key rebuilders of post-war Germany in myriad ways. Scholars have noted that after the hypermasculine Nazi state, post-war Germany found itself in the "hour of the woman" due to women's prominence in the post-war period.[13] Significantly, focusing on post-war German women's plights allowed a welcome escape from attention to war crimes.[14] However the rubble women were not alone in rebuilding West Germany. Elif was just one of many guest workers and migrants, female and male, who not only bolstered West German industry but also set it on a new and irrevocable path. Guest workers played a key role in West German internal discussions, ranging from rebuilding to *Vergangenheitsbewältigung*, or "dealing with the past," and from gender to family discourse.

While most of West Germany, especially industry, had recovered by the 1960s, it was the gendered full employment achieved through the guest worker programs that led to the sense that West Germany was indeed "rebuilt," including socially.[15] For many, increased female employment, especially among middle- and upper-class women, was a symptom of war, and therefore women "returning to the home" should have been a result of peace. Historians have noted that post-war rebuilding did not include a progressive vision of working women.[16] Instead, government policies, such as family allowances for children, protective legislation for female workers, and family law, drafted the idealized image of the male-breadwinner nuclear family. (At the same time, it is noteworthy that some post-war German women questioned men's inherent ability to lead.)[17] Historian Mark Spicka has shown that political campaigns from the late 1940s and early 1950s demonstrated that the Hour of the Woman was short-lived: "[the] conservatism toward gender roles [in the 1950s] suggested that although the *Trümmerfrauen* represented the regeneration of the German nation, they did not signal a fundamental change in public expectations for women and men in society."[18] However, implementing this traditional view heavily depended on the importation of foreign workers, especially women, which allowed many German women to retire from low-skilled jobs to focus on motherhood. Indeed, prior to the guest worker program, demographics dictated that female-headed households until more men could return.[19] The impetus for the nuclear family was then more an ideal than a reality but an important one nonetheless, as it was deemed the sole foundation upon which democracy could flourish. Male-headed families with housewives also provided a stark contrast to the (unrealized) communist family ideal in which gender equity would be achieved, with both parents working, housework shared, and childcare supported by the state.[20] The unstated reality here is that guest workers allowed for the re-establishment of German nuclear families, a new national pride in the economy to flourish, and West Germany to achieve its place of prominence in the capitalist, democratic Western Bloc.[21]

This book looks back on the guest worker program's origins and impetus, initial plans and dreams, and points of first contact and interactions. Here individual microhistories help answer large-scale questions of how the program and its participants' intentions evolved, with particular focus on the small events that could have gone differently.

Some have suggested the guest worker program provides an example of how individual nation states lose their importance relative to supra-national trends such as labour migration and Cold War alliances.[22] Others have wondered whether guest worker history is centred on identity, unable to escape the influence of the nation, and instead part of cultural exchange, hybridity, and transfer.[23] In all cases, though, post-war Europe is an inescapable context. Mass postcolonial migration from Asia and Africa changed the course and composition of European metropoles, engendering new questions of identity, belonging, historical legacy, and atonement while shattering precarious categories, such as "European." Stories similar to Elif's echoed across Western Europe in the 1960s in countries such as France, the Netherlands, and Great Britain. In the German case, it was the "Turks," an amorphous grouping that stood in for all "foreigners," who took centre stage.

Fifty years after the signing of the bilateral guest worker treaty between West Germany and the Turkish Republic, there is still little known about the cases that do not fit into the standard narratives – the women like Elif, the German officials who worried about how the guest worker program might be impacting West Germany's international image, and foreign men who lived in both East and West Berlin. Nascent West Germany could remake itself in the 1950s, build a new nationalism, and atone for its past, claiming to uplift not just the economy but also unskilled foreign workers with its proud traditions of industry and German engineering.[24] At the same time, the Turkish Republic could fulfil its own dreams of modernization and Westernization, renewed after the 1916 coup. Extensive planning and consideration went into the guest worker program on both the sending and the receiving sides, not just at the political and philosophical levels but also in the finest details of regulations and requirements. But the guest worker program did not occur just at the state level. It also occurred at the ground level and was defined not by state-issued memos but by daily interactions between rank-and-file officials, employers, dorm managers, and workers, all of whom broke rules, made up their own, and negotiated these ever-evolving relationships.

Employers played a key role in Germany's post-war reconstruction, especially with its reputation. During the guest worker program, West Germany brought in large numbers of foreign workers, packed into trains no less, on the heels of a recent troubling past. Historians have long grappled with this historical context when considering how West Germany conceived and implemented a post-war program using foreign labour, including selling this program to its own population, to the international community, and to the recruited workers themselves.[25] Contemporary West Germans also had the foresight to consider their historical context. Almost ten years after Elif's arrival in West Berlin, on the other side of West Germany, a representative of Duinger Steinzeugwerk Mühle & Co, an employer of foreign workers, wrote an angry letter to the president of the *Bundesanstalt für Arbeit*, or German federal employment agency (BA). In his letter, he reported with frustration that guest workers bound for his factory had arrived in the middle of the night, forcing them to wait on the station platform for an additional eighteen hours after a three-day train ride.[26] This was not the result of inexperience: the complaint came on 29 July 1973, almost twenty years after the very first arrival of guest workers in Germany. With exasperation, the employer noted: "Surely you will agree with us that such occurrences do not present a good calling card for the Federal Republic of Germany."[27] The employer was not only angry with how poorly workers were being treated but also especially concerned with how this impacted West Germany's post-war image, or "calling card," in relation to non-ethnic Germans' apparent exploitation. He understood and was openly self-conscious of Germany's historical legacy and of the fierce competition to win workers who could have chosen other Western European countries. Much like this West German employer, the federal employment agency's officials – particularly those working from the liaison office in Istanbul – not only actively sought, recruited, interviewed, and vetted workers, but did so with great concern and extreme attention to detail. In other words, the letter did not fall on deaf ears even though traces of concern have not made it into the popular historical record.

Historical Drivers and Contemporary Motivations

In German history specifically and European history generally, historical backdrops are inescapably significant. The post-war guest worker agreements came on the heels not just of the Second World War but also of a legacy of exploitative labour migration for several European powers. Taken together, Germany's history of foreign labour fits neatly into the larger context of Western Europe in general. Analogous to Germany, several Western European powers were importing foreign labour amid a long history of colonial exploitation and violence. Indeed, importing foreign labour was not a novel idea for traditional European powers.

Overseas colonization had long provided temporary, and largely pow-
erless, labour stores for European authorities. During the First World
War, traditional imperial governments, such as in Britain and France,
recruited labour from colonial holdings in places such as North Africa,
Indochina, and China, only to deport the majority of workers when the
war ended.[28] With a similar mindset, Germany had relied on Eastern
Europe for its temporary labour dating back to the 1700s. In the twentieth century, the Nazi state was infamous for using various categories of
temporary, forced, and slave labour, mostly imported from other countries, on an unprecedented scale. In the Nazi era, forced labourers made
up as much as 20 per cent of the German workforce, and few survived
the grueling and inhuman conditions.[29]

    After the Second World War, West Germany again relied on foreign
labour, this time a steady stream of refugees, displaced persons, and
expellees from Eastern Europe. By 1950, West Germany had received
7.9 million ethnic Germans from Poland, Czechoslovakia, Hungary,
and the Soviet Union. In the years leading up to the Berlin Wall's construction in 1961, an additional 3.8 million persons arrived from East
Germany.[30] Concurrently, while other European countries were aban-
doning their colonies, West Germany fostered closer relations with
European colonial powers, continuing to support Portugal and its colonial policies. West Germany also continued close economic, military,
and trade relations with the apartheid government of South Africa even
after South Africa was expelled from the British Commonwealth in
1961. Interestingly, it is within this additional historical context, one of
continuing support for older colonial systems – systems that had relied
on racist exploitation – that Western European nations, including West
Germany, became increasingly dependent on cheap imported labour to
sustain continued economic growth. By 1960, 20 per cent of Germany's
population was made up of refugees from the Eastern Bloc. However,
East Germany's 1961 construction of the Berlin Wall and accompanying ban on *Republikflucht*, or "fleeing the Republic," put a stop to the
hundreds of thousands of refugees and expellees flowing into the West
via Berlin, who had provided an essential workforce.[31] From the late
1940s through the early 1970s, Western Europe was the site of multiple
population movements, as ethnic Germans, refugees, and displaced
persons moved across Europe with numbers rising from 279,000 in 1960
to 1,314,100 in 1966; as decolonization spurred migration from Africa,
Asia, and the Caribbean to France and Britain; and as foreign labourers migrated from northern Africa and Europe's periphery to Western

Europe.[32] Considering this broader historical context, guest worker migration was actually relatively small.[33]

Material conditions and economic concerns permeated every aspect of war-ravaged post-war societies and provided another essential backdrop to post-war migrations. Like many of the volatile economies of the period, the newly founded Federal Republic of Germany experienced an economic crisis in 1950. West Berlin, with its unusual circumstances as a divided city, experienced even greater hardship. When the western Allies introduced the West German mark into the West Berlin economy in 1948, the Soviets retaliated by cutting off all access to West Berlin. The heroic "Berlin Airlift," when American and British forces airdropped food, fuel, and supplies for over ten months from 24 June 1948 to 12 May 1949, saved the western sector. While the airlift sustained the city and ended the blockade, when it was over, 40 per cent of the population was still unemployed.

By the late 1950s, however, post-war European economies, including Turkey's and West Germany's, began to recover. After the Second World War, Turkey transitioned from a single- party dictatorship to a multiparty system, culminating in the Democratic Party's electoral success in May 1950. Under the new Adnan Menderes government in the 1950s, Turkey experienced a push to mechanize agriculture, resulting in widespread poverty among small farmers and rapid and widespread migration into cities and metropolitan centers. In 1954, Prime Minister Menderes visited West Germany to strengthen the bilateral economic relationship between West Germany and Turkey, and, as a result, in 1955 officials signed the German-Turkish Economic Agreement and the German-Turkish Cultural Agreement in Ankara. That year the West German economy expanded for the first time since the end of the Second World War, prompting extreme labour shortages across the country. This trend was common across Western Europe: in 1956 Chancellor Adenauer signed an agreement in Rome that would provide free transport for any Italian worker coming to Germany. To put Italy's agreement with West Germany in perspective, after similar agreements followed, an estimated seven million Italians left their country between 1945 and 1970.[34] Labour agreements were not limited to state-level arrangements though.

In 1955 West German private businessmen and semi-official labour-recruiting institutes began making requests for immigrant workers, and in 1956 the Institute for the World Economy (IWE) at the University of Kiel made one of the first official requests for immigrant workers from

Turkey.[35] The IWE solicited the Turkish Ministry of Foreign Affairs to request volunteer migrants for vocational training. In the same year, the BA reported that Turkish agricultural interns were "very orderly and hardworking and so far have shown no problems. The Turk appears to be ... completely able to fit in and be useful."[36] These initial positive results with unproblematic, solicited workers, however, are rarely remembered, and the pre-1961 migration phase – before the formal bilateral agreement was signed – was strikingly different from the subsequent period of depersonalized mass migration for low-skilled and poorly remunerated jobs that made up the bulk of the "guest worker migration."

Guest worker programs intersected two key post-war phenomena – explosive economic growth coupled with mass migration movements, with each fueling the other in turn. West Germany's post-war period is known as the *Wirtschaftswunder*, or "economic miracle."[37] In fact, by 1958, defeated West Germany's economy was larger than that of war victor Great Britain's.[38] Between 1950 and 1973, German GDP per head more than tripled in real terms.[39] Germany's impressive growth was not necessarily miraculous, though, because pre-war investments in industry and armaments updated factories, the majority of which (83 per cent, in fact) survived the war. After all, in 1945, 55 per cent of Germany's total industrial plant capacity was at most only ten years old.[40] In short, German transportation and housing, not industry, had been destroyed in the war, preconditions that created fertile ground for post-war guest worker programs. Across Western Europe, as available labour supplies – including colonial immigrants, displaced persons, and prisoners of war – dried up, governments increasingly turned to guest worker programs. By the late 1950s and early 1960s, Western European economies were markedly different from earlier in the post-war period as economies recovered. In the new economy, states increased production by increasing the number of workers – a Fordist model that would boom and then bust with the 1970s oil crises.

Another important piece of historical context was the integration of the European economy in this same period. First the "Korean Crisis," or "Korean Boom," created a global goods shortage that encouraged the purchase of West German goods despite post-war resentment of the country.[41] Second, the Treaty of Rome, effective 1 January 1958, created the new European Economic Community (or EEC), linking Belgium, France, Italy, Luxembourg, the Netherlands, and West Germany. Tony Judt argues that the EEC was more important symbolically than economically, as it was "grounded in weakness," depended entirely upon an American security guarantee, and did not offer significantly new innovations.[42] While the terms may not have been novel, this integration, especially creating the conditions for the Common Market and a supranational parliament, was important for continuing and expanding cross-border trading and labour migration, offering reduced tariffs and the free movement of goods, currency, and labour. Post-war recovery for all of Western Europe relied on cross-border cooperation and increasingly on trade with West Germany.[43]

The post-war drive towards growth as well as the labour shortage spurred West Germany and Western Europe to invest at the state level in formal bilateral agreements to import foreign labour, which became a key part of mass migrations from the 1950s through the 1970s. Belgium, the UK, and France were the first to sign bilateral labour agreements after the Second World War when they negotiated with Italy in 1946. In 1948, the Netherlands and Switzerland followed suit. West Germany signed its first bilateral recruitment treaty in 1955, also with Italy. Before the 1960s, Belgium added agreements with Greece and Spain, and France with Greece. Sector-tied agreements were also common in this period with the intent of limiting the impact that migrant labourers could make on their host societies by restricting them to certain jobs and skill levels. The causality of the post-war economic growth is nuanced: did the booming levels of post-war production spur the migration influx, or did the importation of labourers spur the post-war production to new heights?

Supranational organization distinguishes post-war guest worker programs of the late 1950s and 1960s from those of previous eras. High-level organizing characterized this new era: the International Labour Organization (ILO), Organisation for Economic Cooperation and Development (OECD), and Council of Europe all organized bilateral and multilateral agreements that resulted in a free exchange of foreign workers.[44] In the years 1946 to 1960, Western European countries had primarily recruited Italian workers and only in modest numbers; in fact, the number of foreign guest workers in Europe remained largely insignificant until 1961.[45] Also, new in the 1960s was that recruiting countries introduced policies to *attract* workers in large numbers, especially from the more desirable southern European countries of Italy, Spain, Greece, and Portugal because of their European "cultural characteristics" and compatible Cold War political leanings.[46] Another modification in the 1960s was that as the demand for workers increased, recruiting spread to regions not previously considered, including North Africa and Turkey. France, for example, looked to Turkey in 1965 when it could not get enough applicants from Italy, Spain, and Portugal.[47]

Many Western European recruiting countries, however, considered the Turkish Republic and many of the other countries included in this second wave of labour recruitment, such as Algeria, Morocco, Tunisia, and Yugoslavia, less desirable than Italy and the other more "European" countries of the first wave.[48] Scholars are divided on how wary West Germany was of signing a bilateral agreement with Turkey. Some historians have wondered whether the soured relationship between Turks and Germans from the 1970s on caused scholars to project backwards a negative view.[49] Conversely, others have noted that West Germany's initial hesitation about Turkish workers stemmed instead from a German fear that taking in Turks, whom Germans viewed as only "partly European," would open a floodgate for recruits from other non-European countries, such as those in Africa and Asia.[50]

When Greece and West Germany entered into a bilateral agreement in 1960, though, the traditional rivalry ignited and the Turkish diplomatic mission in Bonn accused West Germany of favouring Greece over Turkey – a fellow NATO member. Understandably, Turkish officials were disappointed in West Germany and other Western European countries' wariness, which included grouping Turkey with North African countries instead of with other Mediterranean countries. Turkey wished to be seen as it saw itself – as having an economic system, a defence system, and political values akin to Western Europe's.[51] Indeed, Turkey justified its participation in bilateral agreements domestically by arguing that it was participating in the European political and economic community.[52] The Turkish Republic was also interested in limiting its workers' time abroad so that they could boost the Turkish economy with their newly acquired skills.[53] West Germany did not view Turkey as it wished to be seen, however, and the resulting agreement between Turkey and West Germany placed Turkey in an unfavourable position.

On 30 October 1961, officials signed the formal agreement between the Federal Republic of Germany and the Republic of Turkey, and the BA opened a liaison branch in Istanbul. The agreement was less favourable for Turkey than treaties with other European applicants though. For example, West Germany required that Turkey send a higher percentage of skilled workers than had been required in other agreements.[54] Germany recruited more skilled labour from Turkey than from Greece, Italy, Portugal, and Spain combined.[55] By the end of 1961, seven thousand Turks were in West Germany. West Germany could not afford to remain picky though. As Western Europe recruited more workers, West Germany found itself competing with other European countries, such as France, for workers, adding urgency to its recruitment efforts.

Both German employers and the BA were acutely aware of West Germany's disadvantages in relation to other Western European countries – a lack of colonial labour migration and the Berlin Wall's stemming of Eastern European population flows. West Germany's high turnover and initial rotation system not only were annoying for employers but also prompted additional recruitment and training costs. West Germany had to be proactive in its recruitment and responded by opening four hundred recruitment offices throughout the Mediterranean Basin to attract additional workers. West Germany also used grandiose ceremonies, prizes, and speeches both to show appreciation for the steady flow of workers and to recruit new ones.[56] It was in this particular context of urgency and increasing need that West Germany began its labour migration negotiations with the Turkish Republic.

The agreement between Turkey and West Germany was also a special case. For the first time, the German government was paying social benefits to citizens of another country that itself did not have a social security system. All foreign workers legally employed were entitled to the same pay as West Germans for the same work and to full welfare and social rights, such as child benefit payments for children left behind in Turkey.[57] In the years 1969 to 1973, Turks became the largest contingent of foreign workers in West Germany and also made up a sizeable population in neighbouring Holland and Belgium.[58] In addition to the agreement with West Germany in 1961, the Turkish Republic signed accords with Austria, Belgium, and the Netherlands in 1964; with France in 1965; and, in 1967, with Sweden.[59]

Turkey's political and economic leadership envisioned its own economic miracle in the 1960s, one that far exceeded serving as a passive supplier of low-skilled labour. The Turkish Republic played a large role in shaping the guest worker program because it was seen as an essential part of Turkey's economic, social, and cultural reconstruction after the 1961 modernizing revolution. The bilateral labour agreements were themselves attempts to continue the "Westernizing" project that formed the Turkish Republic's cornerstone at its inception.[60] Indeed, throughout the twentieth century, Turkey took numerous steps, in the words of the political reform movement the Young Turks, to "follow the path traced by Europe."[61] Historian of Turkey Erik-Jan Zürcher has argued that even though more than 90 per cent of Turkey is located geographically in Asia, it is a creation of "Europeans" who shaped the country in their own image, with "Europeans" referring to the elite band of educated men who formed the modern republic in the 1920s.[62]

In the latter half of the twentieth century, Turkish officials furthered Turkey's alignment with the "West," including gaining membership in the Council of Europe in 1949, with NATO in 1952, the OECD in 1961, the Organization for Security and Co-operation in Europe (OSCE) in 1973, and in the "Group of Twenty," or G20, industrial nations in 1999. The "West" also turned to Turkey as an ally throughout the twentieth century, such as when the United States extended the 1947 Truman Doctrine to include Turkey in order to secure the Bosporus Strait. In many ways, the bilateral agreement between Turkey and West Germany fits in with Turkey's twentieth-century trajectory, just as it fits into West Germany's post-war economic recovery. The Turkish Republic saw itself and its citizens as part of a specific modernizing project. By contrast, emigrating Turkish nationals had multiple intersecting identities, such as Alevi, Kurd, or Sufi, and had equally diverse agendas for their move to Western Europe.

Considering Turkey's twentieth-century Westernization and general trajectory of political, economic, and social developments, it is not surprising that guest worker agreements complemented the Turkish Republic's "modernizing" efforts.[63] Indeed, the Turkish Republic elected to participate in the guest worker program with West Germany out of a sanguine view of development and modernization theories that were popular at the time, citing remittances, family unification and settlement abroad, and more highly skilled manpower returning to work at home as likely benefits.[64] Turkish policymakers expected the guest worker arrangement to help develop poor regions; alleviate unemployment; train workers who would later develop Turkish industry; and, through wage remittance and personal investment, invigorate the Turkish economy.[65] The noted sociologist Nermin Abadan-Unat, who conducted a government-sponsored study of Turkish workers in Germany in 1964, concluded that, at the time, the Turkish Republic in fact thought of guest worker programs as an aspect of "social engineering" in the hopes of generating economic and political change for the country.[66] In 1963, Turkey embarked on its first "Five-Year Development Plan," which featured bilateral guest worker arrangements as not only a logical solution to the high unemployment rate but also a way to strengthen ties with Western Europe.[67] Whether or not scholars have historically recognized Turkey's "Western modernity" or considered it a part of the "Western Bloc," significantly, the 1960s Turkish government and federal planners most certainly did.

While the Turkish Republic was looking to its future, the guest worker program provided the Federal Republic of Germany with an outlet to deal with its recent past. Social interactions among ethnic Germans and foreigners, the economic miracle, transnational labour movements, and historical reconciliation all intersected with the guest worker program in important ways. For Elif, for the German employer concerned with Germany's "calling card," and for BA recruiters in Istanbul, the guest worker program provided an important test case for the new Federal Republic. This book offers a closer look at one small population, an eclectic group of workers from Turkey who chose to remain in Germany and to share their life stories in interviews. The chapters provide a bottom-up view of the overlapping themes of post-war Germany. This is a small sample, to be sure. But, despite their initial optimism and self-defined successes, this is not a story of *brav* (or "well-behaved"), well-integrated former guest workers either. True, they are the ones who stayed, made homes, transitioned from migrants to immigrants, and saw the program as an opportunity to conquer. But they were also often ones to break, ignore, and negotiate guidelines and rules. The events of the first three chapters – the recruitment, transportation, arrival, and housing experiences – necessarily lead to the personal and political protests of the final two chapters. This book narrates cases that highlight larger themes – such as the connection between feeling excluded and seeking to escape and the necessity of learning how to work around and bend even the strictest of rules, including the East German border crossing. These idiosyncratic stories demonstrate the inability of complex human narratives to neatly propel a linear historical narrative, government publication, journalist's questions, or politicians' conclusions. And yet these stories have an undeniable importance and influence, as they form the grounds for the evolving debates on post-war Germany's struggles with its historical legacy.

This book demonstrates that important negotiations happened far below the state level: in internal memos, German officials worried about the messages they were sending, about how and whether their plans were being implemented, and they were attuned to circumstances deemed inhumane. Simultaneously, applicants struck deals and negotiated, for example, with local doctors to pass their medical exams; fought with their dormitory managers in Essen, Germany; seduced German women in nightclubs in both West and East Berlin; and joined forces to protest their wages. However, these actions were not always seen, acknowledged, recorded, or remembered. Since the 1980s, German scholars and politicians have debated and at times lamented that ethnic populations exist in a *Parallelgesellschaft*, or "parallel society," in which ethnic or religious migrant minorities live with limited cultural and spatial contact with the majority society.[68] German Chancellor Angela Merkel made waves with her 2010 critique of parallel societies when she announced that "multiculturalism" had "utterly failed."[69] Though journalists seized on this phrase alone, taken in context, her point was that the existence of parallel societies had contributed to integration problems. Indeed, Merkel commented that Germans have had a long and troubled history of deceiving themselves about "their foreigners." The integration debate also cuts both ways, as demonstrated by a 2011 campaign rally with Turkish Prime Minister Recep Tayyip Erdoğan in Cologne, Germany, in which he declared in the heart of the Rhineland: "They call you guest workers, foreigners, or German Turks … [But] you are my fellow citizens, you are my people."[70] The history of contact and negotiations between minority and majority populations continues to intersect with current political debates within the broader historical narrative.

Who Are "Turks"?

One main concern in both political and academic discourse about guest worker studies has been how to talk about this heterogeneous population. Over the years, the term *Türken*, or "Turks," has been used interchangeably with or in lieu of both *Ausländer*, or "foreigners," and *Gastarbeiter*, or "guest workers," as the "others" of West German society.[71] "Turks" has erroneously implied a homogeneous community as well as the status of being forever foreign.[72] Early studies of guest workers and ethnic minorities conducted in post-reunification Germany often focused on xenophobic violence against immigrant communities and commented on now famous photos of the graffiti that read "*Türken Raus!*," or "Turks Out!"[73] However, "Turks" did not necessarily signify people of Turkish descent: the term was often used metonymically, representing the totality of Germany's problems with ethnic enclaves. In 1991, two years after the Wall fell and two years into the ensuing economic crisis, featuring high unemployment in the East, disillusioned right-wing extremists began a series of indiscriminant attacks on refugees, asylum seekers, and immigrants. Violence directed at the ill-defined group "foreigners," as well as at German Jews, increased in step with the recession. The rise of extreme-right voting and government impotence on immigration questions and policies followed.[74] It is important to note that nearly three million Germans protested in major cities in 1992 against violent extremism and in solidarity with foreigners in Germany.[75] However, violent arson attacks on Turkish families, which included the deaths of three Turkish girls in the western German cities of Mölln and Solingen, continued the following year. These attacks on ethnic Turks were particularly troubling, as these families were long-term, legal residents who had felt part of their communities. Significantly, the xenophobic attacks in the post-unification years demonstrated that for some Germans, a diverse group of asylum seekers, Eastern European refugees, and long-term legal residents formed a fictional whole – "foreigners" and often just "Turks."[76]

Just as the term "Turks" has often been used inaccurately, the label "guest worker" is problematic. The nomenclature guest worker is difficult, as the term itself is a misnomer. The workers West Germans began recruiting from southern Europe, North Africa, and the Mediterranean received contradictory messages about the permanence of their stays. Increasingly, they settled and produced children and grandchildren in West Germany, making it their home. Helmut Kohl, the last Christian Democratic chancellor before Merkel, insisted and kept repeating until being voted out of office in 1998 that Germany was "not a country of immigration." And yet as Kohl repeated this mantra, the number of "foreigners" had swollen to nearly 9 per cent of the German population.[77] The state's denial of immigration has had tangible effects – for example, official policies have discouraged guest workers and others from integration and citizenship requirements that were designed to keep certain foreigners on the outside while "blood Germans," such as Russians with eighteenth-century German ancestors, were easily accepted despite their limited knowledge of the German language and lifestyle.[78] However, there are now four generations of ethnic Turks living in Germany, with varying degrees of fluency in both languages and with widely disparate lifestyles and religious, cultural, national, and ethnic allegiances. Studies on Alevis, Kurds, and other ethnic and religious groups break down the category of "Turkish guest worker" in useful ways, balancing the fact that Germany records national origin, not ethnicity.[79] Another important mark of heterogeneity is varying degrees of success and integration: over time, some Turkish-Germans have increasingly prospered – in politics, the arts, and business – while others have remained isolated in monocultural communities in ways typical of large diasporas.

This study follows earlier work seeking to understand the guest worker populations. Sociological studies, anthologies of interviews, and histories of labour and economics began the first wave of scholarship on the guest worker program in the late 1970s and early 1980s. Initially many attempted to contextualize the political and economic immigration narrative in the cultural background of the workers themselves by looking closely at life in Turkey and at family networks there in addition to how transition to Germany played out in the domestic sphere. This initial sociological wave attempted to draw particular attention to Turkish women's lives with feminist scholarship, conducted in German, that at times characterized guest workers or members of their families solely as victims, an attitude exemplified in titles such as "Ignored, Stood Up, Oppressed" and "Where Do We Belong?"[80] This early scholarship focused on the problems of integration and sought to expose the guest worker experience, wanting to speak on behalf of the foreigner population in a call to action.[81] The 1975 film *Shirins Hochzeit*, or "Shirin's Wedding," one of the first films narrated from the Turkish female guest worker's perspective, presented a cautionary tale of a woman's exploitation both in the institution of marriage and as guest workers in West Germany.[82] In Günter Wallraff's *Ganz Unten*, or *On the Bottom*, the German journalist recounted his own fieldwork, during which he wore a disguise for a year to pose as a guest worker, as part of an exposé.[83] It is also noteworthy that the Turkish media emphasized exploitation and poor conditions of guest workers in West Germany, especially after the spread of satellite television access in the 1990s strengthened the connection of ethnic Turkish communities abroad to Turkey.[84]

By the 1980s a solid body of cultural production – from film to *Gastarbeiterliteratur*, or "guest worker literature" – took on the weighty task of conveying a range of experience, complementing existing scholarly perspectives.[85] Turkish-German authors, often writing in German, document their experiences of social, linguistic, and cultural isolation and offer a personal view into the broader demographic and cultural shift.[86] The use of the German language defined both their audience and their desire to record their own histories for a German audience. In turn, social scientists and historians through the 1990s built a robust literature around how groups arrived in West Germany, the types of organizations and alliances they made, their social problems, citizenship and xenophobia in Germany, and what these issues could tell us about how Germany did or did not deal with its dark past.[87] Scholars collected interviews with foreign workers and constructed private archives and museum exhibitions, and the fight for recognition began, especially the recognition that Germany was indeed a "land of immigration."[88]

Many scholars, activists, and politicians throughout the 1980s–1990s centred their focus on a politics of recognition and engagement with the German government's definitions and regulations for being "German." With the Nazi blood-based citizenship laws in the back of many people's minds, the government's responses to non-citizens – ad hoc regulations, ambiguous policies, cultural initiatives, social programs, evolving naturalization rules, and resistance to dual citizenship – were deeply confusing at best.[89] Political discourse on schooling, language acquisition, and social programs for immigrant children were paradoxical: they were touted as important while the state and cities cut their funding and support.[90] Making sense of who guest workers were and why they belonged became infinitely more complicated as the gap in time between initial recruitment (when they arrived in West Germany) and the present (2017) widened. After the program officially ended in 1973 and as populations increased, larger question loomed: the German Left wondered if the state was too tolerant of Islam's "restrictions" on women, such as headscarves, or worse of overt violence in the case of honour killings.[91] The fact that the majority of guest workers from Turkey were Muslim presented perhaps the greatest cultural divide.

European states, especially West Germany, have skirted the term "race" in the post-war period. However in so doing, some slippage between racial, ethnic, and religious otherness has crept into the public discourse. Racial definitions have long been palpable in the German context but also in the postcolonial milieu of Western Europe, which includes both France's *pied noirs* and Britain's racial slur "Paki." Languages present their own boundaries of understanding, communication, connection, and isolation. In terms of industry and globalization, labour migration was a transnational phenomenon, as employing foreign nationals broke down internal barriers in Western Europe.[92] West Germany's guest worker program was a small part of larger global trends during the post-war period, many of which included traversing multiple borders.

Yet the German case remains specific because of Germany's unique history with foreign nationals and ethnicities, causing some scholars to insist on continuities with the Nazi past as a central part of the German guest worker program's history.[93] For others Nazi genocide tainted the concept of "race" in Germany with a specific historical association, causing its use to wane in the post-war period during discussions of guest workers in West Germany.[94] However, connections between West German attitudes towards foreigners and Germany's Nazi experience have remained unavoidable and have constructed guest workers as racial others in ways they may not have been in the 1950s and 1960s. In the 1980s and 1990s as the first historical monographs on guest workers were published, both Klaus Bade and Ulrich Herbert argued that the guest worker program was part of a longer, complicated, and continuous history with foreign labour dating back to imperial times.[95] Herbert argued that it was a problem that Germans did not recognize the connection and continuity with their dark past: "There was no discussion in West German society in the 1960s about the historical fact that the importation of foreign labor during periods of economic boom was rooted in traditions extending back over many decades."[96] However, as Christopher Molnar has pointed out when referring to Yugoslavian guest workers: "While this newfound emphasis on race in Germany's postwar history has been salutary, an approach that puts race and racialization at the center of German interactions with resident foreign populations runs the risk of sidelining the experiences of foreign groups that Germans did not view in primarily racial terms."[97] Turkish guest workers intersect several groups – post-war migrants, Muslim diasporas, and guest worker program participants – presenting a paradox: at times a rupture from and in other cases a continuation of a history of overt racism.

In the 1980s the idea of a "Turkish culture" – a Muslim one at that – emerged in popular discourse as distinct from and dangerous to German culture.[98] At the turn of the century, the German microcensus began counting the number of Muslims in Germany for the first time.[99] According to a 2000 parliamentary inquiry, the number of Muslims – a fictionally homogeneous group – in Germany lay between 2.8 and 3.2 million.[100] Even before the September 11 attacks focused media attention on Muslims, postcolonial migrations, asylum seekers, and guest workers had already settled in most major European cities during the post-war era. Accordingly media and scholarship turned their attention to these immigrant groups and their most visible members, Muslims (from Africa in France, for example, or from South Asia in Britain).[101] However the events of 9/11 increased the scrutiny of Muslim ethnic enclaves and at times the rhetoric around it conflates radical Islam with mainstream Islam in troubling ways.[102]

It was in this context that, in 2005, the Turkish Republic began negotiations for full membership in the European Union. In response, prominent German historians Jürgen Kocka, Hans-Ulrich Wehler, and Heinrich August Winkler declared that "Turks" could not be "European" because of deeply ingrained cultural differences, introducing an ethnocultural definition of Muslims' otherness within a Christian-defined Europe.[103] Among others, Joyce Mushaben has responded to such comments, noting that migrants' religion had not previously been a primary consideration: "Though religion was never a factor in regulating either guest worker or refugee status prior to 1990 ... Since September 11th, [however] political officials have nonetheless conflated religion with other cultural traits used to classify groups as 'worthy' or 'incapable' of integration."[104] This conflation has not abated since: in August 2014, *Der Spiegel*, a popular German news monthly, ran a cover featuring the Turkish prime minister's head set against the flag of the Turkish Republic and above a picture of the Blue Mosque. Beneath the image the subtitle reads: "Is Turkey still a free land?" The title and subtitle are printed in both German and Turkish. The edition also features a special sixteen-page insert solely in Turkish. In other words, almost a decade after the 2005 questioning of whether Turkey was European enough for the EU, *Der Spiegel* produced an inclusive bilingual edition while at the same time running a story once again questioning Islam's compatibility with democracy and, by analogy, with Germany, a stalwart of Western democracy and economics. A major difference now, though, is how the point of view has changed: the 2014 article notes that compared with ten years earlier, when 73 per cent of Turkey's population favoured joining the EU, now only 44 per cent support accession.

The historical legacy of the guest worker program, which recruited and imported workers enthusiastically, must fight its way through an overwhelming contemporary context and ever- evolving geopolitical constellations. Elif's unique story could easily get buried amid media reports on headscarves, as they were not an issue among recruited workers. Elif easily found not only employment but also friends among her colleagues. This book focuses on the first generation in the 1960s and 1970s to provide a grounding perspective through which to consider contemporary media narratives, which can place "foreigners" at the centre of social problems and conflate them with a deep mistrust of Islam. Instead, this account reveals that West Germans feared other things, namely communism, domestic terrorism, and sexual liberation, much more than Islam in the 1960s and 1970s.

This book examines the experiences of Turkish guest workers before departure and on the way to West Germany, as well as daily life once they arrived. The West German officials involved and the attempts they made to control and regulate guest worker immigration, as well as their failures to do so, also play a central role in this narrative. Workers and officials alike took many small steps along the way to make workers' stays in West Germany more permanent. At the same time, guest workers negotiated the process on their own terms, exerted control, and created social lives and spaces in ways not previously recognized. Turkish guest workers' perspectives, which have long been missing from historical studies, are the focus of this book.[105] These immigrants do not fit neatly into historical narratives about postcolonial Muslim migrants, as their relationship with their host country, as well as their citizenship status, was very different.[106] The details of everyday life reflect larger life decisions, provide the background for labour movements, and point to an answer to the question so many journalists, migration scholars, and former workers like Elif have asked: at what point does home no longer mean the place left behind? Workers' first-hand experiences also complicate scholars' assumption that only economic factors motivated migration. It is important to remember that these workers were invited and welcomed and had individual histories as they made new lives in Germany.

The first part of the book focuses on both the Turkish and German governments' intentions, looking first at how the program began and was implemented in Turkey and second at how the first workers applied for and travelled to West Germany. Key arrangements for the program were negotiated behind the scenes, hidden from state-level political discourse, media attention, and the historical record – but, while concealed, these arrangements drove the narrative nonetheless. Both the new West Germany and the reconfigured Turkish Republic of the 1960s could impose their modernizing dreams on to the program. In so doing, post-war Germany, along with its place in the world and its relationship with foreign nationals, also evolved, devolved, and slowly worked its way into the contemporary situation – one of debates on immigration, Muslim minorities, and Germany's role in the new Europe – enlivening press accounts as this book goes to press.

Understanding why Germany has had decades of debates on "multiculturalism" and "parallel societies" starts with asking how Germany's demographic shifts occurred in the first place. In the case of former guest workers, it means considering the information they were or were not given, how West Germany recruited them, and how initial interactions and relationships were formed. Who were the first West Germans they met? The book's first part addresses these questions of recruitment, original intentions, and initial interactions. The first chapter examines the bilateral treaties in greater detail, situating them as a vital part of the long post-war. This chapter also provides a working definition of the group "the first generation," including making a case for the value of focusing particularly on Turks. In short, the first chapter explores the beginning of the guest worker program for Elif and many others, demonstrating how they transitioned from individual applicants into guest workers.

The second chapter focuses on how individual workers reflect on their initial impressions and experiences. Upwards of thirty million European and non-European labour migrants relocated to European industrial centres in the 1960s and 1970s, but this chapter begins with just a handful of ethnic Turks before they departed Turkey. It demonstrates the ways in which applicants attempted to maintain control within a strict, bureaucratic, and at times dehumanizing process. Inherent in oral history is a shift in the focus and perspective of knowledge production, as well as access to exactly the kinds of experiences that are less likely to survive in the archival record – those that are personal, local, and unofficial. Taken together, the first two chapters consider the very important notion of intent or the recognition that applicants, employers, and government officials had plans even if they could not come to fruition.

Significantly, part one positions the beginnings of the guest worker program in Turkey at least a full year before departure for Germany. These workers transitioned in this period into participants in industrialized post-war Europe. The third chapter turns to the German officials stationed at the liaison offices in Turkey, the ones who dealt with Turkish applicants first-hand while receiving instructions from Germany. They stood in the middle between the official regulations and plans and the lived reality that was often makeshift, ad hoc, and just plain chaotic. These beleaguered officials could rarely make both sides happy. Because they were unsuccessful, their efforts often went unseen, hidden from workers, who could only draw their own conclusions about Germany's plans for them, long before departure.

"Guest workers" maintained their moniker even when not at work. The third chapter examines home and private life for the first generation. Life away from work unfolded in vastly different contexts, ranging from workers' dormitories in West Germany to the discos of both East and West Berlin. In the third chapter, workers' accounts of their lives in employer-run dormitories, as well as the notes of an external auditor, speak in tandem with the meticulous records kept by a dorm manager. Pieced together, these details unfold a picture of home life that shows how "parallel societies" did and did not form. In this chapter, I argue that considerations of integration, German identity, and social cohesion were worked out in small daily interactions between foreign workers and German managers, culminating in the larger issues and debates of the later 1980s. Workers' reactions to their living situations and social experiences tell a lot about West German society's ability to adapt to the major demographic shift occurring in its midst.

The second part of the book shifts the argument from intentions to realities and the creative ways in which particular guest workers acted out and fought back against their isolation and frustration with their situations. They formed new and remarkable alliances – mutual coalitions that served all sides. Personal and political negotiations on an everyday level demonstrated, before many even realized it, that they had embarked on a permanent life and investment in Germany.

The fourth chapter is a unique narrative of West Berlin-residing foreign workers, in this case men who crossed to East Berlin for social lives with East German women. Therefore, this is also a story of East German women's actions and desires. Studying these two marginalized groups together changes Cold War history and the multiple, even symbolic, borders involved. To the East Berlin women, these foreign men served as a conduit for hard-to-obtain goods and even, through marriage, a way out. Ironically, these "Eastern" men represented Western consumer culture and found greater social liberty behind the Iron Curtain. In this chapter, I argue that these seemingly trivial social interactions reveal layers of meaning and agency and challenge the narrative of the tightly closed border and traditional political Cold War histories. Taken together, these examples change what we know about how guest workers lived and interacted with West and East Germans, who were and were not connected with the official program.

The status of guest workers evolved over time. They transitioned from Germany's guests to "German workers," especially through labour activism. The fifth chapter provides a counterexample of integration through a discussion of labour activism by intended and unintended German and non-German workers' coalitions. Significantly, the early 1970s saw the beginnings of foreign worker-based labour movements that no longer distinguished foreign workers by nationality and included the first signs of solidarity among foreign and native-born workers. This chapter focuses on Turkish guest workers' experiences in the workplace and, in the early 1970s, their increased interest in workers' rights. In the case of labour activism, ethnic origins became less important in light of potential gains for all workers, hinting at workers' long-term investment in Germany. I argue that before the 1973 recruitment ban, which many credit with prompting former guest workers' permanent settlement in West Germany, labour activism signalled social citizenship, or the desire to stay, invest, and develop lives in Germany permanently.

At its core, this book aims to fundamentally shift the history of the guest worker program, considering multiple, sometimes conflicting, viewpoints in conversation rather than two sides locked in debate about integration or multiculturalism. Before parting, Elif said to me, "Thank God that we didn't speak German [well] then ... because then I would have understood everything, and it would have bothered me."[107] Her future in Germany and her role in its history were not certain. Instead they developed over time. She concluded: "[At] a certain age, people mull their lives over ... your thoughts work through your past ... When you don't consider your past as personal history and family history, then you can't build your future."[108] This book's exploration of individual histories enriches our understanding of guest workers' struggles as well as their achievements, while shedding light on the complexities of some immigrants' strategies for negotiating an uncertain status, which sometimes involved devising innovative ways of manipulating alliances with ordinary citizens and governmental representatives in ways enabled precisely by their uncertain status in their new world. In short, recounting and analysing these personal histories culminates in a richer understanding of two rapidly evolving nations and their struggles to build a new future, just as the individual actors negotiated their own daily battles. At the same time, this investigation takes seriously the fact that the complexity of individual lives often is irreducible to clear representations of social movements. The remarkable individuality within this group of immigrants, in other words, means that their diverse stories do not fit neatly into the confines of clearly marked political movements.

PART ONE

1 "Don't be late!" Giacomo Maturi, *Hallo Mustafa!: Günter Türk Arkadaşı ile konuşuyor*, (Heidelberger: Dr Curt Haefer Verlag, 1966), 9.

1

The Invitation

"Don't be late!" admonishes an illustration from a 1964 instructional booklet, *Hallo Mustafa! And a heartfelt Welcome to Germany!*, designed for guest workers headed to West Germany (see figure 1). In the image, the anthropomorphized clock face uses raised eyebrows and a frown to convey dismay and concern – with one finger wagging in warning and the other showing the way. The wagging finger illustrates the stereotype that Germans find Mediterranean men lacking punctuality. Beneath the clock, workers carrying briefcases run full tilt, with one man actually pushing another, in the direction indicated. The palpable nervous energy and urgency reflect the early 1960s guest worker arrangement between West Germany and Turkey quite well. The illustration also signals anxiety and desperation – West Germany's intense need to expand the program while competing with other European countries for a shrinking labour pool coupled with workers' own impatience and eagerness to seize an opportunity.

Marketing involves manipulation, a drive to connect with a person's desires and impulses, and this image is no different. It casts the early years of the labour arrangement in a distinct light – one of frantic desires. West Germany invited workers with various messages – conveyed by the media, by German representatives in Turkey, and in application and orientation materials – all of which impacted Turkish workers' initial relationships with West Germans and interpretations of their new role as guest workers. West Germany, the modernizing Turkish Republic, and individual applicants approached the program with their own ideas about how to make the situation work for them, regardless of the messages around them. Examining the invitation addresses elusive questions of why an immigrant decides to leave and what West Germany had in mind when inviting these guests. Far from just recruitment based on a treaty, German officials oscillated their positive and negative views of and messages to workers, playing on the word "invitation" itself. As workers' initial excitement and positive attitudes soured, their cynicism about the strict application procedures increased, long before they ever arrived in West Germany.

This chapter traces two intersecting phenomena: how West Germany and the Turkish Republic negotiated the bilateral labour agreements and, at the same time, how rank-and-file German officials and individual Turkish applicants negotiated the application process and new relationships through smaller interactions over an extended period of time. The larger institutional structures and the daily, one-on-one interactions combined to make post-war guest worker migration unique. Despite the careful planning and strict rules of the West German BA, the individual level often functioned quite differently and in surprising ways for applicants. After a brief historical overview of the guest worker program's origins, this chapter illuminates the plans, frustrations, and interactions of the applicants who navigated the German Liaison Office in Turkey for months or even a year before departure. Before the application process began, though, West Germany and the Turkish Republic had to come to terms with both the historical and contemporary forces that drove the guest worker program's evolution.

Recruiting the First Generation

In 1964, BA director, Anton Sabel, celebrated the departure of the ten-thousandth worker from Turkey just three years after the official program had started. Sabel travelled to Istanbul to express gratitude for Turkish workers in person, saying: "We are thankful for all the relief to Germany that the Turkish workers' departure allows. We are trying to shorten the waiting period."[1] Sabel also wanted to assure the newly departing Turkish workers, as well as the greater Turkish public, that workers in West Germany were leading comfortable and prosperous lives, even enjoying the same rights as West German workers. As an added bonus, Sabel mentioned West Germany's post-war *Frauenüber-schuss*, or "surplus of women,"[2] noting that a German girlfriend was a real possibility and ignoring female applicants in the process.[3] One Turkish newspaper even quoted Sabel as saying, "Many foreign workers are marrying German girls."[4] Relationships, especially marriage, with German women suggested settling down in West Germany, an idea that was quite at odds with a supposedly temporary labour program.

Sabel did not touch on West German employers' demand for Turkish female workers, which were ever increasing. However, similar enticements of a fun and exciting life in West Germany for Turkish women would have been considered scandalous in Turkey's traditional society. Abadan-Unat noted that first-generation guest workers left a Turkish society that had a strong sense of tradition, religion, and family life, firmly engrained with distinct gender roles.[5] Sabel's comments, as well as the preceding state-level negotiations, gendered the guest worker program male in a troubling way that differed greatly from the realities of the program. Indeed, archival records and official documents rarely consider the ways in which male and female guest workers did and did not have different experiences along gender lines. However, Turkish women also went to Western Europe in sizeable numbers, and some were openly excited about it as interviews such as Elif's make clear.

Sabel's words of enticement were markedly different from both the state-level negotiations and the general wariness West Germany had previously expressed about Turkish workers; in fact, they were quite invitational. What mattered most, though, is that for many Turkish recruits, Sabel and his message represented the public face of West Germany – one offering welcome, encouragement, and solicitation. Elif's and many others' recollections of enthusiasm and dreams for a better life in West Germany make sense in the context of Sabel's public sentiments. For those who had been considering working in West Germany, or who had been wait-listed, Sabel's news was encouraging it was the reassurance that workers needed to sustain them through the tedious, bureaucratic, and expensive application process, one offering few guarantees. Yet the positive press was hardly needed: at the time of Sabel's visit in 1964, more than 150,000 Turkish workers were already waiting to leave for West Germany.[6] In the period between 1961 and 1973, the Liaison Office in Turkey processed on average more than 50,000 workers per year.[7] However, the story of foreign workers in West Germany cannot be told with numbers alone. The official history of the treaties and contracts signed are only part of the story: there were also words of welcome as well as big dreams and plans. The initial moments of contact, exchange, and negotiation between German officials and Turkish applicants provide the context needed to understand how Turkish guest workers interpreted their German counterparts.

Post-war economic miracles were not just the history of West Germany or of the Marshall Plan but also that of many migrants who sought new futures in Western Europe after 1945.[8] Indeed, it was the individuals moving across the constructed borders of "East" and "West," as much as state-level officials, who engaged in post-war "modernizing" projects of their own.[9] Across Western Europe, significant demographic changes occurred in the post-war era as individuals turned to immigration and emigration as a way to secure better financial futures. In June 1946, Italians left for work in Belgium. In Britain, immigrants arrived from the Caribbean and staffed the country's trains, buses, and municipal services. The Dutch government encouraged workers from Spain, Yugoslavia, Italy, Turkey, Morocco, and Suriname to take jobs in the Netherlands' textile, mining, and shipbuilding industries. The physical border crossing of Turkish workers into Western Europe was a tangible symbol of the movement of Turkey's labour force and economy in the direction Turkish modernizers had hoped – they were literally moving to the "West."

West European nations welcomed these immigrants enthusiastically in the early years. "Up until now, [foreign workers] have been in an experimental phase that has led to positive experiences on both sides. But how should it continue?" asked the noted Italian immigration scholar, Giacomo Maturi, in the early 1960s.[10] He continued: "It was a bit surprising when the millionth worker was greeted in 1964. This act was the start of the question on the part of all interested parties, if an extended influx of workers was desired, and if so, what could be done for them."[11] In short, his focus was on how to accommodate the large influx much more so than how to stem the tide.

Words of welcome also extended to government-published instructional booklets, though they came laden with normative messages. *Hallo Mustafa!* as well as other West German publications for guest workers – whether for recruitment, as guides to life in Germany, or meant to explain workplace rules and regulations – turned author's opinions, attitudes, and preconceptions into a singular German view, just as they addressed all Turkish workers as a monolithic group. They also played no small role in setting up expectations on both sides. Figure 2 appeared in the Turkish language edition of *Hallo Mustafa!* after a paragraph that emphasized success dependent on good behaviour and patience: "I wish you much success with your plans especially the possibility to earn lots of money, but remember, it is not always smart to demand an egg when you can, through the same means, have the entire

2 "Imagined riches."

3 "Confusion over contracts."

Source: Maturi, *Hallo Mustafa!*, 12, 17.

hen tomorrow. Don't be impatient and in a rush ... At work, one must reign in his temperament and feelings."[12] The author pointedly concluded: "you Turks are hot-blooded."[13] The image and message are both optimistic and cautionary: unimaginable riches are easy to come by if only one can control one's ethnically defined "temperament." Instead of the egg, the worker could have the hen – a symbol for steady, reliable wealth accumulation. The smug grin, rolled-up shirt sleeves, and loosely flapping house slipper portray a sense of accomplishment not toil and provide no hints of the workplace inequalities that would come to the fore in the 1970s as discussed in the final chapter of this book. The men are not dressed as workmen, but rather in shirt sleeves presenting an image disconnected with the nature of the work most guest workers endured.

The manual is filled with cartoon illustrations lending it a playful tone and presenting guest workers as confused, smug, or homesick depending on the topic. The tone of the manual makes the situation seems less dire and certainly more casual than the intense application procedures and grueling train ride to West Germany most had to endure, as discussed in the next chapter. In an illustration about contracts and wages, a very serious issue, a cartoon presents a patronizing tone that portrays the foreigners as naive, slow, or even child-like. In the image a man with a gaping mouth scratches his head while his friend looks on in a crouched, almost fearful position. As we will see in chapter 3, extra fees tacked on in workers' dormitories and, in chapter 5, Elif's description of the various and perhaps purposefully confusing payment system of piecemeal work, these issues were no laughing matter and employers were not the kindly father figures presented in instructional materials. Unlike the image of the man with the piles of money in figure 2, the two men in figure 3 sport bushy eyebrows, mustaches, and, instead of neckties, are wearing the more traditional woolen vests more commonly worn in Turkey than Germany. The illustrator made certain telling choices in these portrayals of foreign workers.

Unlike the portrayals in *Hallo Mustafa!*, the first generation of Turkish guest workers was not a unified group; they came from different places, had different education and skill levels, had different family situations, and included women as well as men.[14] Here, the "first generation" refers to those who were born in Turkey and came to West Germany as formal applicants of the bilateral guest worker program during the official years of the program, 1961–73. For the most part, this group of Turkish workers was travelling to West Germany for the first time, many with little knowledge of the German language, people, or customs, an aspect that set guest workers apart from former colonial subjects travelling to colonial metropoles. This first generation included both male and female guest workers, with the number of female applicants increasing over time. A 1975 BA report stated that the proportion of Turkish female workers abroad increased from nearly 8 per cent in 1961, and to 24.4 per cent of all Turkish workers by 1973.[15]

Though their percentage was relatively small, Turkish women's migration was not negligible.[16] West German employers recruited women guest workers heavily, as they set aside "women's work" in the lower-paid "light wage categories" for foreign women, a move that helped German women return home to build nuclear families with male breadwinners. This 1960s exodus of Turkish women was unparalleled and unprecedented and produced major changes, including new-found economic independence for Turkish women, the replacement of extended family networks by nuclear families, and new marital strains and conflicts.[17] It is important to note that these women were not spouses following their husbands to Germany but workers with contracts. In fact, most of the Turkish workers in the early 1960s travelled alone, without their spouses, children, or extended family, though several also ended up following spouses, family members, and acquaintances.

The first generation of Turkish guest workers was also distinct from populations of both ethnic Turks and Kurds who emigrated to West Germany and Western Europe in general after the 1980 military coup in Turkey. Up to three hundred thousand Turkish citizens came to Europe as either refugees or political asylum seekers in this period and made claims on the West German state that were quite different from those of the invited guest workers who preceded them.[18] Despite the distinctions between the various groups of Turkish citizens who travelled to West Germany, as well as the distinctions among the various groups of guest workers, there was an interesting slippage among the constructed categories of "Turk" and "guest worker" – monikers that served as shortcuts in official discussions, in the media, and in the West German public consciousness.[19]

On the other hand, Turkish guest workers' uniqueness was also debatable. Turkish workers had a lot in common with other migrants in post-war Western Europe, too. Recruitment agreements were typically similar among various nationalities, with similar information about wages, types of work, places of work, work hours, housing arrangements and expenses, and transportation.[20] They had the same medical exams, received the same instructional booklets, rode on the same trains, lived in the same dormitories, worked the same jobs, and eventually fought alongside other nationalities for better working conditions and wages. This unified experience might also explain the often-unqualified use of the term "guest worker." It was also only rarely that cases of Turkish cultural or religious considerations came to the fore, such as considerations of a strict Muslim diet (one without pork). Much to workers' dismay, in fact, their culturally specific ideas of modesty and homosocial spaces were not always considered, as evidenced by, for example, the medical exam.

Navigating Departure

Perhaps more than push-and-pull factors, individual choice, ambition, and opportunity are all inherent in any voluntary migration. One Turkish man, Murat, said he came to West Germany as an official guest worker because of poverty and unemployment at home: "This is the main reason that everybody comes here, but some people lie about it. They say they did this, they did that ... It's all a lie. The only reason to go to [West] Germany, to go abroad, is unemployment ... A person with money in his pockets, doing well in his business, couldn't stand the difficulties of a foreign land."[21] Indeed, deciding to leave home, and especially family, was not a decision taken lightly. One woman, recalling her parents' departure, said: "I remember very well the day that my father left for Germany ... People came to say goodbye ... My mother and I were alone in Ankara ... [When my mother joined him a year later] I was dropped off at my grandmother's. It was the most painful day of my life ... In Turkey, everybody told us, 'Your mother and father are sweeping up money from the ground in Germany.'"[22] In these cases – a man looking to find riches, another hoping to avoid hardship, and a family willing to endure separation in exchange for economic security – Turkish guest workers sought their own "economic miracles" by going to West Germany. This section takes a closer look at application materials for Turkish workers to assess what information applicants had as well as the German attitudes implied in the materials given – in short, how Germany invited its guests.

The German and Turkish employment agencies set up an elaborate, orderly application procedure for processing the large, steady stream of potential Turkish workers. Yet workers' recollections, as well as memos from the employment offices, reveal several areas in which this application process broke down. Poor planning, miscommunication, and cultural insensitivity plagued those applying to the program. Nevertheless, Turkish applicants found ways to navigate a confusing and overly bureaucratic process, even bending rules if need be, offering evidence of the control that applicants were able to exert in a situation in which they just as easily could have been exploited.

Despite official attempts to standardize the application process, there was great variation and constant modification. For some workers, the process was tedious and lasted many years – years of appointments, long lines, repeated examinations, and frustration in general. At the same time, other workers skipped exams and were able to speed through the process. Published application guidelines described a bureaucratic, orderly process, yet according to interviews with former workers, these published guidelines were hardly representative and reveal a mismatch of intentions and agendas. The application procedure rarely resembled policy makers' detailed plans and published instructions. It is not that the West German officials provided a "right" way of doing things, and that the Turkish applicants tried to get around it, but rather that all involved found ways to negotiate the process on their own terms where possible.

Working in Germany began in Turkey and entailed multiple steps. The first step was to contact one of the German Liaison Offices, which were located at first only in the capital of Ankara and in Istanbul and later also at a location on the Aegean coast, Izmir, and in a Black Sea coastal town, Zonguldak, as well. Applying in person was a requirement, necessitating a long, expensive trip for many, especially for those living east or south of Ankara in a country spanning 302,535 square miles. The Liaison Offices exclusively controlled recruitment, taking over from earlier, less formal agreements and developed instead an extensive, standardized screening and placement procedure.[23] The Liaison Office accepted and arranged the transportation and placement of approximately 70 per cent of applicants through just two branches – the Istanbul and Ankara offices – creating a large, bureaucratic bottleneck.[23] Approximately 640,000 Turkish men and women applied at either the Istanbul office (from 1961 to 1973) or at the Ankara office (from 1963 to 1967).[24]

To guide workers through the process, West German officials published instructional and orientation materials. What these materials mostly describe, though, are West German attitudes towards the program and its applicants. More than just instructional booklets, orientation materials were also a way for West German officials to present a stylized view of the new West Germany as host. Orientation materials also revealed the relationship West Germany wished to develop with its guest workers – one of German dominance. *How Does One Go to Germany to Work? Living Conditions in the Federal Republic of Germany* is a booklet less about life in West Germany, as the subtitle suggests, than a list of rules on how to apply for the program in Turkey before departure. The tone of the booklet is equally important, as it emphasizes the BA's absolute authority; as one example, the preface notes that it was forbidden to seek a job from a private person.[25]

Other orientation materials, such as the *Hallo Mustafa!* booklet with the clock graphic that opened this chapter, took on a more cheerful and pedantic tone. *Hallo Mustafa!* was a 1966 publication with identical editions in four different languages: Turkish ("Hallo Mustafa"), Italian ("Hallo Mario"), Spanish ("Hallo José"), and Greek ("Hallo Spiros")."[26] Positive interactions with West Germans were a key element of this booklet: "I know that you had concrete goals as you left your homeland for the foreign. You want to earn money ... But one also *lives* in the period when one is toiling away ... One looks around and sees fellow men, who also see, notice, greet and speak to him or her."[27] In contrast to the frustrating and dehumanizing application process, this book countered ideas of exclusion: "Your rambles through our towns are like visits in a zoo or in a museum ... But you should not feel alone. Today I want to welcome you. We work and live side by side."[28] Most important, it underscored West Germany's desire to have these workers and to invite them: "I want to tell you something in good faith that you have probably already noticed: good workers are needed here; you are needed, and most likely not just for this year."[29] Despite such words of welcome and concern, including Sabel's mention of marrying a German girl, there was little evidence of formal steps taken to address integration in West German society.

Indeed, orientation materials that hint at a more permanent life in Germany sent a confusing double message. Although most instructional manuals rarely discussed the length of guest workers' stay in West Germany, *Hallo Mustafa!* did comment that workers' stays could be more permanent: "Here you can start something and if you are tenacious and a little bit adaptive you can make plans for the *long term*, and you will certainly not be eternally a foreigner or a guest, but known as an equal and esteemed colleague."[30] Such messages of European unity and of long-term plans in West Germany conflicted with the messages both of an application process that scrutinized "non-Europeans" and of the guest worker program's founding rotation principle. The 30 October 1961 German-Turkish agreement stated that Turkish workers would be in West Germany for exactly two years. However, already in 1962, officials considered striking the limitation on the stay in West Germany, citing orientation costs and problems with integration in factories.[31]

In the agreement's 30 September 1964 revision, officials jettisoned the rotation clause, and no other limit on the stay in West Germany was included in the contract.[32] Equally important, suggestions of a more permanent stay might also offer clues as to what applicants might have had in mind about their future homes in and plans for West Germany.

Words of Welcome

Many orientation materials emphasized a post-war nod to a common European community, similar to the Turkish Republic's view of itself as European. *Hallo Mustafa!*, especially, emphasized mutual understanding after the war: "We want to be good friends. We are not just fellow citizens of the world but also of this small Europe, which we all want to rebuild in peace together, simply because we belong together … We are at home in Europe: we are neither foreign nor guests."[33] Such comments of reconciliation are indicative of the initial spirit of the early years of the guest worker program. In its instructional materials, West Germany revealed efforts to reclaim its history and a sense of nationalism. Certainly, through the guest worker program, Germany could not just rebuild its economy but also revise its historical image and trajectory in the eyes of the international community. In the case of *How Does One Go to Germany to Work?*, the front cover features grand buildings, majestic mountain ranges, and a great thinker, highlighting the positive aspects of German history and society and evoking the popular idea that German is at its heart a land of *Dichter und Denker*, or "poets and philosophers" (see figure 4). Interestingly, the booklet's back cover features a quote from Atatürk, or "Father of the Turks," who founded, Westernized, and secularized the Republic of Turkey. The Ataturk quote *"Türk, öğün çalış güven,"* or "Turk, be proud, work, trust!," connects Turkish national pride to work and, significantly, to trust – a main message of many instructional materials. The booklet *Would You Like to Get to Know Germany?* features women and men in traditional dress dancing a folk dance, harkening back to a pre-twentieth-century Germany, and begins with a brief introduction to German history, from the Holy Roman Empire through both world wars.

Application materials, as well as the program in general, allowed West Germany to recast itself in its own best image. Many booklets addressed issues in Nazi Germany in elliptical fashion, intimating a continuity of democracy and self-determination even in the Third Reich. When discussing the interwar period, *Would You Like to Get to Know Germany?* vaguely stated, "The Saar Basin that was to be subject

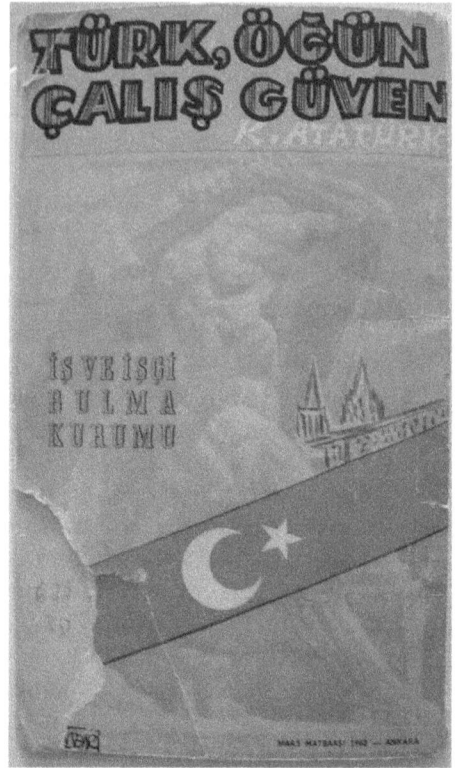

4 "How does one go to Germany to work? Living conditions
in the Federal Republic of Germany."

Source: İş ve İşçi Bulma Kurumu Genel Müdürlüğü Yayınları [Labour
Office Directorate Publication], no 28. (Ankara: Mars Matbassı,
[National Library Ankara] 1963), DOMiD, 637 SD.

to an international administration under the League of Nations in
1919, was returned to Germany following a plebiscite in 1935."[34] Historians would take issue with this presentation of the Nazi takeover
of the Saar Basin. In a similar fashion, *Today's Germany* ignores twentieth-century German history altogether, choosing instead to feature
images of centuries-old architecture while discussing older history or
contemporary prices, tourism, and social life. A note from the pub-
lisher on the inside cover points out that the "Federal Government

of Germany" called for its publication, underscoring the role that the West German government played in attempting to orient not just foreign workers but also, perhaps, the country itself to its new leadership position of post-war uplift.

German Bureaucracy Meets Turkish Cunning

Tedious bureaucracy as well as lists of steps to follow and requirements to meet dominated the predeparture period. First workers had to go to the German Liaison Offices in Turkey, where "committees of qualified members" would select workers through a precise and systematic process.[35] German employers would first communicate their wants and needs to the BA, whose employees would then notify the various branches in Turkey. Second, "a committee of at least two people" would consider candidates to see whether they matched the "desired age, education, and experience requested by the German employer."[36] Third, candidates who matched were then sent letters of invitation, and, fourth, within ten days of receiving the letter of invitation, candidates had to report to the local employment office at their own expense. If applicants did not report within ten days, they would risk losing their place and would have to start the application process over again from the beginning. The extremely limited advance warning made it impossible for some workers to make the deadline. Finally, an additional committee, of at least three staff members from "suitable bureaus of the employment agency," would determine the particular position assigned to a potential worker by taking into consideration the wishes of the German employers and whether the candidate had the appropriate age, education, skill level, physical build, and even "personal appearance and attitude."[37]

Determining personal appearance and attitude added an element of the subjective to the application process, one that implied West Germans' interpretations of potential Turkish workers' character. "Those considered inappropriate," the instructional guide warns, "will not be chosen and the referral process will be stopped. The selection committee's decision is final."[38] For example, a criminal record would prevent a potential applicant from being eligible. The booklet notes that applicants proven to have committed any of the following crimes would not be considered because they were "inexcusable": embezzlement, theft, bribery, rape, and other such "disreputable crimes."[39] Therefore, the BA sought to have workers who were not only skilled in a desired profession but also of a certain presumed moral character. Although the committee often had no basis on which to make such judgments, the booklets also warned against general moral and cultural deficiency.

Though instructional booklets might not have had much information about future employers, they did offer clues as to how employers and the German recruiters perceived Turkish applicants. Perhaps unsurprisingly, the published directives focused on the German employers' points of view, wants, and needs. Instructional booklets were also filled with admonishments of "Turkish" mindsets and behaviours based on stereotypes, such as when authors discouraged tardiness and stated that criminals need not apply. Above all, they noted, bribery would not be tolerated: the authors emphasized that the BA's services were free and that officers would not take money from Turkish workers seeking employment or from German employers looking for workers.

Admittedly, bribery and barter were somewhat common aspects of Turkish bureaucracy at the time. Indeed, contrary to West Germany's state policies, in interviews, former workers talked openly about the role of bribery during the application process. For example, Hasan, who went to work at Ford in 1962, said that when his blood was taken during the medical exam, he gave the man fifty to sixty lira to "make sure it was clean."[40] Another worker, Adil, recalls that he went to a man in his village and asked him to come up with a letter stating that he had worked for him for two years.[41] Mehmet, who was injured in the military and had lost the use of his hands, had his friends "harass" a German doctor. This German doctor had previously told Mehmet that no one would possibly hire him in such a condition, but later (after the alleged "harassment") the doctor signed off on a forged medical record. As a result, Mehmet made it all the way to West Germany, but his employer subsequently fired him when he discovered that Mehmet could barely use his hands.[42]

The BA was well aware of bribery's role in Turkish bureaucracy. A 1961 report noted: "Bribery does not evoke a moral dilemma for Turks; they do not have any moral qualms [about it]. Whoever lets himself be tricked is considered the dummy."[43] How prevalent a role bribery or harassment might have played is not clear; however, the fact that both Turkish publications and German internal memos mention bribery documents officials' concern. Turkish and German authorities' attention to bribery could be considered either as playing on stereotypes or as an awareness of a certain Turkish cultural sensibility – a recognition that such practices took place in Turkish bureaucracy and were simply an aspect of a different bureaucratic system.

Skirting rules, bribing doctors, and assisting fellow applicants were common and stemmed from a more community-based culture than that found in Germany. One former worker, Erol, recalled from his medical exam that the men in line helped one another, sharing, for example, urine samples if someone knew of a problem; these men helped others at the risk of their own positions as applicants. Another man had friends fashion fake tooth fillings for him from bottle tops. Moreover, in sharp contrast to the lengthy and detailed official application, one former worker had a friend set up his application for him within only a week's time with the help of a forged document:

> [A] friend … told us that if any of us wanted to go to Germany, he could arrange it; he knew someone who could send us there. I didn't quite believe what he said, but at the same time I wanted to go to Germany. He took us to the Employment Office … [then] the man he knew took me to the German Liaison Office … The people working there knew about my friend's friend, and they welcomed us. This guy told the civil servant working there to send me to Germany. They said, "Your wish is our command." They immediately filled out an application with an old date on it, and I signed it. I got my invitation within a week and started doing the paperwork.[44]

In this case, an applicant number, an assessment of his moral character, professional abilities, age, and general appropriateness did not matter – he was connected. In short, for many workers the printed instructions were false, irrelevant, ineffectual, or ignored at some point. Significantly, workers' ability to ignore or modify instructions and call on networks of friends and family for help is evidence of how they manipulated the situation instead of simply being manipulated by it.

Bureaucracy's Burdens

Appointment through official channels was an involved, multistep process, at least according to published literature. Workers who were accepted via the official channels would first receive a letter of appointment, which provided the first and only information about their future work in West Germany – the name and location of the position; the hourly wages; the amount of deductions for taxes and health insurance; information about overtime wages, yearly vacation, and social help; whether room and board would be provided; and, if applicable, what deductions from wages would be made to cover these costs.[45] Even though the published instructions state that information about assignments in West Germany would be given in detail, in reality, it was unlikely that applicants would know much about their placement in advance. Second, workers who accepted these conditions then had to provide additional paperwork: proof of a clean criminal record, proof of smallpox vaccinations, birth certificates, passport pictures, and letters of recommendation from previous jobs.[46] They also needed to obtain a passport, visas (for Yugoslavia and Bulgaria, which they would pass through on the train), foreign currency (in Deutsche mark or US dollars), and a physical. For workers who had never before left the country, obtaining a passport meant having an original copy of their birth certificate, a certificate of completion of military service, a completed passport application, and the application fee – items that they may or may not have had or been able to find or afford. Obtaining the necessary documents could not have been an easy task – one could get a passport only from Ankara or Istanbul.[47]

The application process was a large commitment of time and money, as well as a great personal financial risk. Applicants began at a local office where they had to fill out paperwork in person, in which they listed their profession, education level, and (for men) whether military service had been completed. The goal was to obtain a "worker's card," an appointment date at one of the liaison offices, and a placement number. There was little flexibility in the appointed time and place and little understanding of the expense involved in travelling to a liaison office. Adil recounted that he had to borrow money to travel to Ankara once he got his appointment: "We had no money. I went to the village merchants … and asked them to loan me 100 lira. No one gave me the money. [Eventually] a friend of mine managed to get the money for me so that we could go to Ankara."[48] Travel to Istanbul could be even more expensive because of the western location, and room and board along the way had to be considered as well, as the trip could take up to eight days in some cases.

For workers who were unemployed, application expenses would have been extremely difficult to secure. For employed applicants, taking time off to meet appointments and procure documents was equally difficult. Application fees did not cover additional expenses such as the medical exam, the passport application, and postage. The total of the application procedure was on average 181 Turkish lira or about 13 dollars in 1963.[49] This was not a small price for a Turkish worker to pay in the early 1960s. To put the application costs in perspective, the wages listed for a Turkish male worker were hourly rates of between 2 and 2.8 German marks (DM) and for female workers, an hourly rate of between 1.5 and 1.7 DM.[50] In other words, a woman would have to work about 32 hours in West Germany or 128 hours in Turkey to earn the amount equivalent to the application fees.[51]

Adil's experience of borrowing money to be able to go to the Liaison Office was fairly common. In her 1964 study, Abadan-Unat found that workers typically paid for travel to the Ankara or Istanbul Liaison Office by borrowing money or by selling off their belongings, an irrevocable commitment to the chance for a better life in West Germany.[52] Even after arrival at a liaison office, applicants had to stay in hotels or pensions during the ten to twelve days of bureaucracy. After the application was completed, the wait was still not over: the typical period between the date of application and the departure date was between one and three months.[53] As applicants flooded employment offices, delays in the application process resulted from the beleaguered and understaffed offices. A memo to the BA complained that the staff in Turkey was overwhelmed, lacked office space, and at best could hope to reduce the period between signing the contract and placement to between six and eight weeks.[54] The German Liaison Office did not collect data on applicants' trips from their hometowns and villages to liaison office branches, and workers' recollections provide only a vague sense of the costs involved in applying. For many, applying for work in West Germany was a risky and serious investment in an uncertain future. Workers' insistence in their recollections decades later that they made the right decisions must also be considered in light of the sacrifices they made simply to apply.

Published guides emphasized that workers had little say over their placement. Employers' demands determined the direction of causation: the BA was not looking for jobs that matched workers' skills but rather for employees who matched the jobs offered. Candidates could either list one single profession or state that they were open to any profession. If the latter was the case, however, they would have to take the work assigned to them, and they would be forfeiting their rights to protest if they later found a job in Germany that better suited their education and vocational training. The profession listed could impact one's departure order, and many applicants knew this. If two workers applied on the same day, a worker who had a profession that was currently in demand would be given priority and sent first.[55] "Additionally," the booklet states, "Germans might be looking for a specific age, education level, and work experience."[56] In other words, applicants who matched specific, requested descriptions would be given priority as demand arose. Consequentially, workers might have tried to list what they hoped would be a more desired profession, but picking the wrong profession could potentially trap an applicant in an endless waiting process as jobs were continuously opened and filled – a process that offered little transparency for applicants. Workers were, therefore, at the mercy of the market-driven demands of German employers, creating a frustrating, helpless, or hopeless situation for many who could be left waiting for years.

In practice, though, many application procedures were for naught, as workers' recollections stand in stark contrast to the officially archived materials. Former workers, in fact, rarely mention placement numbers or orderly procedures at all. Instead, they recall chaotic scenes and confusion at the employment office and at the departure point. Erol recalled that a man used a megaphone to shout instructions to thousands of workers waiting in line, and instead of calling the names of workers with appointments, he called company names. "The Bremen something factory," Erol paraphrased, "to the dockyards ... to Opel in Rüsselheim, to Volkswagen in Wolfsburg, to Mercedes, and so on and so forth."[57] Moreover, even successful assignment was not always sufficient. Even though Erol had already been assigned a position at Siemens and was ready and waiting to leave, Siemens management did not take him. Apparently Siemens had already filled its personnel quota. To put it in context, Erol had quit his job, travelled to Istanbul, and gone through a year-long application process, only for Siemens to turn him away at the point of departure. Erol's example demonstrates that employers were also working around official procedures, in which the BA mandated that workers be selected and ordered based on their skill set, position on the wait list, "appropriateness," and other tedious decisions German Liaison Offices had made.[58]

Yet the instructional books, such as *How to Go to Germany*, did not address cases like Erol's; in fact, it does not mention quotas at all. Instead, the author urged Turkish applicants to consider the West German employers' concerns: the author warned that, during the month-long application process, one should not give up and *"disappoint the wishes of the German employer,* especially without prior notification."[59] Much to the dismay of people like Erol, there was no consideration of how West German employers might frustrate applicants.

There were multiple ways to subvert official rules and several channels existed for arriving in West Germany. One of the most significant was the "nominated appointment," or *namentliche Anforderung*, in which workers persuaded employers to hire friends or family members by requesting them by name, regardless of their standing on the waiting list.[60] The Liaison Office had the ultimate control over appointments and had little patience for those unable to comply with its rigid regulations. Applicants who travelled to West Germany through unofficial channels as tourists often encountered visa problems, as was the case with Ms Arikan who travelled to West Germany as a tourist and found a job only to be fired for not having a work visa.[61] Furthermore, the BA noted that it would not be held responsible if after a worker received a letter of appointment, it was found that he or she had failed the medical exam, did not have the profession required, had not or could not obtain a passport, had been convicted, or had left the country in an illegal way.[62] A clear tension existed between West German employers' impatience for workers, applicants' strong desires to depart Turkey, including enduring the tedious application or subverting it, and the West German officials' simultaneous desire and inability to control and regulate the program.

The Medical Exam

Though the medical exam was just one part of a larger application, former workers talk about it more often than any other aspect of the application. The medical exam was an extremely negative experience for most applicants. More than simply a visit to the doctors, many applicants experienced the physical as a deeply personal violation at the hands of a foreign man, who was speaking in a language they did not understand. In interviews, almost all workers recall the exams as uncomfortable and even strange. Perhaps workers wished to express their greater anxiety about the move to West Germany through a description of this initial violation in a semipublic space. According to historian Mathilde Jamin, the experience of the medical was at the very least a culture shock in which workers were interviewed in a group, in their underwear by doctors and translators, without consideration for having male doctors for men and female doctors for women – both men and women were present.[63] In short, the physical was a disconcerting experience in light of the Turkish cultural consideration of modesty.[64]

However, none of the discussions in the employment office files mentions handling problems with cultural norms of modesty that such exams might threaten. In other words, they did not discuss what potential workers would think of such exams or how to address potential problems that might arise. Cultural norms about modesty (different from those of Western Europe) made having such a private exam in a group setting or undressing in front of a member of the opposite sex – or even in front of just a stranger – an extremely personal if not traumatic experience for many potential workers. The procedures were unfamiliar for most, especially the women, who made up about 30 per cent of all Turkish applicants. Elif recalled her medical exam thusly:

> [The] things they did were very strange ... The women were all together in one room in just their underwear. We were almost naked and went to the examination like this. They didn't have extra changing booths. We waited inside of a big room all in a line, we were almost naked ... The doctor was a man and the translator was a woman ... I didn't really have a problem with the doctor being a man. A doctor is a doctor whether he is a man or a woman. If the doctor had been a Turk, we might have been more relaxed. The translation took a long time.[65]

Elif mentioned twice that they were "almost naked," because they were in their underwear, implying that she found this state of undress unacceptable and perhaps demonstrating a modesty different from that in Western Europe. She also pointed out that the doctor's foreignness made them even more uncomfortable. When asked what other women thought of the medical exam, Elif recalled: "I have to point out that, because we were from Istanbul, we were more relaxed and it was to our advantage. In the later years, those coming from Anatolia had a different lifestyle ... There were women [not from the city] who were seeing a doctor for the first time ... So I couldn't say it was the same as what they experienced. We were more comfortable."[66] Elif's comments highlight the gendered aspects of the examination, which must have been extremely difficult for women who had never been to a doctor before and most likely had never worn a bathing suit or been seen in public in less than full dress, which might have been the case for women from Anatolia, the interior of Turkey.

The Liaison Office also noted that women who came from Anatolia were different. Authorities specifically stated that Anatolian women needed to have their medical exams immediately to determine whether they were "suitable."[67] One woman who came from a small village and had previously worked in a cotton field applied together with a friend from her village. She noted that her friend was not chosen because she was illiterate, so she had to continue the application process on her own.[68] Female workers remained in high demand – a demand that was exacerbated by the fact that many of the female applicants were in fact deemed "unsuitable" during their medical exams.[69] It is interesting that both Elif and the German employment officials had the same stereotype about women coming from Anatolia – that they were different. Yet these Anatolian women were there in the same employment office as the women from Istanbul, making the same westward trip and travelling alone, even if they had entirely different reasons for going.[70]

The medical exam was not necessarily easier for male applicants, who often describe the exam as invasive. One worker said he had to get completely naked to have his genitals examined. He noted that he was uncomfortable being examined together with twenty-five people in one room where all of them had to take off all of their clothes.[71] Another male worker recalled his medical exam as intrusive and difficult: "They had us take off our pants and made us bend over so they could examine our anuses with their fingers ... [There was a] German doctor, Turkish doctor, and of course there was a translator. [*Was it difficult for you?*] Of course it was difficult. I almost changed my mind and decided not to go to Germany when they had me take off my pants and made me bend over, but a girl came up to me and said that there was nothing wrong with what they had been doing."[72] The woman's reassurance suggests that many men thought the exam was not a typical or normal procedure. He does not comment on what he thought of the woman's presence when he was in such a vulnerable, exposed state. He goes on to comment on how strict the medical exams were, pointing out that the slightest problem would mean failing: "People who had both high and low blood pressure failed the checkups. Anyone who had signs of infirmity or who had more than three cavities failed. They didn't care if you were tall, big-framed or not."[73] Strikingly, in light of such a careful medical exam, the same man also noted employment officials did not test his technical skills at all, implying that the medical exam was much more important than how vocationally qualified he might be. West German officials gave these medical exams priority over vocational exams – whether out of fear of overburdening the West German health care system, a desire for the strongest workers, or a more biased view of Turkish health care – which suggests that they thought something was at risk with these workers. Furthermore, despite otherwise detailed instructions on all other parts of the application, workers did not know what to expect from the medical exams at all, and most were surprised and extremely uncomfortable when doctors crossed the boundaries of their personal modesty.

Even more confusing were illustrated instructional booklets that presented false representations, as was the case with *Hallo Mustafa!*[74] Here the medical exams, as well as potential housing arrangements and social life, were presented in cartoon form in addition to text. The illustrations in the booklet, however, did not resemble anything like what workers would actually encounter during the medical exam before leaving Turkey or after arrival in West Germany. Figure 5 portrays the medical examination as a light-hearted encounter with an at-ease, whistling patient face to face with a whimsically smiling doctor, both exuding calm and nonchalance.[75] Significantly, this doctor and patient are both male and standing alone; the patient still has his pants on, or at least pulled up, while the doctor exams his chest.

By July of 1971, the medical examiners of the German Liaison Office were examining more than seven hundred applicants per day.[76] It is doubtful that the experience of the medical exam improved with such a high volume of exams taking place. The very personal aspects of the medical exams and the complete lack of acknowledgment of the gendered differences of the application and transport of workers were glaring omissions in published instructions. Instructional booklets had little information to offer about what this experience was like.

5 "The medical exam."

Source: Maturi, *Hallo Mustafa!*, 26

Harsh Realities

There were many bumps on the road to West Germany. The application process included many mistakes and opportunities for grievances. First, the language barrier provided a constant source of confusion. A 30 October 1962 memo from the Federal Employment Office notes that workers' contracts were not clearly translated into Turkish from German, leading to misunderstanding and conflict.[77] In addition, the contract itself had a confusing layout. It had two columns, with writing in German on one side and in Turkish on the other. West German employers did not know Turkish and would fill out only the German side of the contract, leaving the Turkish side blank.[78] The result was that Turkish

workers who could not read German had no idea what they were signing: "As a result of this omission the guest workers cannot have a clear
idea about the working conditions offered to them."[79] This memo came
a full year after workers had been signing contracts without knowing
what awaited them upon arrival in West Germany, especially in terms
of wages and job descriptions.

Workers signed their contracts in groups of ten within ten to fifteen
minutes. The short period in which workers signed their contracts
implies that applicants gathered insufficient information about the location and nature of their jobs.[80] Moreover, the majority (59 per cent) of
workers Abadan-Unat surveyed left for West Germany within two days
of signing their contracts, limiting their ability to find out more about
their assignments and make departure plans. Travel costs were an additional point of contention: Turkish authorities wanted the contracts to
state clearly that German employers were to pay for the trip between
Istanbul and the city of employment and that they could not deduct this
cost from employee's wages at a later date. They note that confusion on
this point had "quite rightly [caused] much discontentment among the
guest workers," implying that, up until this point, German employers
had in fact been trying to deduct travel costs from workers' wages.[81]

Moreover, even ten years after the initial agreement between Turkey
and West Germany, delays were still common in the application process.
In a 1970 memo from the Federal Employment Office to a West German
company, officials wrote that it was difficult to get the workers picked
out, contracts signed, and workers sent on their way in a speedy fashion, and they suggested that it would be simpler for everyone to take
care of the paperwork with one contract, and for workers to travel en
masse instead of being arranged singly.[82] Confusion, delays, and problems on both the sending and the receiving ends not only slowed the
application process; they also offer evidence that the detailed instructions issued to applicants were a fiction.

Turkish applicants and West German and Turkish officials all dealt
with application problems by bending rules and skipping application
procedures, often out of necessity. There is evidence that West German employers simply ignored rules that did not suit them – just as
Siemens abandoned Erol at the departure point. One former worker,
Rezmi, noted that while waiting at the departure point in Istanbul, he
was one of 180 workers who were simply handpicked by a BMW representative.[83] Contrary to the official warnings to not "disappoint German employers" by backing out without proper notification, cases like

Erol's and Rezmi's, in which employers picked workers like livestock, led to resentment among workers who had endured the long application process. West German employers were obviously not held to the same standards, and workers noticed. Erol remarked that the Turkish government sold its workers to Europe like "cattle at the market" and that it made him think about how "black slaves were smuggled from Africa."[84] Even a West German employer's association noted that the recruitment of guest workers in Istanbul was like a "slave market."[85] Erol was perhaps additionally bitter because the round-up point for departure, the Vinegar Seller's Station, was located across from the busy Golden Horn harbour in Istanbul – an extremely public and potentially embarrassing place to be on display for employers' selection.

The Turkish employment agency expressed concerns over procedures to German officials. Indeed, officials constantly debated guidelines through letter exchanges. In the case of the medical exam, the Turkish side resented the follow-up exam by a German doctor, which it considered a "sign of surveillance and mistrust."[86] The Turkish side wanted to be more independent from the BA in the processing of workers. Furthermore, the Turkish agency apparently complained that the medical exam was too expensive for the uninsured, to which the Germans retorted, "The German side has no control over the fact that the applicant has to pay for the examination in the hospital, which, for uninsured workers, can cost up to 200 Turkish lira."[87] Moreover, Turkish officials had originally planned for there to be seventeen different liaison offices, spread throughout every region of Turkey.[88] Their German counterparts, however, found this unacceptable and logistically difficult and were successful in having the number reduced to four: Izmir, Ankara, Istanbul, and Zonguldak, with centrally located Ankara being the easternmost location. This logistical decision surely negatively affected the initial goal of helping the impoverished regions (which were mostly east of Ankara) through the guest worker program in addition to increasing travel costs from the most remote eastern regions.

In sum, the modifications and negotiations, which resulted from interactions between different employment offices, in addition to the exchanges between the officials and the workers, broke down the streamlined, orderly appearance of the application process that the published manuals, media, and politicians suggested. Instead of an idealized German bureaucratic control, a constant negotiation between two different systems based on different motivations – control versus subversion and cheap labour versus economic uplift – drove the guest worker program's initial years in Turkey. State-level negotiations mirrored ground-level interactions by two extremely motivated but also potentially dissonant groups – German officials and Turkish applicants.

In the end, despite their concern, Turkish officials were able to wield extremely little control over the application process, especially the selection of workers. For those who were not accepted because they either failed the medical exam or did not have the necessary skills, returning home was not always feasible. The majority (90 per cent) of the applicants had applied anonymously as unskilled workers. The West German Employers Association noted with concern that a harsh reality was in store for those who were rejected.[89] It commented, "those who have saved up for years and sold all of their goods down to the last goat in order to go to Germany, the praised land, are now, after the necessary rejection, thrown back to zero if they have to return home."[90] Workers took a leap of faith when applying to work in West Germany. They were unable to rely on their government to guide them through the process, and they could not rely on published German instructions to make applying easier either. The next chapter continues to explore these themes by focusing specifically on the train transportation for Turkish applicants to West Germany and how their experiences en route created the homogenized category "guest worker."

2

In Transit

In the early morning fog that blanketed the Salzburg train station, a reporter from *Salzburger Nachrichten* (*SN*), Werner Kobes, impatiently awaited the overdue Hellas–Istanbul Express, more commonly known as the "Guest Worker Express."[1] The train primarily carried Turkish guest workers, but it also picked up travelling vacationers in Yugoslavia and Greece on the way to West Germany. Local authorities had granted Kobes, as a reporter for *SN*, permission in June 1969 to experience the infamous train first-hand to answer the following questions: "Does the 'Guest Worker Express' ... really resemble a cattle transport for the civilized people of the twentieth century? Is it true in all honesty that no 'normal' traveller would dare to ride this train? Is it really as bad as reported?"[2] Indeed, for Kobes simply boarding was a "nearly unsolvable problem," because there was apparently not a centimetre of free space.[3] The Salzburg Rail Administration had warned Kobes about overcrowding, and the train's conductor, instead of helping the bewildered reporter, simply shouted, "If you really want to board, well then go ahead!"[4] Once he had squeezed on, Kobes found himself "hurdling" over luggage and people and scaling "barricades of luggage, trash, pillows, bedding, broken bottles, sacks, boxes and even a [blind] old man." Kobes described his "safari" as an adventure of climbing, twisting and turning, and, above all else, dodging a mass of humanity – men, women, and children of all ages – who had "strained expressions" while trying "to sit with at least some part of their bodies."[5]

Kobes's initial questions and subsequent article highlight the various ways guest worker transport was logistically problematic. In his article, Kobes pointedly compares the state of the guest worker train with a train for Germans, noting that just before the "Guest Worker

Express" arrived he had witnessed the punctual departure of a "German train" with passengers stretched out in comfort. But Kobes's critique goes beyond the logistical with an uncomfortable historical allusion – comparing guest workers' trains to "cattle transport."[6] His report is an example of the international media's gaze trained on post-war West Germany's dubious arrangement for foreign labour transportation.[7] Kobes used his observations to show the public the train's dire conditions and, in so doing, prod German National Rail authorities into addressing them. Kobes's report fails to reveal that West German officials were actually aware of their unwieldy transportation problems and even fretting in internal memos over how to manage them humanely and efficiently, particularly in light of Germany's recent troubling past. Such media reports were also unable to explain how, just a year later, in 1970, almost 1.5 million Turkish workers were waiting to depart for West Germany on these very trains, a journey that would transform individuals into guest workers.[8]

This chapter turns to departure and arrival. Many books and films feature German train stations with exhausted and bewildered passengers stepping foot for the first time in West Germany.[9] Scholarly literature about post-war foreign labour in West Germany often begins with narratives of *arrival* in West German train stations, overlooking how these immigrants actually got there and implying that their narrative started in West Germany and not before. This chapter argues that the process began even earlier and that the train journey itself was an important part of "becoming a guest worker." Train travel functioned as a symbol of economic recovery and dynamism in West Germany in contrast to Turkey's stagnation, just as train travel has historically stood for modernity and progress.[10] For critics, train travel was problematic, functioning as an enduring symbol of Germany's dark historical legacy. For travelling workers, however, train travel symbolized opportunity, hope, and adventure. This rail travel was, as new labour historians would argue, an important site of working class creation: upon arrival, these individuals stepped off the train as "guest workers."[11] In the case presented here, the three-day train ride to West Germany was yet another crucial step in the development of a larger, classed, and homogenizing experience: as we saw in the preceding chapter, applicants had to successfully manoeuvre a year-long application process, vocational testing, multiple medical exams, various appointments, and tedious visa applications before boarding. The train trip continued the process of orientation to a new life in West Germany and applicants clung to goals of success and adventure in spite of overcrowded, dirty, frigid, and at times inhumane trains, setting the stage for a fifty-year coexistence of Turks and Germans.

The previous chapter focused on the expectations of applicants on both the German and the Turkish side. This chapter turns to the first tangible interaction, the first parts of the guest worker program once it was set in motion. It examines the individuals – ranging from travelling applicants to intergovernmental officials – who were impacted on both sides of this nascent, post-war, transnational labour migration. Here guest workers' own excitement, expectations, and recollections fill in the standard narrative. Individual workers' construction of new social identities as guest workers emerged from a combination of West German officials' careful planning, the plans' subsequent unravelling, and the awkward negotiations of the recent German past.

Careful Planning Breaks Down

The terrible scenes and conditions Kobes described and questioned were certainly not what West German officials had planned or were aiming for. The Istanbul Liaison Office of the West German employment agency (BA) painstakingly debated every aspect of worker transportation to West Germany – from the travel provisions' calories to the number of train seats, recording minutiae in its files. At exactly 6:33 p.m. on 26 September 1961, the first official group of Turkish guest workers – a group of sixty-eight workers, headed to the Cologne Ford factory – arrived at the Munich Central Station.[12] The German Liaison Office in Istanbul planned the trip with precision, noting a full two weeks before its departure that the group would arrive in Belgrade at 11:30 p.m., leave Belgrade at 12:45a.m., and arrive in Munich at exactly 6:33 p.m. The escort for the trip, Mr Ibrahim Etzer, reported, "The trip from Istanbul to Munich passed without particular incident. The stop at the border and customs stations did not take more than the usual time."[13] However, this initial trip was not representative of the many that followed. From 1961 to 1973, around 866,000 Turkish workers came to West Germany; up until 1970, three-fourths came by officially organized train "transports."[14] Different agencies and national train administrations shared, or attempted to share, the responsibility of guest worker transportation with limited success, and, as the number of travelling workers increased, organization between agencies suffered.

However, the federal employment agency was certainly not indifferent to its recruits.

Detailed travel instructions demonstrated the agency's concern for its workers. *I'm Going to Germany*, an instructional pamphlet distributed to recruits, stated that trains would depart for West Germany from Istanbul at one o'clock in the afternoon daily, that the trip would last forty-four hours, and the trains would arrive in Munich at eight thirty in the morning.[15] A different pamphlet, *How to Go to Germany*, laid out the details of workers' packing allowances, down to how much cheese and olives (one kilogram) and how many cigarettes (ten cartons) were allowed.[16] It is difficult to know how officials distributed these instructions, how many workers had access to them and how many actually read them; one contemporary study noted that only 58 per cent of workers recalled such instructions.[17] Nevertheless, the pamphlets demonstrate a striking attention to detail. The BA also invested a great deal of time and money in securing nutritionally appropriate (e.g. 1,111.4 calories) provisions.[18] (Various West German firms also courted the agency for the lucrative deal of supplying provisions.)[19] A state laboratory in Munich even tested the nutritional, satiation, and germ values of provisions.[20] After the inaugural trip in September 1961, the official travel provisions included: "150 to 200 grams of cooked mutton, 150 to 200 grams of ground beef meatballs, 100 grams of baked mutton liver, 1 kilo Turkish bread, 1 pear, 1 apple and 500 grams of grapes, 2 small green cucumbers and 20 olives, 60 grams of cheese, 2 hardboiled eggs, 2 tomatoes, 3 yeast pastries, rice-stuffed grape leaves and, for drinking water, two 10-litre containers that could be filled."[21] In another demonstration of concern, a travel escort requested additional provisions and noted that it would be more appropriate to offer after arrival, instead of coffee, "a thinned yogurt drink," referring to the common Turkish drink *Ayran*.[22] (The yogurt drink was unknown in Germany, signified by several handwritten exclamation points next to the request.)[23] Cultural considerations of palate and dietary restrictions demonstrated West German officials' commitment to addressing more than just the functional aspects of the trip to West Germany.

On paper, officials also showed great concern about what was in workers' baggage. In their internal memos, for example, German and Austrian customs officials were apprehensive about the threat foreign sausages posed, in this case the Turkish spiced sausage – *sucuk* – which is similar to pepperoni, but made from lamb or beef.[24] German Rail repeatedly requested that the BA remind workers before departure, especially if they were Turkish, that they could not bring foreign meat products into West Germany.[25] Internal reports also reveal that custom officials would stop and thoroughly inspect all trains at the border, which would take hours if guest workers could not curb their "unusually large amounts" of baggage and foodstuffs.[26] Often such threats were idle: the reporter Kobes noted that an Austrian customs official had told him that it simply took too much time to "climb over the barricade of luggage in the aisles" and that the resulting delays would be "unbearable."[27] In other cases, travelling workers tried to take advantage of the situation to smuggle goods past customs officials, though they were not always successful. Customs officials discovered tobacco, spirits, and carpets, as well as huge sacks of potatoes and an entire train-compartment's worth of tanned hides that guest workers were trying to bring with them.[28]

To further complicate matters, BA officials who managed the departure from Istanbul did not necessarily enforce their own official baggage guidelines. One official noted that it was his policy to have passengers occupy fifty seats and leave twelve seats per car for luggage.[29] There was leeway in baggage storage, he argued, because "not every Turkish worker packed alike." Workers coming from Anatolia (who were about 30 per cent to 50 per cent of passengers), he explained, tended to carry a bag or small sack, while only 40 per cent of them carried a suitcase.[30] On the other hand, workers from Istanbul apparently averaged two suitcases apiece.[31] More than just casual about the regulations, this official was sympathetic to the fact that workers needed to pack clothes for an entire year: "Many of the Turks are in no position to spend the money they have earned in Germany for clothes," he noted, "[especially] when they would rather use it to take care of their families in Turkey."[32]

Many of the everyday aspects of guest worker travel were simply out of the BA's or applicants' control. First, there were simply too many people: BA officials accepted the majority of applicants, approximately 70 per cent of those who applied, and arranged their transportation to West Germany through either the Istanbul or the Ankara BA Liaison Office. Second, the BA faced the additional thorny situation of moving workers across borders and having to work with other national rail administrations, customs officials, and food-and-water suppliers. BA officials could neither standardize transportation nor guarantee that arrangements would be carried out as they had planned. International cooperation was not a hallmark of guest worker transportation. The German Employment Office in Istanbul sought to arrange guest workers' travel together with German Rail, Turkish Rail, Yugoslav Rail, and Bulgarian Rail administrations. National rail administrations, including the German National Rail, were either unable or unwilling to supply trains that could travel from Istanbul all the way to Munich.[33] Not only were neither Turkish Rail nor Yugoslav Rail willing to commit direct trains to Munich,[34] but no rail administration was willing to offer its best trains or enough cars either. The *Frankfurter Allgemeine Zeitung* reported in 1965 that because of a lack of cooperation there would be no relief in the near future for train travel in the Balkans: "German Rail knows the intolerable conditions of certain Balkan trains only too well ... For months they have attempted to have the train administrations in Yugoslavia, Greece, and Turkey contribute additional cars."[35] When the BA requested more train cars from Turkish Rail, Turkish Rail replied that it simply did not have extra cars to spare for the transport of workers to West Germany, as their extra train cars "were meant for tourists and not workers."[36] Either foreign rail administrations were uninterested in supporting the guest worker process or their hands were tied due to local economic concerns.[37] Therefore, according to an international agreement, each national rail administration would commit a certain number of cars for travel through its districts[38] – workers would travel part of the trip in one wagon and then change cars in another country's station until they reached West Germany.[39] Chaos ensued.[40]

Travelling workers bore the brunt of the disorganization: "Fight scenes over reserved seats" was a headline in the *Rheinische Post* in 1965 about a train in which travelling vacationers and foreign guest workers came to blows over reserved seats.[41] In one case, a train travelling from Istanbul to Munich stopped in Belgrade, where workers poured out of the train as soon as it stopped despite instructions shouted from a megaphone to stay on the train. As a result, twelve Turkish workers were left behind when the train continued on shortly thereafter.[42] In another case, sixty workers ended up scattered through a train amidst non-guest-worker passengers while a translator tried to "round them up" with a megaphone.[43] Workers, especially women, often reported having to stand in the trains because of a lack of reserved seats.[44] Officials could rarely guarantee the reserved seats for which passengers had paid, leading to frustration on all sides.work[45]

National rail administrations also reneged on commitments, making massive delays common.[46] By 1964, notes such as this were familiar: "The Yugoslavian train cars that were meant for today's planned departure did not arrive again."[47] Moreover, even when trains did arrive as planned, the number of cars and seats could range widely – from between 824 to 912 seats, for example.[48] Problems with arranging workers' timely departures from Istanbul continued for years,[49] and as late as 1970, workers could change trains and find no cars waiting for them, resulting in a "catastrophe" in which workers were required to press into already-full cars and stand the rest of the way to Munich.[50] In other cases, Yugoslav Rail employees would take Turkish workers out of their designated cars in Belgrade and distribute them in the remaining cars, forcing BA officials to search for them individually on the train platform in Munich.[51] Or the Yugoslavian police would co-opt a guest worker train for their own purposes and insist that their passengers be accommodated on already-full trains.[52] The BA noted with frustration that other countries' officials were "not innocent" in causing problems.[53] The BA had planned for efficiency, yet circumstances proved out of its control and travelling workers gathered repeatedly negative impressions of their handling.

The political and Cold War borders constantly reminded travelling Turkish workers of their dependence on West Germany for westward travel, another condition that solidified their new status as guest workers. West German officials had to gain Turkish workers entry to the other countries along the way in a Cold War context that could not be ignored. From time to time, foreign police thoroughly searched guest worker trains, reportedly looking for "refugees."[54] In addition, foreign consulates were hardly designed to process the vast amounts of paperwork necessary to secure travel visas for such a large population; visa delays were so bad that they could cause an entire trip's cancelation.[55] (In 1962, the Bulgarian and Yugoslavian consulates could process only twenty-five visas a day, creating a huge bottleneck of waiting workers in Istanbul.)[56] The visa delays caused up to three trains to be cancelled per week – at the very time that the German Liaison Office in Istanbul was trying to increase workers' departures. The BA appealed to the visa offices to treat Turkish guest workers as an exception "to not negatively impact the West German economy."[57] The visa delays caused more than congestion in Istanbul; they also affected workers' ability to make transfers to their final destinations upon arrival in West Germany.

Delayed departures often caused unplanned arrivals on weekends, when employers' representatives were rarely available.[58] As a result, many workers spent their first night in West Germany in the Munich train station.[59] One official noted: "The trains that arrive in Munich extremely delayed cause foreign workers to reach their final destinations after midnight. According to state-level employment office reports, this [late arrival] has led to great difficulties … I think it is necessary that the passengers who would reach final destinations after Munich between the hours of 1 and 5 a.m. as a rule should spend the night in the transfer station. The frequent train delays call for a revision of the distribution of arrival and provisions."[60] In hindsight, the amount of detail in both travellers' instructions and internal memos about guest worker travel is noteworthy but ironic considering that officials could not even guarantee all workers a *seat* on the train to West Germany, much less tackle the thornier issues of borders, visa processing, and the resulting delays. Workers ultimately bore the discomforts of the trips' disorganization, regardless of the cause, and were among the first passengers to traverse the new Cold War borders. Their entrance into the West German "economic miracle" was riddled with meaning.

Material Conditions and Responses

Not privy to the BA's angry letter exchanges, workers experienced the trip as it happened and drew their own conclusions. Travelling workers could not possibly have adequately prepared for the difficult journey to West Germany, as detailed instructions from the BA could not address unpredictable logistical problems or poor conditions. "The trip was like a cattle transport," a former worker, Yalcın, noted, "Everyone was nervous. No one knew the language. There was a translator who was watching over the whole train and acting like a superintendent [saying] 'Don't get up; stay in your seats'"[61] Elif recalled poor provisions: "It was a three-day [train] trip … [Our food] was a package that had canned goods … but there were no can openers. It was terribly planned."[62] Having already completed a tedious, year-long application process, workers endured the three-day train ride under horrific and exhausting conditions. Despite efforts to make the transition to West Germany as smooth as possible and to address critiques, arriving workers faced disappointments that coloured future relationships and threatened to tarnish West Germany's post-war image forever.

However, the BA's Istanbul Liaison Office, not indifferent to material conditions, often distinguished itself from the main office in Nuremberg in its concern for travelling workers. Individual officers, who had been living and working in Istanbul for years, openly worried about their applicants. When, due to missing cars or limited seating capacity, workers could not depart as planned, official BA policy dictated that they be "sent home" and given a new departure date, which could be up to three weeks later.[63] However, officers posted in Istanbul reported back to the BA in Nuremberg that applicants, especially those from Anatolia, had already travelled long distances to Istanbul (up to 1,700 kilometres) and had done so at their own expense, making a return home impossible.[64] During departure delays, the Istanbul BA Liaison Office sympathetically offered an extra food packet and a small amount of money in compensation.[65] One official even demonstrated his familiarity with Istanbul when he stated with apprehension that early morning departures would not work because the shared taxi *(dolmuş)* service, upon which many depended, did not run through the night and would force workers staying in Istanbul's outskirts to leave their residences in the afternoon the day before their departure to arrive at the train station on time.[66] "In my opinion," he noted, "it is not reasonable to have Turkish workers [leaving their homes] 8 to 10 hours early so that they then have to wait at the train station an additional 13 to 15 hours."[67] Employment bureau officials tried to keep the trip to West Germany orderly and humane by paying attention to detail where they could, such as in providing travel instructions, planning travel provisions, and organizing trip escorts. However, officials' inability to translate such attention to detail into practical implementation had consequences.

No aspect of guest worker transportation highlighted the confusion over responsibility, the employment bureau officials' impotence, and guest workers' inhumane train conditions more than trains' water supplies. German authorities expected that any train's local rail administrations would logically have adequate water supplies and clean facilities. "Not only is providing water a part of train service, [especially one] that is traveling for 53 hours," wrote an Istanbul BA official to headquarters in Nuremberg, "but also the cleanliness of the toilet and replenishment of toilet paper and of soap [is expected], just as it is common *on every long distance trip in Germany.*"[68] However, the problem was that this trip was not in Germany and that this train was designated as a *Sonderzug*, or "special train," only for guest workers. For drinking water, West German officials in Turkey issued water bottles before departure, instructing passengers to fill them before leaving and refill them as necessary during the trip.[69] Once en route, however, passengers rarely had a chance to refill their water bottles.[70] Because there were multiple bureaucracies involved, the problem of supplying water for the trains had no easy solution. "Trains that are coming from Bulgaria and Yugoslavia," an official in Istanbul reported to Nuremberg in 1965, "either have no water or only have limited water supplies."[71] Water containers on the trains that passed through the Balkans were not refilled during stops there, even when travel escorts insisted.[72] According to the train schedule, train authorities should have refilled water containers at stops in Svilengrad, Sofia, Belgrade, Zagreb, and Resenbach.[73] The only explanation given as to why the bottles were not refilled in the Balkans was that it was a time-consuming process, implying indifference.[74] BA officials continually reported problems with water and sanitation until as late as 1970.[75]

While the lack of water caused serious sanitation problems, officials appeared equally concerned about keeping trains clean. BA officials in Nuremberg hired travel escorts (one per two hundred applicants) to accompany travelling workers not only to handle group tickets and logistics but also to use megaphones to ensure "discipline" and "cleanliness."[76] Furthermore, condescension, especially in attempts to regulate behaviour on trains, poisoned the relationships between travelling applicants and their hosts. BA officials distributed paternalistic instructions admonishing passengers not to throw trash from train windows, to keep the toilets clean, and to be sparing with the water.[77] They warned against disembarking en route to "get water or to go shopping" and against damaging doors (by "shutting them violently") or windows (by boarding through them); passengers were also to stay in their seats and "take care of their health" during the trip.[78] Such instructions were naive at best in light of the substandard conditions on the trains.

Bureaucratic mismanagement had tangible and dangerous results for travellers. In one case, guest workers "stormed" a train when it arrived in Zagreb. The escort reported: "In the process, not only the doors, but mainly the windows were used to board. It was an appalling scene, as women and men climbed in like wild animals. It was as if a catastrophe had broken out and everyone wanted to come into the safety of the train."[79] The same train was also "confused with" one meant to take Greeks and Yugoslavs who were on vacation back to West Germany, and no one could prevent these additional passengers from boarding as well.[80] When the German escort tried to address Yugoslavian passengers, who were apparently "obtrusive" to travelling Turkish women, the difficult passengers replied, "This is Yugoslavia. You can't say anything here!"[81] During the rest of the trip, the cars were overstuffed and the aisles filled with luggage and people, just as Kobes had reported. The escort hoped that at the Austrian border, he could have the rail police deal with the extra passengers, but to no avail. The conductors, train police, and border police did not find it "worth their while" to deal with the situation on the train, and the escort, who was the official representative of the West German Employment Office, was only able to observe with horror.[82]

Despite the well-documented logistical problems, the BA and other administrations not based in Istanbul continued to blame "Mediter-ranean people" for problems en route. Implicit in the discussions of train sanitation was a commentary on the cleanliness of Turkish workers and of the cultural differences between Turks and Germans more generally. "Even though I am aware that some passengers are unfamiliar with the basin toilet," noted an Istanbul Liaison Office offi-cial, "the blame for the filth cannot be placed solely on the passengers [especially when] ... *Sonderzüge* [or "special trains"] from Bulgaria and Yugoslavia have absolutely no water or only very little."[83] The BA met with German Rail to improve the conditions on the trains and requested that the water "actually be supplied according to plan," as well as other solutions such as larger trashcans to prevent travellers from throwing their trash from the windows of crowded compart-ments.[84] For months the employment bureau fruitlessly continued to pass on to German Rail unanswered requests for water, toilet paper, and soap.[85]

Workers suffered because German Rail primarily provided the BA with small, slow, poorly provisioned local trains, which were hardly appropriate for long-distance travel. German Rail continually offered the slow-moving "B3y train" for guest worker travel. During the over-fifty-hour trip, the B3y had problems not just with water but also with heat, light, and a lack of storage space for luggage, and it was also extremely uncomfortable for passengers.[86] Workers complained about travelling for three days on bench seats without headrests, which was especially problematic for those sitting in the middle or on an aisle.[87] In response, German Rail lamely proposed attaching a headrest as a "com-fort improvement," but it is unclear if this was ever implemented.[88] This train became so synonymous with guest worker travel, that a display of its seat is included in the section on the guest worker program in the German Historical Museum in Berlin.

An Istanbul BA official responded with frustration to German Rail's offerings: "When, due to a lack of toilet paper, newspaper and packaging must be used [in the toilet] and there is no water to flush, it is no wonder that the toilets are stopped up and the filth reaches an unimaginable degree. So far, my comments on these problems have hardly had any impact."[89] Instead of addressing logistic problems, however, German Rail seemed primarily concerned with damage to their trains for which they blamed the passengers, specifically the ethnic Turks. German Rail told the BA in Nuremberg that the state of the guest workers' trains was unacceptable and, furthermore, a danger to public health: "Particularly the trains that are used for Turkish guest workers arrive in Munich in an indescribable state. I have attached a photo that unfortunately cannot entirely describe the extent of the unhygienic conditions on the train. Our workers repeatedly refuse to clean these unbelievably dirty trains. Several workers became sick to their stomachs when cleaning. Some of the cleaning ladies reported to have been bitten by fleas. State Health Department doctors ... report that cleaning these trains could cause an epidemic."[90]

Interestingly enough, while the employment bureau in Nuremberg was writing to German Rail about the poor conditions on the trains, it seems that German Rail was writing the employment bureau to complain. The employment bureau responded, in an internal memo in 1964, that it would request that travel escorts emphasize cleanliness to passengers en route and, more important, noted that if German Rail refused to clean the trains or refused to provide train service, it could interrupt recruitment.[91] In the eyes of the workers and the outside world, the same employment agency that issued instructions about how many olives one could pack seemed unable or unwilling to make the connection between the lack of water and the inhumane conditions on the trains or to take responsibility for it. However, the program depended on intergovernmental cooperation that never came to fruition. The BA failed to get its partners to commit to their plans.

After a year of discussion, BA officials broached the subject at an international conference for guest worker travel, noting that other rail administrations could no longer be delinquent in providing the necessary water, as it was clearly needed for sanitary reasons. Strikingly, in 1969, Nuremburg BA officials finally admitted that trains were not being filled with water or cleaned properly in an effort to keep delays to a minimum.[92] But this admission came too late. Starting in 1970, the German Employment Office began using airplanes to transport workers, especially female workers, to West Germany.[93] While the era of guest worker train transports was officially over, the relationships and negotiations that had occurred leading up to this point had a lasting impact.

Shaping West Germany's International Image

During the program's tenure both West German employers and the BA were forced to address Germany's historical legacy and assess their own roles in a new German narrative of imported foreign labour. The Second World War and the Holocaust tainted Germany's international image, influencing how many contemporaries and present-day scholars would approach Germany's guest worker program. Two perhaps surprising counternarratives complicate the dominant negative perceptions of guest workers in post-war West Germany. First, West German employers and officials recognized and responded to the image of West Germany they were portraying to the international community and to the German public.[94] Second, the focus of the subsequent section, workers' recollections undermined the trope of the "naïve, passive migrant" who was unwittingly exploited by the West German state. In both cases, the actors play to an outside audience as much as for themselves. Indeed, the employers, BA officials, the German public, and the applicants alike were cognizant of their own agency within this important test case and, significantly, within the creation of the historical record.

The eyes of the international media motivated West German employers to consider how the guest worker program and its problems could cast all of post-war West Germany in an all-too-familiar bad light. West German employers, the ultimate destination of travelling workers, were not indifferent to workers' transportation problems and grew impatient, though it was not empathy alone that motivated them. As noted in the introduction to this book, one West German factory owner complained that when his arrived workers had to wait an additional eighteen hours on a train platform, the BA was not presenting a "good calling card" for West Germany."[95] As evidenced in their own internal memos, employment bureau officials did indeed agree that guest worker transportation presented a negative image of West Germany and its post-war institutions, yet they remained largely impotent when it came to addressing the larger issues.

Eerie comparisons with pre-1945 scenes also troubled many West Germans who witnessed guest workers' arrival. When delayed applicants arrived at the Munich Central Station (the first stop in West Germany for workers arriving from Italy, Greece, Turkey, and Yugoslavia), German Rail would not allow them to loiter on the platforms.[96] As a result, the police escorted workers to a former air-raid shelter, causing traffic delays and, more important, parading "marching columns" of bedraggled people through the streets – a disturbing image for the post-war Federal Republic.[97] In an attempt to address this problematic public image, authorities took advantage of a subterranean air-raid shelter that was directly beneath the Munich Central Station. At the end of arrival platform eleven, there were stairs leading directly into the bunker, which authorities had retrofitted to serve as a waiting room. The Munich station bunker was not only convenient but also kept arriving guest workers out of sight of the general public.[98] The shadow of Germany's recent past was all too prominent for all involved. The train trip to Germany not only shaped the guest workers' identity as a category but also reinforced Germany's identity and reputation in negative and certainly unwanted ways.

One travelling worker, Cahit, changed into fresh clothes and shaved before getting off the train in Munich in 1964, hoping to be greeted by German girls. Instead he was led into the bunker. "They said, 'You will sleep here, and tomorrow you will go to Berlin.' We actually thought there would be German girls. It was a shock."[99] Speaking about his night in the Munich bunker, another worker, Erol, said: "We got off [the train in Munich] around morning. When we got off the train, they treated us like we were a bunch of bums … [The] Turkish workers who came from Anatolia … were wearing çarık [rawhide sandals] on their feet and yorgan [traditional quilt bags] as clothing. We formed a double line [we lined up in pairs] and followed a translator who had a megaphone … [We] were treated like soldiers, lining up. Under the station there were small dark rooms [cellar]."[100] However, the Munich Central Station was not an entirely negative experience. First-aid stations assisted travellers and organized clothing drives together with local charities and the Red Cross to outfit arriving workers, such as the workers from Anatolia, for Germany's climate.[101] The efforts of the Munich Train Station's staff to aid arriving workers demonstrate a level of concern for the workers that sharply contrasts with their negative experiences during the trip.

Guest workers' train travel had an even more direct historical connotation for West Germany in its nomenclature, especially considering the role of "transports" – a euphemism used by the Reichsbahn to refer to forced removal and mass transportation by cattle cars with inhumane conditions to collection and death camps – during the Holocaust. Strikingly, the BA continued until 1955 to refer to post-war guest workers as *Fremdarbeiter* (the same term used for foreign forced labour before 1945). The West German press even continued to use the term well into the mid-1960s.[102] *Gastarbeiter* (guest worker) and *Ausländische*

Mitarbeiter (foreign co-worker) were examples of terms deemed more palatable and appropriate for the new Federal Republic and were introduced in the 1950s as acceptable alternatives. And yet, almost two decades later on 21 September 1972, the Union for Wood and Plastics wrote to the Federal Ministry for Labour and Social Affairs to formally request a name change for guest worker train transportation. The union suggested that the historically loaded term *Transportlisten* (transport list) be replaced with the term *Sammelreiseliste* (group-trip list).[103] The union laid bare the negative historical connotations: "When humanitarian conditions are a given, then naturally the terminology should avoid being, or at least be acknowledged as being, the same as used by the SS and the *Reichsbahn* for "Deportation," for prisoners and for *Fremdarbeiter* ... We recognize that the employment bureau attempts to make the trip as pleasant as possible ... therefore, the contradiction is all the more crass for the promotion of our job market that, up until arrival, human conditions have fallen by the wayside."[104] The union's reference to the promotion of "[the West German] job market" highlights the importance of the international gaze. As a result, on 24 October 1972, the federal employment agency sent a memo to all foreign liaison offices as well as to national labour offices noting a terminology change for all dealings with foreign workers' travel to West Germany. It wrote, "The term *Transportlist* [transport list] will be immediately replaced with *Sammelreise* [group trip]; *Transportleiter* or *Transportbegleiter* [transport guide] replaced with *Reiseleiter* or *Reisebegleiter* [trip guide] ... *Transportteilnehmer* [transport participant] with *Reiseteilnehmer* [trip participant] and so forth."[105] However, by 1972 it was too late to take into consideration the historical connotations of guest worker transportation, as the damage had already been done. Many of the various individuals involved had already chosen their answers to the Austrian reporter's initial questions. Travelling workers were especially aware of the roles they were playing in post-war Germany's evolving history.

Turkey's Departing Workers

In spite of the difficulties of the application process, a lack of clear information, and, for many, the extreme discomfort of the medical exam, the guest worker program remained immensely popular for years, with more applicants than officials could process. At the end of 1970, the federal employment bureau reported that 94,167 Turks, 20,036 of whom were women, had left for West Germany.[106] Altogether, 316,436 foreign workers entered West Germany in 1970. However, the number of Turkish guest workers who entered West Germany was always just the tip of the iceberg because it never represented those who were waiting for departure. In 1970, almost 1.5 million Turkish workers were waiting to go to West Germany.[107] According to a 1974 Istanbul University study, more than 300,000 applications piled up yearly while placements remained under 100,000 a year.[108] By July 1973, the last year of official recruitment, approximately 750,000 Turks had emigrated to West Germany through the legal channels set up by the federal employment bureau.[109]

Like Germany, the Turkish Republic had careful plans and research to justify sending its citizens to West Germany. Contemporary reports from the period, such as the 1970 report by Turkish social scientist Ahmet Aker, offered cautionary tales about the program that largely fell on deaf ears. Aker's study of departing Turkish workers concluded that, contrary to government plans and proclamations, the best-educated, most-skilled, and fittest workers were departing Turkey.[110] In his study, Aker outlined all of the positive outcomes that Turkish government officials had cited as reasons to participate in the program and then disputed them. Aker found that instead of exporting unskilled labour, Turkey was losing citizens with higher average education rates (when compared with the rest of the country, which was only 55 per cent literate) and that more than 90 per cent of applicants surveyed were not unemployed, but rather had jobs sometimes as recently as up to three weeks before their departure.[111] Aker warned of an impending and dangerous deskilling in Turkey's remaining industrial sectors. He also dispelled myths of workers reinvesting and invigorating the Turkish economy. The incoming personal savings and remittances were not enough to establish large-scale industrial enterprises in Turkey without partnerships or corporate arrangements, many of which had tragic results: "Entering into partnerships with locally established entrepreneurs has often led to the liquidation of the returning [worker's assets] and the evaporation of his savings through fraudulent bankruptcies engineered by the more experienced established partners."[112]

The migration to West Germany was also part of a larger east-to-west migration in Turkey that was leaving the easternmost regions poorer and more desolate than before, in direct conflict with initial aims of the agreement: "[Turkey's] poorer regions seem to be acting as training grounds for labour that will then seek employment in richer areas – a task

they are least equipped to do and can least afford ... [Turkey is export-
ing] skills that are already of short supply within the region itself."[113]
Departure from Turkey was risky and melancholy not just for the individual but also for the prospects of Turkey's development and economic
future, according to the contemporary studies. In short, in light of such
evidence, the Republic of Turkey knew as early as 1970 that its plans
and ideas had been debunked but did little to acknowledge this. Despite
such advisory reports from contemporary social scientists, the migration of workers to West Germany had become a movement that Turkish
government officials could not stop, just as the West German officials
had trouble regulating it. At the same time, many departing workers
turned blind eyes to cautionary tales, even when they were reported
predeparture.

The Turkish press also increasingly criticized workers' poor conditions and treatment in West Germany, even as early in the program as
1962.[114] Yet even if those back home could not see tangible results of success, or of failure for that matter – even as late as ten years after the program started – literally millions were waiting for their turn to depart.
Turkish workers made up their minds to go to West Germany, refusing
to see the contemporary evidence that the program was not what they
had hoped. Whether they decided based on media reports, information
published by the employment office, or because or even in spite of what
they might have heard about life in West Germany, the decision was
theirs. In most cases the opportunity to make more money – Turkish
workers could expect to earn in Germany four times as much as what
they could in Turkey – trumped other concerns.[115] The bilateral guest
worker agreements set up migration to a nation that was vastly more
prosperous than the one from which the migrants came. Therefore, it is
important to examine what steps, if any, government agencies on both
sides took to address the implications of this financial inequality, not to
mention the potential problems that different cultural norms, religious
traditions, and huge language barriers could cause.

Becoming a Guest Worker

Guest workers fit uncomfortably into existing analytic categories (e.g.,
diaspora, immigrant, and working class) while still overlapping with
these groups. Any coherent narrative of "guest workers" will be a constructed fiction because paradoxes abound. Kobes pointedly blamed
the German National Rail directly, and the BA indirectly, of deliberately

overlooking inhumane conditions, while in fact the BA was mired in negotiations with various organizations in an attempt to address poor conditions for which it felt responsible. This narrative moves away from the initial wave of sociological and ethnographic studies that emphasized hardship and joins more recent scholarship in recognizing workers' agency – skirting rules and holding onto their initial excitement and ambition.[116] While post-war West Germany was unable to let go of its past, the travelling Turkish workers interviewed here refused to let go of their future.

This section turns to guest workers' recollections and highlights their ambitions and disappointments, offering insight into unexplored aspects of becoming a "guest worker."[117] The interviewees were workers, not authors or scholars, and their narratives begin in Turkey with their initial decisions to leave, their application procedures, and their train travel to West Germany. In the same interviews, though, workers' recollections about their initial excitement for a new life in West Germany accompany if not trump the poor experiences, recasting their narratives as ones in which they retain historical agency. "As I was looking out of the window of the train, noticing that we were crossing the border from Turkey into Bulgaria, I thought, I will return in five to ten years a millionaire," recalled Cahit.[118] In spite of poor conditions while they were in transit, former workers often insist upon having had a sense of adventure, excitement, apprehension, and – above all else – ambition in their initial decision to move to West Germany. Erol, who commented on the chaos at departure in the previous chapter, noted that he also wanted to come to West Germany for adventure, especially to meet women. He described the misery of his trip to West Germany, thusly: "They placed bags in our hands together with plastic water canisters at the Vinegar Seller's Station, and with them we boarded a local train. There were no compartments; it was open. It was a three-and-a-half day trip by train. Excuse me please [for saying this] but there was no water to use for cleaning one's backside [after using the toilet]. We were also unshaven … We took turns sleeping in the aisles on newspaper and in the places meant for luggage. We arrived in a state of agony and torment."[119] Yet Erol also highlighted his excitement: "There was a guy with a Wilkinson razor … and we shaved with it before we got off the train in Munich. After all, we had come for the women; so to look good, to look handsome, we shaved with the bottled soda pop that we had picked up in Yugoslavia."[120] Even in the face of inhumane conditions, Erol anticipated no problems in achieving his personal goals. He noted that he had gone to West Germany for an urban lifestyle – to see the latest fashions (especially the disco boots) and nightlife; it was an adventure, and he considered the poor treatment just a hiccup in his larger ambitions for success.[121]

Turkish guest workers sought their own economic miracles by going to West Germany, but the decision, application, and trip there changed them and their extended families irreversibly before they even entered the country. Despite the obvious economic reasons for going to West Germany, the decision to stay and create a new life there resulted from a series of negotiations before departure and along the way that extended beyond the economic.

Even when eschewing positive narratives of excitement and ambitious goals, workers who recalled negative experiences often chose to accompany them with comments on how they negotiated the conditions, revising their history with their own recollections. One man, M., began with a common narrative: he came to West Germany in 1962, leaving his wife and children behind with the plan to get a vocational education for two years and then return to Turkey; he worked for Ford in Cologne for four years.[122] "Forget about [speaking] German; the workers were the kind of people who barely knew Turkish," he commented, continuing, "the Turks' mental state was bad. Including me, no one got what he was hoping for. However, returning to Turkey would have been humiliating: Being unsuccessful ... was a shame so we had to stand being there." One place M. found solace was in a newly founded Turkish association, where he would play his *bağlama*, or saz (a long-necked lute, traditionally used in Ottoman and Turkish music). He gained the reputation and title *aşık*, or troubadour, which he denied, saying, "I am not a poet."[123] But he recalled climbing up the stage at the Turkish association one night and announcing to the clapping crowd that he was going to "tell them an epic about our coming to Germany." He continued: "Let's call it 'Germany Epic.' They clapped a lot. I wasn't prepared at all and said, 'Forgive me if this doesn't rhyme.' I closed my eyes and started playing. I sang about the day we left Turkey from the Vinegar Seller's Station, the difficulties we had in Zagreb, changing trains on a winter day, and the day we came to the Cologne train station. We heard the harmonica playing, but we couldn't figure out what it was. It turned out that they were welcoming us with a band."[124] Of all of his memories, M. chose to begin "Germany Epic" with his departure from Istanbul and travel to West Germany. His story begins in Turkey, and his first vivid memory is the changing of trains in Zagreb. For him, and many others, the train trip to West Germany represented a point of personal transition into someone and something else; it was an emotional, personal, and transformative journey.

Conclusion

After arrival in West Germany, guest workers were not necessarily surprised by the substandard living arrangements and difficult work conditions that awaited them. The train trip offered workers the first clues to their future treatment as guest workers, and the travel conditions also predisposed them to certain views of West German employers and authorities, which would come to a head years later in labour conflicts and national debates. Applicants could use the application and travel period to focus on their goals for life in West Germany and, as will be seen in the next chapter, "stayed" despite the poor conditions – after all they had gone through to get to West Germany, why would they leave? The train trip also illuminated the dynamic of the entire guest worker program for years to come – good intentions on the part of officials followed by a lack of implementation. And yet intergovernmental exchanges, plans, and failures cannot possibility capture the subjective, transnational experience of individual guest workers, whose narratives began even before they boarded the first train. This population, haphazardly thrust together through common, often-miserable classed experiences, formed a new vanguard of global labour migrants as post-war West Germany tentatively and self-consciously stepped back into the spotlight of Western industrial production in the new Cold War order.

Post-war guest worker programs between West Germany and southern European and African countries offered a lens through which to evaluate Germany's evolving relationship with foreign labour and its historical legacy. Within these considerations of historical continuities versus ruptures, though, existed individuals with their own agendas who disrupted dominant conceptions and expectations. The questions the Austrian newspaper asked remain relevant, but there is more to the story. Whether the BA and West German employers were acting out of empathy or were driven by a perceived evaluating international gaze is unclear, but they did acknowledge their roles and responsibilities towards guest workers in ways not previously highlighted. Guest workers, too, defied existing narratives and analytic categories, as they transported their "life space" – the site of conscious actors functioning within their cultures and communities – over borders and as situations evolved.[125] These workers created an interesting hybrid working-class and immigrant community. This community remained consistently unstable, as it was in motion and under constant redefinition from multiple sides. The various actors involved – whether they came from the media, official positions, workplaces, or the applicant pool – were cognizant of their roles in the continuing debates over Germany's legacy, its new commitment to democracy, and its sense of atonement for the past. The train journey had transformed these individuals into the complex and constructed category of "guest worker," but workers' own plans and dreams defied pat categorization. "In this train, you see, anything is possible," the conductor told Kobes, and he was right.[126]

3

Finding Homes

"Home life as it is understood in Central Europe might ... have been unknown to many [guest workers] ... when they first took up residence in the Federal Republic of Germany," notes social scientist Ursula Mehrländer in her 1974 study on foreign workers' living conditions.[1] For Merhländer, industrialization preceded cultural development, including a sense of *Wohnkultur* – the uniquely German concept of "home culture," encompassing a range of meanings from home decor to domestic culture. Mehrländer's point was that economic development was linked to cultural refinement: "Because of their socio-economic background, the majority of foreign workers will have had no opportunity to be influenced by these factors as far as ... way of living and home life are concerned."[2] However, once employed as industrial labourers in West Germany, these workers could reach a higher living style: "[The] need for cleanliness, order and decoration in the home ... have to be interpreted in part as a direct result of industrial activity and factory discipline."[3] As Mehrländer's pedantic tone implies, the guest worker program was much more than a contract for labour. It also included a search for home, as well as ever-evolving social identities and relationships, not just between employers and employees at work but also in domestic and social realms. How foreign workers lived and socialized in West Germany was as important, if not more so, as work life for reflecting new relationships between Germans and foreign workers in the post-war period.

For many workers, housing in West Germany, which was often employer-owned dormitories, defined their lives much more than their jobs did.[4] In interviews, memoirs, novels, and films about life in West Germany, workers mention their dormitories much more often than their workplaces.[5] The West German federal employment agency required employers to supply housing, but employers only loosely, if at all, followed up on this regulation.[6] In his state-sanctioned study of workers' housing in North Rhine-Westphalia, Ernst Zieris found that the West German housing market could not handle the influx of foreign workers, leading to extreme cases of improvisation such as housing workers in garden huts, cellars, and attics.[7] Mehrländer's 1974 study also reported a wide range of housing that included hostels, private rooms, and barracks. Most interesting, though, were the tight quarters: a third of those she interviewed shared rooms that were less than fifteen square metres, while 60 per cent of interviewees shared rooms that were less than twenty square metres.[8] On the whole, workers felt their rent was too high and the furnishings substandard.[9] Even worse, isolating foreign workers seemed to be by design, as the idea of housing temporary foreign workers together with German workers was not what the BA had in mind.[10]

This chapter addresses failed attempts at and missed opportunities for informal interaction between Turkish guest workers and their hosts, specifically the Germans who managed their housing. Similar to the train ride to West Germany as discussed in chapter 2, workers' life spaces existed far from the shop floor. In many ways, employer-owned dormitories could have provided at the very least the perfect incubator for the types of daily interactions and cultural exchange necessary for mutual understanding and, at best, integration. Instead, poor interactions between West German dorm managers and foreign residents exacerbated misunderstandings and resentment, driving the two groups even further apart. Housing arrangements also fueled workers' need for escapism in their private lives. As we will see in the next chapter, many workers went as far as East Berlin to find a sense of self and to escape from their social realities in West Germany.

In this case study, flawed arrangements and miscalculations contrast with meticulous records and good intentions. Unfortunately, however, managers' substantial efforts and attention stemmed from desires to control and judge workers, not to engage with or integrate them. Ironically, few positive interactions occurred between Turkish workers and those closest to them – West Germans who interacted with them daily in their dormitories. In short, though the bilateral agreements required employers to provide housing, there were few attempts to provide real homes. Moments of assimilation, integration, and social cohesion could have germinated in the daily close contact, but they did not, eventually contributing to larger political issues, including the labour activism of the 1970s (as we will see in chapter 5) and the social debates of the late 1980s and beyond. Workers' reactions to and negotiations of their stressful housing situations demonstrate coping mechanisms for a post-war society that was unable to come to terms with its new and major demographic shift.

Max Frisch famously described the guest worker program with his oft-quoted saying "They called for workers, but people came," and Frisch's comment succinctly raises the issue of what workers are when they are not *at work*: what it could mean for a guest worker to live and not just work in West Germany.[11] Both employers and workers tried to negotiate how guest workers should spend their time while not working, including navigating social lives in West Germany. Workers struggled to create their home lives and negotiated private time and spaces in the face of severe restrictions. Yet the status of "guest worker" proved to be a category that workers could not escape at the end of the workday or at home because workers' treatment outside work reinforced their positions in society. Despite their categorization, guest workers arrived in West Germany with their own notions of self-determination that challenged power relations both at work and "at home."

Housing among the Rubble

"It is a problem to find good and cheap housing in Germany today," reported the 1964 instructional booklet *Hallo Mustafa!* "I can understand your worries, Dear Mustafa," the author continued, "but you must also remember that twenty years ago, Germany was a pile of rubble."[12] Indeed, Germany's recent past did provide a troubling aspect of guest worker housing.[13] Destroyed cities and housing shortages, the ever-increasing population of diverse foreign workers, and the historical burden of Germany's recent past combined to form the dynamics of the new West German nation. A West German newspaper's announcement that "the treatment of guest workers would be regarded a test case for the sincerity of Germans' commitment to democracy" points to the historic burden placed on the shoulders of ordinary West Germans.[14] Indeed, amid massive post-war migrations, for West Germany in particular, the post-war period was meant to be a rebirth from its dark past – a moment in which West Germany was conscious of its perception on the world stage.

The palpable presence of the past and the concern over Germany's international image perhaps explain why, according to Karen Schön-wälder, there was little open conflict among Germans and foreigners, embarrassing national anti-immigrant campaigns, or other public out-breaks of "residue from the past."[15] This public silence meant, however, that Germans' attitudes towards the large influx of foreigners were perhaps internalized and pushed to the private sphere. The issue of housing foreign workers provides insight into the interactions between West Germans and foreign workers behind closed doors – clues to West Germans' thoughts about their new neighbours and the reverse.

Workers' dormitories, barracks, and makeshift housing have an enduring and problematic history in Germany. In the nineteenth cen-tury, the Krupp Company built workers' colonies to provide housing (as well as parks, schools, libraries, and recreation grounds) as part of a larger worker welfare and insurance plan. Included in Krupp's good-will, however, was a plan to maintain control over workers and their lives to prevent the "misuse" of leisure time, produce better workers, and thwart labour organizing.[16] Workers' housing took a troubling turn when guest workers' employers in the 1950s and 1960s reused housing that had been used for prisoners and slave labourers during the war, leading some to wonder if Germany could break away from an inherently xenophobic tradition of *Lager*, or camps.[17] Historian Ulrich Herbert wrote that workers' facilities were historical placeholders, in which workers were part of a troubling replacement process: "Many towns and villages had camps of barracks that had been occupied by a succession of outside laborers ... [including] work detachments of the National Labor Service ... in the 1930s, then *Fremdarbeiter* [foreign workers] during the war, later on by (largely Jewish) DPs, and finally by expellees from the East, only to be utilized starting in the early 1960s as camps for *Gastarbeiter* [guest workers]."[18] This succession implies that guest workers participated in a linear history of exploitation and perhaps were even interchangeable with the preceding forced labour. However, post-war West Germany had little in common with the nation-building, imperialist, racial agenda of the previous regime.

More generally, housing shortages were not unique to foreign work-ers: after the Second World War, twenty million Germans were home-less because the vast majority of destroyed buildings were apartment houses.[19] Allied bombing raids had destroyed up to 80 per cent of resi-dential areas in some cities.[20] Good intentions did not matter either: the 1949 constitution guaranteed the rights of *Vertriebene*, or ethnic German expellees, and yet they were just as unlikely to have proper housing even well into the 1960s. The expectation for *Vertriebene* was that they would move elsewhere in West Germany, for guest workers, however, the expectation was that their accommodations would be continuously reused by subsequent waves of workers following the rotation principle. From the beginning, housing for German workers was distinguished from housing for foreign workers, with lower expectations for foreigners' housing; housing for mixed populations of German and foreign workers was not considered.[21] As in the preceding centuries, guest workers' employers used housing, in addition to work, to form relationships with their foreign employees – a relationship that lay somewhere between Krupp's paternalism and forced labour's extreme utility.

Because many foreign workers' dormitories were on company property, the distinction between work and home blurred. "The dormitory was on the factory property and was fenced in with barbed wire," one former worker said. "Except for the translator, no one was allowed in. Only the director was German, and the rest were all foreign women, many from Turkey."[22] Other workers' dormitories were, conversely, isolated from work and surrounding towns, leading to feelings of seclusion. Elif recalled: "[We worked] eight full hours, plus an hour to travel there and an hour to travel back. Ten hours you are on the go and then when you come home, you are not at home but rather in barracks ... it was military-like."[23] Employer-controlled housing, in addition to rigid work schedules, contributed to workers' sentiments that employers managed their entire lives. Such work and living arrangements also limited contact with local German residents. Historian Heide Fehrenbach writes that post-war Germany's racial re-education did not come solely from official programs but also from social interactions with occupation troops and from observations of social relations among multi-ethnic American occupation forces.[24] However, guest worker housing prevented such social interactions between West Germans and foreign workers; instead, it kept workers out of public view and, therefore, was perhaps complicit in sustaining negative attitudes about a largely unknown population.

Life in the dormitories was also as stressful, if not more so, as life at work because of the mental toll that the structure and isolation from society exacted. Elif reported that she used her active imagination to make dormitory life more liveable: "I lied to myself back then. I thought [to myself], 'Elif, imagine you are at a boarding school and in the mornings you go to the factory and that means [you are at] school, and evenings you come back to the boarding school, everyone together.' Otherwise you can't stand it. You have to always lie to yourself."[25] Elif told me that one of the most famous authors of the guest worker experience, Emine Sevgi Özdamar, worked at the *Telefunken* radio and television factory in Berlin with her and also lived in her dorm.

Özdamar's popular semi-autobiographical novel, *Die Brücke vom Goldenen Horn*, or "The Bridge of the Golden Horn," is one of the most well-known recollections of guest worker dorm life. Özdamar herself arrived in Berlin at the age of nineteen as a guest worker. In the novel, the protagonist, also a single woman from Turkey, speaks of life in the "*Wonaym*," mimicking a Turkish mispronunciation of the German word *Wohnheim*, or dormitory. The novel's main character describes life in a typical employer-owned dormitory: "I lived with many women in a women's dormitory; *Wonaym*, we said."[26] She continues: "We all worked in the radio factory … We got up at 5a.m. In the rooms there were six beds, always stacked one on top of the other."[27] The word *Wonaym* plays on the idea that workers were not quite at home, unable even to pronounce where they lived.

Dormitory standards, however, evolved through a process of negotiation over the course of labour recruitment in the 1950s and early 1960s. The German government wanted to ensure that workers would have housing waiting for them in Germany and made employers responsible for providing it. In 1954, the German Commission for Employment in Italy, the first country to enter into a guest worker agreement with the Federal Republic, set the precedent for future arrangements. In this initial agreement, the German-Italian commission made providing "adequate housing" for workers a condition upon which obtaining workers was dependent.[28] To clarify what officials meant by "adequate housing," in 1959, the government updated the 1934 Law of Housing Regulation to include the following specifications: rooms could have a maximum of six people and had to provide an "airspace" in bed of at least ten centimetres above each person, a lockable cabinet, a place at a table, a place to sit down, and, in the dorms in general, a toilet for every fifteen people.[29] These requirements provided a minimum standard at a time when employers had to find a pillow for every head and housing for a large population very quickly. German officials demanded that employers provide housing because they were not only concerned with workers' well-being but were also apprehensive that foreign workers would stress the already-overburdened post-war housing market. Indeed, German officials approved of hiring foreign workers at least partially because they could be seasonal workers and, therefore, housed in barracks or other such structures that lay outside the standard housing market.

Making employers responsible for housing resulted in great variety of housing options.[30] Some employers resorted to makeshift housing, especially in the initial years, including condemned houses, cellar apartments, attic apartments, garden huts, retrofitted production plants, warehouses, and management offices.[31] As might be expected, many workers found such makeshift housing unsatisfactory, and complaints of poor accommodations prompted the West German government to invest in additional accommodations: in 1960, the government agreed to invest one hundred million German marks in the construction of *Ausländerwohnheimen*, or "dormitories for foreigners," and in 1963 it invested an additional two hundred million German marks.[32]

Starting in October 1960, the federal employment agency allotted financial support for the construction of housing for guest workers with the idea that it could later be used, without significant renovation, as more permanent housing for the general population.[33] The BA planned to distribute these additional funds with specific stipulations. For example, the dorm's property should be "secure" for the foreign workers yet should not be too isolated from the German population. Also, and more ambiguously, the housing was supposed to satisfy the foreign workers' "special needs" and, most important, offer a "homelike environment" that would enable an "individual lifestyle."[34] Foreign workers' "special needs" remained an unarticulated phrase, and the employment agency never specified how these regulations were to be enforced.

"Special needs" could be a reference to the religious requirements of Muslim workers. A mining company noted, for example: "Prayer rooms were prepared for our Turkish residents. Special toilets were also arranged for this group of workers."[35] Both the prayer rooms and the "special" (presumably "Eastern-style" in-floor) toilets' proposed construction suggest that these employers were attempting to demonstrate cultural sensitivity. However, such reports are rare. In the end, there is no evidence that policy makers tried to enforce these standards, especially after 1961, when the population of foreign workers increased exponentially. Whether intentional or unintentional, guest workers rarely lived in constructions that provided the stipulated "homelike environment" or enabled an "individual lifestyle." In fact, temporary solutions lasted for years. The Volkswagen Company in 1962 lodged four thousand Italian workers in forty-eight wooden houses and, by 1966, six thousand workers in fifty-eight houses. For nine years Volkswagen stuck with a provisional arrangement that was designed during the initial months of recruitment.[36]

Stressful living conditions, such as overcrowding, compounded the pressure stemming from the adjustments that workers had to make – such as learning a new language, dealing with new customs, and working especially long hours. Despite negotiations between employers and the employment agency over housing requirements, workers' wages, and other details outlined in contracts distributed to workers in Turkey before departure, there were few guarantees after arrival in the Federal Republic. Indeed, Cahit reported that when he and his cohort arrived in West Germany, they had nowhere to live: "We found that our companies didn't even have any accommodations for the workers who had come before us. For eight months we didn't have any place to sleep; they let us sleep here and there. I stayed in a church."[37] The stay in the church, however, was temporary: "After two to three months, a group of sixty to seventy Turks joined us. But unfortunately the church had to let them go because they [the new group of Turks] were making too much noise. The Turks didn't want to accept the rule that you have to be quiet in a church. I continued to stay there alone. They didn't let me go because they liked me very much."[38] In short, Cahit apparently stayed because they "liked" him.

Finding housing outside factory-owned dormitories was difficult not only because of a general housing shortage in post-war Germany but because of negative impressions of foreign workers – not everyone was as well liked as Cahit. *Hallo Mustafa!*, for example, informed foreign workers that they faced enduring stereotypes: "I know that most Germans refuse, or only reluctantly rent rooms or apartments to foreigners. There are still many stereotypes at work and, here and there, also a certain animosity and contempt [towards foreigners]."[39] Yet at the same time, *Hallo Mustafa!* reaffirmed and excused the very attitudes that made finding housing a challenge for many: "[But] I would like to tell you openly that we sometimes shake our heads when we come across many foreigners' customs in relation to their homes. The order and cleanliness leaves much to be desired."[40] The "we" in "we sometimes shake our heads" presents a unified German perspective just as it portrays a monolithic group of foreigners. The author goes so far as to explain that living in a civilized manner is a characteristic that many foreign workers lack because they do not come from a "highly developed" country in which a certain affluence is taken for granted: "I can understand that in your climate the home and its inviting warmth and coziness do not play as large a role as in our latitude [or part of the world]. It would be too much to ask of many poor people to expect a sense for 'culture of the home' [*Wohnkultur*] comparable to that in a highly-developed country with certain prosperity."[41] The author, as in Mehrländer's 1974 "scientific study," implies that guest workers cannot understand *Wohnkultur*, lending an ethnic Germanness to a warm and cozy home life, and an inherent excuse for accompanying housing discrimination. The "poor people" and "highly-developed country" remarks in *Hallo Mustafa!* set up a class contrast between the Germans and their foreign guests, falsely putting all Germans in the latter category and all foreign workers in the former. The same author – who prefaced the housing section by stating that Germany was a pile of rubble twenty years ago and was currently in the midst of a housing shortage – nevertheless draws on the grandeur of either an earlier era or an imagined future.

Indeed, the author's implications coincided with a new post-war chauvinism, or the idea that West Germans could understand the recruitment of foreign workers as evidence of their own civic, economic, and cultural superiority. Schönwälder has pointed out this new post-war nationalism: "Germans were invited to interpret the recruitment of thousands of foreign workers as evidence ... of their role as a leading civic force in Europe and even as political educators."[42] This sense of German or European superiority also extended to Turkish workers, who themselves had expected more from West Germany. When a Turkish representative of the German Federal Trade Union audited various workers' dorms, he noted that he found the kind of housing one might expect of an "underdeveloped country" but certainly not of the Federal Republic of Germany.[43]

Despite being an instructional pamphlet, *Hallo Mustafa!* certainly did not provide a clear picture of life inside workers' dormitories. Illustrations and photographs in the booklet show pictures of men sleeping alone in spacious rooms instead of the more common bunk beds, with six people to a room. An illustration from *Hallo Mustafa!*'s housing section portrays a worker in bed alone, looking longingly at a picture, presumably of his family back home, whom he supports from abroad – and to whom he will presumably return (see figure 6). He has a plush duvet and a shelf of books above his head – not realistic expectations for guest workers. In contrast, it was much more common for workers to live in small, crowded spaces, as seen in a photograph of a Ford dormitory from 1963.[44]

Erol described his dorm room, which he shared with three other people, as being much like one in the photograph: a tiny, sixteen-square-metre

6 "At home."

Source: Maturi, *Hallo Mustafa!*, 427.

space with bunk beds, sinks, and a double-door cabinet. For Erol, life in the dorms was a psychological nightmare; he could not sleep at night and attributed this, at least partially, to "the smell of bad breath and feet."[45] Unfortunately, even though overcrowding taxed dormitory resources, the population of foreign workers was ever increasing.[46] Employers faced the task of housing an overwhelming and ever increasing influx of workers – workers who had waited for years to get a chance to come to West Germany and, therefore, would accept most anything. Initially, both workers and employers tolerated subpar housing: both thought it would be temporary, and they were eager to earn money and begin production, respectively. Problems arose, however, as temporary fixes became permanent situations.

Life inside the Dormitories: Chaos and Control

In 1971, the German Trade Union Federation (the umbrella organization for organized labour) sent a representative to evaluate Turkish workers' dormitories and to speak with residents, dorm managers, and translators. Mete Atsu, himself a bilingual Turkish man, was sent to dozens of dorms in the Ruhr River region of West Germany, a major industrial centre. Atsu found that, in the decade since employers had begun recruiting Turkish workers, neither conditions nor employers' willingness to address problems had changed. The inspection of the workers' dorms revealed, for example, cases in which there were no refrigerators because of the lack of adequate power supply, no cooking facilities altogether, or kitchens with lidless trashcans that resulted in bug- and vermin-infested rooms and cooking areas.[47] In one dorm, instead of cooking areas, there were expensive canteens, where workers' passports were held when they incurred debts.[48] Atsu found another dormitory near Aachen to be "abominable" because there was only one shower for 150 people and only one stove for 40 people. To cook or to wash, one had to go from one barrack to another, and residents had no choice but to store food together with shoes and dirty clothes in small cabinets in narrow, four-person rooms.[49] Yet at the same time, Atsu reported that another dormitory in the Aachen area resembled an "Intercontinental Hotel" and that workers had no problem finding and working with the translator there. Such great variation suggests not only that worker housing was the luck of the draw but also that the federal employment agency – the same agency that subjected potential workers to lengthy, expensive, year-long application procedures and multiple medical exams – had no real control over the conditions of workers' lives after their arrival in West Germany, just as it did not during travel to the country.

As variable as the dorms themselves, the dormitory managerial staff proved to be an eclectic cast of characters who often exacerbated already-stressful situations. In the "Frederick the Great" dormitory, named after the king of Prussia, the translator was, fittingly, a former military officer who behaved like a "nobleman," insisted that workers stand at attention when addressing him, and requested that workers refer to him in the "noble form," or the third person![50] However, despite his self-importance, he did not feel personally responsible for handling workers' problems. It is doubtful that this officer-cum-translator was a typical managerial representative; however, it was common for translators to think of themselves as unaccountable for workers' complaints or situations. One former worker reported that her dorm manager was like a "Gestapo Frau" who would wake the female workers early in the morning with a "shrill whistle."[51] All the women of this dorm who had one-year contracts sought to change dorms after their contracts ended.

The dorm "Dove Street" had a housemother who was paid to keep the dormitory clean but also took it upon herself to maintain strict order: the residents were forbidden from visiting with other residents in their rooms. When Atsu visited the Dove Street dorm, he commented that the housemother was treating grown men like fourteen-year-old boys and that the residents resented the restrictions on their personal freedom. Revealing perhaps more about himself than the dorm, Atsu commented in his notes that such an arrangement – one that stifled personal freedom – was potentially dangerous and could evoke radical violence: "It is already psychologically false to let these grown men, who have been separated from their families for years, live in close quarters ... with a woman who is responsible for order. When it one day leads to rape or some similar conflict, no one would be surprised."[52] Animosity between dormitory managerial staff and workers was not only common but also, at its core, a conflict over mismatched ideas about who should control life inside the dormitories.

Typically, large dormitories had a managerial staff of as many as fifty people, consisting of translators, managers, maintenance, and a cleaning staff that performed minimal tasks such as taking out the trash. Management sought to provide an orderly and sanitary environment that could foster good workers. Dorm management set up rules and regulations for all residents as well as penalties for noncompliance. Trying to provide a "homelike environment" was not the dormitory managers' main concern. A typical example of dormitory rules illustrates restrictions that were meant to maintain order:

> Damaging or dirtying the rooms or the furniture in them is not allowed. It is specifically not allowed to hang anything on the walls or to pin up pictures inside of the lockers. Smoking in bed is not allowed, nor is throwing trash from the windows. It is forbidden to wash clothes in the room. Visitors are only allowed between the hours of 10 a.m. and 10 p.m., and every visitor must sign in and sign out again with the dorm manager. Female visitors are forbidden with the exception of wives who come during the allowed visiting hours as noted above, and who are admitted with the approval of the dormitory management.[53]

However, workers might have viewed not being able to pin photos on the wall or bring home a girlfriend as an affront to creating the residential atmosphere, or *Wohnkultur*, that they wanted and needed.

Furthermore, dormitory directors and translators often took advantage of the language barrier. Not only did few residents have the German language abilities necessary to speak directly to a dorm director or to those who could solve dorm-related problems, but there were also translators and directors looking to capitalize on the situation. In one case, workers reported to Atsu that a dorm director collected DM20 to arrange for vacation tickets to Turkey but passed on only DM10 to the translator and pocketed the rest. In another case, a translator charged extra money for helping to complete salary forms.[54] Workers also complained of contract violations, such as sleeping four to a room instead of three or paying DM48.50 instead of DM40 as stated in their contracts.[55] In an interview, one worker reported that the stoves in the kitchen, once free, had begun to require DM0.10 coins, suggesting that the dorm manager was looking to profit or at least use workers to defray maintenance costs.[56] Another reported that he paid DM0.50 to use a stove burner for half an hour in addition to DM30 per month for the rent of the hotplate.[57] In the factory he earned only DM2.80 an hour.

Management personnel also threatened to send workers back to Turkey – or otherwise misused their positions of power – if residents did not follow directions exactly.[58] Though dormitory translators were meant to be impartial conduits, workers accused them of representing only management's interests.[59] From the management's point of view, guest workers came to Germany primarily to work, not to live. Even in the "home" management thought of them as foreign workers, not as residents or tenants and certainly not as their guests or neighbours.

Dorm managers revealed their thoughts through their close monitoring of dormitory activities. Management took both its position and its sense of mission to maintain order very seriously. Correspondingly, workers felt that they were constantly watched. Özdamar's novel hints at the psychological effects of this surveillance when, for example, the main character believes that even her mother in Turkey could monitor her through the public payphones on German streets. This constant surveillance made guest workers more than just employees: they were management's wards. Indeed, dorm managers figured prominently within former workers' recollections, because, much more than simply looking after maintenance problems, they regulated every aspect of dormitory life according to their own ideas of order. In Özdamar's novel, a kitchen scene of multilinguistic cooperation among women comes to an abrupt halt when the dorm manager walks in:

> It looked like a Turkish shadow-puppet play: the figures came on stage, everyone speaking in her own dialect; Turkish-Greek, Turkish-Armenian, Turkish-Jewish, various Turks from various locations and of various social classes with their various dialects. They all misunderstood one another, but they continued talking and acting in turn. The women of the *Wonaym* [dormitory] handed each other the knife or the pot, or pulled up a sleeve so that it didn't fall into a pan. Then the dorm manager came, the only one who could speak German, and she checked to see if the kitchen was clean and tidy.[60]

There was a conflict of interest within the lively "Turkish shadow-puppet play," in which the workers were seeking to build community while the dorm manager was checking on sanitation and order. This symbolic divergence of purpose formed the core conflict within dormitory life – the difference between the creative and personal process of making a home and the functional task of providing housing and maintaining subjective ideas of order. The post-war housing deficit, overall poor planning, and miscommunications between management and residents – all the issues that plagued guest worker housing – were matters that could, in theory, have been solved. However, the fundamentally different mindsets about the function of a dormitory, as shown in the mismatched expectations of the residents of the dorm and the dorm management, presented a problem that could only worsen over time.

Management's Point of View

To see a dormitory and its workers through the eyes of a dorm manager is also an attempt to understand dorm life as managers did. In the case of the North Rhine-Westphalia dormitory "Bergmannsheim, Westfalen I" – a large, all-male complex of several multifloor houses – the managerial staff kept meticulous records of dorm activities in its daily log. Staff members went on morning, midday, and evening shifts and painstakingly noted dorm activities and maintenance problems. It was uncommon for the management log to refer to workers by name. The word "*Gastarbeiter*," or guest worker, appeared in the notes in lieu of people's names. Yet from time to time the dorm manager appeared uncomfortable with this expression as well: in a few entries, the word "*Gastarbeiter*" is crossed out and the phrase "*ausländische Mitarbeiter*," or "foreign co-worker," is written in its place. This self-conscious action was a small clue that the dorm manager was himself not certain what his relationship to the foreign workers living there was and had no idea how long they would stay.

The manager's log entries paint a dreary picture of month-long heating and plumbing problems and dark hallways:

> October 12, 1970: the heat is not working; the lights in the bathroom do not work.
> October 13, 1970: the toilets were stopped up.
> October 14, 1970: the heat is not working, after trying to repair it, sent a report.
> October 15, 1970: the heat is not working, tried to repair it and was successful.
> October 16, 1970: the heat is not working, took a look and repaired it.
> October 20, 1970: in House 8, stove 1, 4, and 5 are not working; in House 9 the hall lights were burnt out, replaced four light bulbs.
> October 26, 1970: the heat is not working, tried to repair it, was unsuccessful and reported it; light in the entrance hall was burned out, replaced it … lights in the bathroom burned out, repaired them.
> October 27, 1970: hall lights burned out, repaired it. Toilet was stopped up, repaired it.[61]

The log noted maintenance problems typical of housing of this scale. However, daily reports of no heat indicate that the dorm management was either extremely understaffed or delinquent in addressing problems. On 8 October 1970, the log began with a note that the heating was not working, and this note was repeated almost daily, as shown above, until 16 November.[62] On 19 November, the report stated that the heat was not working and then, in the same entry, complained of workers burning packaging (presumably for heat): "Heating leaky; packaging burnt."[63] On 23 November 1970, there was a note that no lights were working in the entire Building 6.[64] On 24 and 27 November, and 1 December, near-daily reports of no functional heating resumed. From 2 to 7 December, the log listed a miserable litany of problems: windows were broken; a table had "fallen apart"; a door handle was missing; four of five stove burners were not working; and, in one dorm, none of the urinals were working, the sinks did not drain, and, as usual, the heat was not working.[65]

However, the December housing reports also noted the following transgressions and fines, mixing maintenance with supervision:

Morning shift, Dec 2, 1970
Checked all dorms for *cleanliness*.
Dorm 10, Room 108, the floor was unclean and a fine was issued;
Dorm 10, Room 103, floor dirty, fine issued;
Dorm 10, Room 113, floor unclean, fine issued
Room 97, issued a fine for everyone for "lack of order" [*Ordnungsstrafe*]
Dec 4, 1970
Dorm 10, toilets were dirty, told them to clean up their own mess, and threatened to fine everyone if I found it dirty again.
Dorm 2, Room 5 … Hasan deliberately damaged his cabinet door, must pay 20 DM [German marks]
Morning shift, Dec 7, 1970
Dorm 8, Kitchen was deliberately left dirty, because the trash can was empty!!
Everyone must be issued a fine.[66]

Comments like the kitchen was "deliberately left dirty," "Hasan deliberately damaged his cabinet," and workers should clean their "own mess" show that management was directly, and perhaps subjectively, blaming the workers themselves for maintenance problems. The writer's frustration, seen in both his threats and his tone (and in the multiple exclamation points that dot entries), reveals the animosity between staff and residents. Similar comments about fines continued daily for the subsequent twelve months. The dormitory log had a dual function of reporting repairs and tracking misbehaviour and penalties. A 24 February 1971 report of "power out again, called maintenance, but no one came" is followed by the comment "made multiple rounds and checked for quiet and cleanliness."[67] Despite being unable to repair the heating, management demanded order.

Yet workers might have found it paradoxical that patterns of poor maintenance persisted despite the strict regulation of the workers' cleanliness and behaviour. The responsibility of the dorm managers to maintain liveable conditions (including providing for basic human needs such as heat, security of property, and sufficiently maintained plumbing) fell by the wayside as management primarily focused on a desire to police and fine workers for "unclean" conditions. Even if managers thought that maintaining sanitary conditions was just another part of their job, their ability to fine workers for transgressions while the managers themselves were not penalized for their own inabilities to maintain the dormitory created a skewed power dynamic. In sum, policing trumped addressing maintenance problems: workers had to pay fines for having dirty floors in their unheated dormitories. A tenant-landlord relationship, in which residents were in a position to make demands of the dorm management, did not exist. The fines, threats, and dorm managers' close observation of workers and how they spent their free time all imply that dorm managers did not think of these residents as tenants to whom they had a responsibility to provide services.

Despite the responsibility dorm managers assumed to monitor workers' activities, they appeared less inclined to deal with infractions such as theft among workers. Remarks that residents had sums of between DM25 and 500 stolen, often from their cupboards, dot the management logs. The dorm manager, however, did not make a connection between reports of theft and complaints of broken doors and locks on the cabinets. A 17 February 1971 entry stated that a cabinet was damaged and the lock missing but does not consider that a robbery had taken place. Instead, the report noted that the man would have to pay for the damages: "In room 88 the cabinet door was purposely damaged and the lock is missing. He will have to pay for this himself!"[68] Possibly the most heartbreaking account was that DM920 – quite a nest egg – had been stolen from between the pages of a "Neckermann Catalogue," a well-known wish book that represented, for many, the possibilities of what the investment of their time in West Germany was worth.[69] The log did not demonstrate interventions or attempts to control theft or even, more generally, any sense of empathy for the loss. On the contrary, descriptions of theft were accompanied with subjective comments such as "criminal most likely Italian."[70]

It is unclear whether management was accusing workers of damage because of prejudice, workers were damaging property out of frustration with their housing situation, or the incidents were coincidental, though workers did feel they had reasons to protest their conditions. Workers also rebelled against their living situations in more organized ways. In the 1970s, after workers had spent more time in Germany, activism increased in the form of protests against conditions at work and at home, the topic of chapter 5. Workers were particularly vocal about their housing situations. One example is the following list of demands made at an Opel dormitory:

1) Colleagues from shift A and shift B don't sleep in separate sections of Dormitory 90. Shift A and Shift B [workers] should be placed so that they don't disturb one another when they come and go.
2) There is no warm water in Dormitory 82 (for the shower).
3) Three colleagues have to sleep together in a two-bed room in Dormitory 90. That is too many!
4) In the dormitory in Evertal Street 46/8 a German colleague has a room to himself. And he has white bed linens. Why don't the Turkish colleagues [have these things]? We would also pay more for the rent [for these things].
5) We need a mail box in Dormitory 82 and 90.
6) We need a phone booth in Dormitory 82 and 90, in case something happens in the night and we have to call a doctor quickly.[71]

Activism became a way for guest workers to find a voice and agency in West Germany – denied at work and in their dormitories – and, more important, to effect real change in their lives. Indeed, in the early 1970s, both workers' conditions and workers' protests against them began to gather media attention, bringing the debate about guest workers' conditions to the broader German public.

On 1 January 1971 the West German television station *Westdeutscher Rundfunk* broadcast an exposé about a guest worker dormitory. The report revealed poor conditions for workers and large profits for management: for example, at the same time that the company was making large profits by overcharging on the rent, the windows had holes in them. Workers in the dormitory also did not have the basic rights to come and go freely or to receive visitors, and a fence prevented seeing into or out of the surrounding grounds. In the television exposé, a reporter interviewed a company representative, Dr Georg K, and asked him how five water faucets and twelve showers, of which only eight were currently working, could possibly be considered sufficient for the 678 workers living there. Dr K defended the company by complaining that the dormitory was rather expensive because the upkeep costs were high, such as the cost of employing the fifty or more dormitory managers. In response to the accusations of poor lavatory conditions, Dr K scoffed and responded defiantly that the company often had to spend money to replace the toilets because, he complained, "these people" don't know how to use them and break the toilets by standing on them. Workers' protests about conditions in the dormitory not only drew media attention but also, ultimately, resulted in fines for the dormitory management.[72]

Dissatisfaction over employer-provided housing led to lasting resentments among guest workers, especially over how much employers were profiting from rent. "A Room is More Expensive than a Whole Apartment," read a headline in the 21 October 1962 edition of the *Kölner Stadt-Anzeiger*. The article noted that employers charged rent by the bed and not by the room, noting that employers could make a killing – as much as DM240 for a room with six beds and a table, a price that could have also secured an apartment.[73] The longer workers lived in "temporary housing," the more resentment and grievances over wages and discriminatory treatment grew, fueling larger, more organized protests in the early 1970s.

Workers' Social Lives

"I wasn't just concerned with making money," reported Erol. "Accumulating culture was also important to me," by which he might have meant learning more about West German nightlife. In his recollections he recalled nightclubs, like the "Big Apfel," and the latest hairstyles and fashions their denizens wore, especially the high-heeled boots.[74] Erol's co-workers were also constantly telling stories about their adventures in German discos, adventures that were living up to the dreams they had envisioned on their long train rides from Turkey. Erol's narration of his goals for his stay in West Germany, as well as other tales of exciting social lives, incongruously accompany the first generation of guest workers' grim descriptions of difficult conditions in West Germany. At the same time that workers recall their ambitions and adventures, they describe living in overcrowded dormitories that had strict rules – rules that especially regulated private life. In interviews, former guest workers emphasize the limitations of and surveillance on their housing, as well as their sense of adventure and freedom when not at work. Workers' dormitories were sites of constant control and negotiation between dorm managers and residents over the meanings and uses of "free time" and "private life."

Workers had smaller, more personal protests as well – in the ways they lived their lives. Though these actions were smaller than those that attracted media attention, they were just as large in the effects on their lives. Amid control and regulation, tight quarters, and petty theft, workers made dormitories their homes when they took steps to create a social environment, carved out private time, and broke rules about visitors. Workers defiantly ignored the directive about visitors, especially of the opposite sex. "Did the first round and everything was quiet," the manager of a male dorm writes when reporting almost exclusively on social behaviours. He continued: "On the second round, chased people out of the television room, where burning cigarettes were thrown on the floor. In room 125 there was the same [non-resident] woman as on Friday, and I had to get rid of her ... with difficulty. [On another floor] cards were being played at high stakes. It was broken up after I threatened punishment. The trash container was turned over. Culprit unknown.[75] It is doubtful that residents did not know that women were not allowed. More likely, they did not care. Try as the manager might to "chase" people out of the television room and get the "same woman" to leave, workers maintained enough control over what they did in their free time by ignoring the "threatened punishment."[76] While the dorm manager might have seen himself as a warden, by using words like "culprit," he was apparently an increasingly unconvincing authority figure. In many cases, workers reported creating a home life out of their limited time and space regardless of the rules, exerting their own sense of self-determination over the controlled atmosphere.

Workers' dormitories broke down traditional ideas of public and private spheres by making home life a public, observed, and regulated affair. Workers' defiance against regulations was an attempt to reclaim this space and time and, in so doing, to have control over their lives. Indeed, for many residents, dormitory life was an important source of social activity. Some workers reported that roommates functioned as substitute families and sources of comfort. (Elif, for example, is still in close, almost-daily, contact with former dormitory roommates.)[77] Canteens and common rooms were often a place for drinking beer, watching TV, playing cards, and listening to music from home. Dorms also became outlets for workers to experiment with new freedoms. Male and female workers reported going out to discos with their roommates at night. "You have to go to the places where people meet, where it is possible to have spiritual and physical contact with them," Erol commented. "And since young people spend the weekends at matinees, night clubs, and discos, we felt we had to go there to have social contact ...We changed our clothes and hair styles ... [Long] hair was in, and high-heeled boots and the like, that was how we would go to the discos. [It was] not only to meet people but also to improve our language skills."[78] Erol and his friends went out to discos to feel a part of the larger society.

Particularly for female workers, who were about 30 per cent of the total population of foreign workers, the ability to live autonomously in a foreign land or to earn one's own money afforded a previously unknown lifestyle.[79] It would be inaccurate to suggest that all Turkish women had serious restrictions on their personal freedoms from which they were released (or not) upon arrival in West Germany. Turkish guest workers were a linguistically, religiously, and ethnically diverse group that drew from both cosmopolitan centres and Anatolian villages. However, anthropological and sociological research has suggested that, for at least some Turkish women, there were serious limitations on private life because of familial and social restrictions in Turkey.[80] At the same time, immigration scholar Umut Erel has written that it is too narrow a view to discuss female migrants as necessarily passive and limited: "Assumptions about migrant women's culturally reified passivity and reduction to family life are problematic, [and reproduce] ... oppressive truths and social realities ... [They] fix migrant women as passive and within the private sphere, while ignoring their intervention into community building and both participating in established public spheres, as well as *creating their own public spheres.*"[81] In their own recollections, female guest workers connected how they spent their free time in West Germany to expressions of self – as adventurous or glamorous. Indeed, for some women, despite the highly regulated life at work and in the dorms, West Germany did provide a new and even liberating lifestyle. Elif recollected:

All [the other women in the dorm] were for the first time in their lives working [for themselves] and were earning money, and they did not know how to handle money. They [had] never learned it ... Luxury, for example: what is luxury? For example, an evening dress – not [for] a disco but [for] a dance salon. On the weekends we went dancing, naturally. Sometimes in a group, sometimes [we were] three people, sometimes a big group was planned. Every time we explored a new dance salon, with a different name. And so on. And these times [we] had lots of friends, coworkers, [who would buy] an evening dress with their own money to go dancing.[82]

Sociologist Nermin Abadan-Unat concluded that, through working in West Germany, Turkish women developed a sense of independence and gained control over their financial decisions. Furthermore, she found that women who worked outside the home had more rights in decision making as well as more authority that manifested itself mainly in access to consumer goods. However, this "pseudo-independence," warned Abadan-Unat, did not necessarily lead to a new lifestyle and "real self-confidence."[83]

Not all women were as successful in creating their own public spheres and living the carefree life Elif describes. Everyone dealt with his or her new situation in Germany differently. Some workers, both male and female, rarely left the dorms. Elif commented that some female workers never went out: "And some also were simply not for spending any money at all – they never went dancing. They were afraid. [Their lives consisted of:] factory, dormitory. Dormitory, factory. We also sometimes tried to force them. [We would say:] 'Come along, just one time! Just once [so that] you can experience something. But it'll be interesting.' But no ... They were afraid."[84] When asked what these women were afraid of, she responded: "Oh, of the foreign, unknown country and other expectations in their heads. And some came only to work and earn money and for other reasons ... But some never visited a disco; [they were] always in the dorm. Boring. But that was their decision. Can't do anything about that."[85] In Elif's portrayal of dormitory life, earning one's own income meant being able to choose what to do with one's free time. For many of these women, buying an evening dress had a double meaning: first, that they had the spending money to afford it and second, that they did not need permission to go out dancing. "Some also went out every evening," Elif noted. "[They were] extreme ... Suddenly there was lots of freedom [for them]."[86] Elif suggested that, as guest workers, these women had newfound social freedoms. Their work in West Germany, therefore, enabled workers to create new families and to reinvent themselves by taking advantage of autonomous and anonymous living in addition to new economic freedoms. This ability to reinvent oneself was often a sign that one was living a temporary existence, one in which consequences did not matter.

Turkish guest worker migration demonstrated both challenges to and consistencies with gender roles that were more complex than the binary opposition Elif presents of adventurous versus boring. Turkish women left behind in villages with their children were often under the thumb of their in-laws. Their husbands rarely returned, started second families in West Germany that absorbed their money, and basically abandoned their Turkish families to a twilight existence.[87] Furthermore, some Turkish women who followed husbands to West Germany as guest workers ended up on their own.[88] One woman recalled a dormitory roommate's story thusly: she had followed her husband to Kassel, West Germany, but lived in the dormitory in a four-person room while her husband was living with a West German woman. One day her husband came to the dormitory to get her, and even though her roommates told her she should leave him and find something better, she did not heed their advice and left with him.[89]

Single Turkish women in West Germany also faced enormous problems, and many of their fond memories could be stories about the past they created for themselves to explain the present. Significantly, when Elif recalled the early years of her life in West Berlin, she emphasized her new earnings, how she spent her free time, and her feelings of independence instead of any indignities suffered. Elif's positive spin on her experience could be the creation of an idealized past (e.g., she never mentioned what happened with the boyfriend she followed to West Germany). However, Elif's and other interviewees' interpretations of their own pasts, especially in terms of their social lives, are perhaps their way of reclaiming their experiences and reconstructing their histories. Foreign men and women had trouble with life in West Germany, and for the women this was compounded by gendered experiences. Contemporary social scientists note that workers in company housing suffered from isolation, lack of privacy, racism, and deprivation spurred by the desire to save as much as possible to support family back home.[90]

Control of Workers' Private Lives

Dormitories housed mostly single workers and more men than women. By 1968, among unmarried Turkish guest workers in West Germany, 52 per cent of the women and 64 per cent of the men lived in company-provided dormitories.[91] (Female workers remained at about 25 per cent of the total population of Turkish workers in Germany during the 1960s.) Perhaps the fact that dormitories were largely male contributed to how dorm personnel thought of their residents, imposed rules, and considered what services they were obligated to provide. The surveillance of workers, especially the male workers, included regulating intimate relationships: dorm rules clearly stated that female visitors were not allowed.

Dormitory management also regulated traditional expressions of masculinity: men were scolded like children, were fined for not cleaning, faced strict curfews, and were banned from having visitors. At the same time, stereotypes about aggressive sexuality among male guest workers abounded. For example, in 1963, 160 people signed a petition against the construction of guest worker housing near Karlsruhe. The signers complained not only that the construction unappealingly looked like barracks but also that it housed only men and that the lifestyle and temperament of the Mediterranean male guest workers would be bad for the community and "especially bad for children."[92] However, it was not only Germans who had stereotypical views of "Turkish masculinity" or "Turkish sexuality." In interviews, male workers themselves bragged about their sexual exploits with German women, as will be seen in chapter 4.

Dorm managers and instructional booklets even sought to regulate the intimate relationships of foreign workers. "I don't want to make any intimation, dear Mustafa, there are many family fathers, who actually are so well behaved, but most of the young people look to spend their free time in the possibly pleasant company of a female," begins the section on "free time" in the worker's manual *Hallo Mustafa!*[93] Interestingly enough, this instructional pamphlet on life in Germany coaches these male family breadwinners on how to pick up German women in their spare time.[94] Indeed, the booklet assumes that adultery was the norm and that it was best to accept it. The author takes the time to wish workers luck and to warn them of such licentious activities' potential dangers: "I wish you lots of luck and joy with this; perhaps you can make your dreams come true here. I must, however, also warn you. It is not true, that women are always the best use of time. Every meeting with a woman demands tact and good manners. I would also like to warn you about sexually transmitted diseases, but that matters mainly for a specific category of women."[95] In this particular case, the statement "perhaps you can make your dreams come true" is not connected to earning large sums of money but rather regards sex. This passage represents the extent of employers' comments on and involvement in the transnational family situation of their workers. Some married men who came to Germany rarely returned to Turkey and chose instead to start new families in Germany, leading to the financial and personal ruin of wives and children left behind.

The pamphlet's flip comments about adultery and dating advice fail to recognize the role that migration and the businesses themselves played in separating families. Instead, applicants were warned that German social life was a "source of danger." "It is not possible for a young person not to think about women," explains *Hallo Mustafa!*

> But different countries have different customs and also the women here often have different lifestyles from the women in your country. You will have your own experiences, but please be smart and careful. That can be the best way to a normal introduction into the German social life but can also be a source of danger and complication. I can't give you any advice. You must keep your eyes open and manage [make your own way]. A reasonable plan for free time is a necessary complement to work life; it can give you happiness and self-confidence and make it easier for you to build a new existence here.[96]

One can only wonder what would be an example of an abnormal as compared with a "normal introduction into the German social life." The author is perhaps alluding to a post-war perception of German women's sexuality, especially the high incidences of dating occupation troops.[97] Concerns about the introduction of "different customs" and vague "complication" undermine the author's friendly suggestions and encouragement of leisure time: after all, these are not simply interactions between men and women but interactions between foreign men and German women. The author also warns foreign workers to keep their jealousy, temperament, and impulsiveness in check when dealing with private affairs.[98]

In contrast, for an example of a "reasonable plan for free time," the authors included a photograph of appropriate social co-ed behaviour. In this photograph, a table helps to separate the men and women. Prominently displayed Coca-Cola bottles provide a non-alcoholic beverage option; the men are dressed in coats and ties, symbolizing upright behaviour; and the photo offers singing as an appropriate (and platonic) way to spend time with the accompanying women.

Conclusion

However, it was not only through exploring nightlife or shopping for chic outfits that workers sought to assert autonomy and control their lives. Other workers defied the guest worker identity in their own ways. For example, one man, Adil, was determined to maintain his identity as an intellectual: he read books from sundown to sunup, and at work he would try to sleep, asking a co-worker to wake him if anyone came by.[99] It did not matter to him how tired he was; he spent what little free time he had creating a life in keeping with his own view of himself. Asked whether he ever went to a bar, he answered: "No, no, I didn't have any kind of bar life in Germany; the others went. At the most I would go to the cinema or go to a nice restaurant with a friend. I would take a trip if I was in a bad mood. Then I would get in my car and drive on the autobahn and sing at the top of my lungs."[100]

Whether imagining that one's life was different (as Elif did when she pretended to be a girl at a boarding school), exploring a new disco every night, reading until sunup, or driving on the autobahn, foreign workers had a need for escapism – a tool used not only to create a social life or home life out of limited free time and space but also to endure a difficult life of long hours, cramped quarters, and isolation from family and society in general. In interviews, most former workers shed positive light on situations, especially in reference to free time, and try to demonstrate how they controlled their situations. Even in retrospect, Turkish workers actively attempt to influence their life histories.

Focusing on life outside work provides a way to view the process of importing labour from the inside out. German officials' attempts to provide temporary housing reveal (conscious or unconscious) efforts to ensure that workers had only temporary stays in West Germany. Officials' attempts to provide and regulate appropriate housing for foreign workers broke down when the responsibility was assumed by others, such as employers, dorm managers, and translators, many of whom tried to do things as quickly and cheaply as possible, played power games with workers, or, more troubling, the game of "civilization." Despite dorm managers' attempts to control even the most intimate details of workers' lives, guest workers managed to exert control over their own lives in their free time and often through expressions of their sexuality, as will be explored in the final chapter. In this chapter, guest workers' ambitions and rebellions, whether in their home lives or their social lives, reveal ways in which male and female workers were able to maintain a sense of self within a highly controlled and regulated process. In the dormitories, workers created their own spaces with their own imaginations and defiance. These attempts are also transparent in revealing, foremost, that the workers were opinionated, not passive, in their situations. They shaped their homes – an aspect that is often ignored in descriptions of workers' poor housing and bad conditions. Perhaps Özdamar's term *Wonaym* is not a mispronunciation but a transliteration in which workers represent their German home in their own new language.

Over time, workers changed their housing as they needed to, such as when a family member joined them and they needed a larger place or when they wanted to change jobs. The instability of workers' housing led to an inability to truly settle in West Germany and inhibited integration into society. It also led to the "ghettoization" of Turkish minority populations, which resulted in problems in the 1970s and 1980s.[101] The longer guest workers stayed in West Germany, the greater their dissatisfaction with their housing arrangements and their position in society. The BA's housing guidelines were not regulated, and, in addition to a continuing shortage of reasonably priced housing in West Germany, foreign workers faced prejudice when they attempted to find private accommodations. As dissatisfaction with housing grew and as workers decided to stay in West Germany longer, worker protests over housing also increased, as did the likelihood of workers seeking personal lives away from work or of joining more broad-based labour activism as ways to commit to a better and more permanent life in West Germany.

PART TWO

4

Contested Borders

"We went to dance," Cahit reminisced in 1995 about his nights in East Berlin in the 1960s and 1970s.[1] Cahit left Turkey for West Berlin in 1964 on a two-year contract but settled permanently after falling in love with an East German woman and starting a family. "[All] the Turks went to [East Berlin] to find women and flirt," he reported.[2] While it is a bit hyperbolic to claim that all Turks socialized in East Berlin, Cahit had a point: a great many Turkish nationals crossed from West Berlin to East Berlin regularly, with ease, and for years. Cahit was just one of many who maintained a cross-border relationship from the 1960s through the 1980s. These border crossers presented an interesting paradox. West Berlin society deemed them suspicious as foreign and "Eastern" – a cultural and ethnic distinction that created social outsiders. At the same time, the East German State Security Police, or *Stasi*, found them suspect because they not only came from West Berlin but also, in the eyes of the *Stasi*, embodied Western capitalist culture and as such offered a figurative and literal escape to the West. Guest workers' experiences in and perspectives of East Berlin complicate the divided city's story, as many of them saw the new and experimental state as a space to explore and enjoy greater social autonomy and acceptance among Germans, especially in contrast to feelings of social isolation in West Berlin.

This is a story of paradoxes – of suspicion and acceptance, of love and manipulation, and of transgression and compliance. However, male Turkish guest workers in East Berlin were also interesting for their ordinariness: in East Berlin they were a ubiquitous and accepted part of the cityscape. For decades, a large population of West Berlin-residing Turkish nationals built social lives, business deals, intimate relationships, and transnational families across divided Berlin. Men such as

Cahit and their unusual cases provide a window through which to view the Berlin border, its crossing, and its definition. Traditionally, economic and political histories have dominated the narratives of divided Berlin and the Cold War writ large.[3] This particular history of guest workers in Berlin tells a new narrative of divided Berlin, specifically how porous its borders were. This perspective reveals points of contact between foreign nationals and East Germans; the East German state's opinion of the guest worker program in West Germany; and, significantly, moments of integration and acceptance. Various personal interactions reveal different and moving allegiances, sometimes based on attraction and other times on exploitation.

This chapter presents this group from multiple vantages, each with its own bias – the recollections of border crossers, the concerned *Stasi*, and East German women whom the border crossers courted and sometimes married. This chapter draws on the *Stasi*'s documentation of Turkish citizens in East Germany. Using the files held in the Archives of the State Security Police of the Former German Democratic Republic (BStU), this chapter considers the *Stasi*'s point of view in identifying "suspects" among guest workers in its jurisdiction. This police surveillance folds guest workers into the larger narrative of the East German state's gaze.

After a brief look at the larger historical context, this chapter explores guest workers' roles in divided Berlin through three themes: lovers, border crossers, and transgressors. The first theme, "lovers," provides access to the private, intimate realm – a sphere with which historians of totalitarian states have long been fascinated.[4] The idea of *Eigensinn*, or "self-will," has dominated discussions of how individuals negotiated the dictatorship at the grassroots level.[5] Johannes Huinink has highlighted "individual spaces for action," in which German Democratic Republic (GDR) citizens negotiated personal dealings in ways that demonstrated their ability to exploit situations and behave tactically, not just accept dictates and conditions. He points out that they always had "the potential to shape things themselves."[6]

The intimate, sexual relationships of this chapter not only represent individual space but also more closely approach a home life, in a private bedroom that the employer-owned dormitories of the previous chapter denied. The encounters in East Berlin, whether fly-by-night or long-term, offered welcoming embraces and even, ironically, more privacy than could be found in West Germany, the true "host country." Yet a sense of home was found across the border, under the watchful eyes of the *Stasi*. Some couples went to great lengths for relationships that defied borders and showed an alternative social organization to the state. Other lovers' motivations were more elusive and answers to these questions remain speculation: Were these trysts part of East Germans' plans of escape or of exploiting access to Western goods? Did these cross-border lovers seek sexual outlets they could visit and leave at their own discretion or were they searching for long-term partners?

The second theme, border crossers, reflects a unique and often bizarre social and cultural cross-border world. This section includes those who crossed the border for love as well as many other reasons. Their experiences' complexity offers myriad vantage points on relationships between foreign nationals and East Germans (including the *Stasi* officials tasked with tracking them) – all of which add a new dimension to our understanding of both the guest worker program and Cold War narratives. These untold stories provide a fuller and, at times, paradoxical picture that demonstrates that the closed border was indeed crossed, that Turkish nationals and Germans socialized, and that these relationships threatened the GDR as well as pat concepts of what constituted the West and the East.

The final theme, transgressors, delves into a deeper level of human psychology – the complicity of collaborators, including *Stasi*-recruited Turkish nationals. In truth, transgression is a theme woven throughout this chapter, as it is implied in myriad borders that are crossed – politically, culturally, bodily, and linguistically. Just crossing the inner-Berlin border was a transgression in the most literal sense. The search for fun, some freedom, and sexual and domestic comfort was another type of transgression, especially in light of the restrictions on private life West German employers imposed in their workers' dormitories. However, there is also a deeper level of transgression at work here, one more akin to betrayal, in the overt breaking of laws, flouting of regulations, and cooperation and formal collaboration with East German authorities to report on countrymen. Betrayal, complicity, and coercion combine to some degree in transgression and collaboration. While not operating with total free will, collaborators were, at some level, both choosing and manipulating their collusion with the state. Questions of whether love is true and why people betray also dovetail with ideas of nationality and belonging. In short, these border crossers were constantly renegotiating their statuses. They were both Eastern and Western; they were insiders in private relationships with Germans, outsiders as foreign nationals, and – as collaborators – insiders within the *Stasi* who tracked their countrymen.

Historical Context

The border between West and East Germany, with Berlin as its symbol, defined the Cold War locally and internationally. West Germany diplomatically isolated the GDR, while East Germany locked its own citizens in. When the two German states were founded in 1949, the contestation over who could be representative of "Germans" also began, adding a political classification to the blood-based one. The Federal Republic asserted that only it, with its freely elected government, could legitimately represent Germans. Indeed, the West German government could not, it argued, even recognize the GDR as a state.[7] When other states entered into diplomatic relations with the GDR, the Federal Republic reacted with countermeasures, breaking off diplomatic ties and politically isolating the GDR until the end of the 1960s. East Germany, in turn, also expressed the desire to unite all Germans, but only under the flag of socialism. However, the socialist state began to lose its population as it lost its appeal. Once the socialist planned economy proved to be inefficient, partly because of the heavy burdens the Soviets placed on it, many East German residents fled for financial, political, and family reasons. *Republikflucht*, or "fleeing the republic," as the East German state referred to those emigrating to the West, caused the population drain that prompted the Berlin Wall's construction in 1961. The question of who and where the "real Germans" were, in addition to the Wall's connection to the guest worker program, was eerily prescient of the post-Cold War debates about German citizenship for guest workers and their descendants.

On 13 August 1961 the East German authorities constructed the Berlin Wall to stem the outmigration of their citizens. In the sixteen years before the Wall's construction, 3.5 million people had fled from the East German Republic. The West, however, considered this outmigration representative of people voting with their feet. Previously, West Berliners had also regularly travelled to East Berlin: in fact, until August 1961 about 80 per cent of the West Berlin population had visited East Berlin at least once a month.[8] The inner-German border had an undeniable appeal for West Germans, and by the end of the 1950s, it had become a well-established tourist attraction, where tourists would hike, picnic, and take photos.[9] From the very first instance, the GDR saw "border tourism" as a provocation and an attempt at propaganda for the "better Germany" by the Federal Republic.

The Berlin border closing had a large economic impact on West Germany, and West Berlin in particular: it thwarted the hundreds of thousands of refugees and expellees who had provided much-needed daily and seasonal labour. Berlin Wall historian Frederick Taylor has pointed out that the Wall's construction in fact prompted the guest worker program's expansion by thwarting West Germany's steady labour supply from the East.[10] Yet West Berlin waited until 1964 to invite guest workers, as the city wanted to appear self-sufficient at all costs, especially as observed from the East.[11] In other words, both West Berlin's initial hesitance and its later participation in the guest worker program were Cold War responses, and foreign nationals were unwitting pawns in political manoeuvres.

Like much of post-war Europe, East Germany imported foreign workers to assuage its industrial labour shortage. Beginning in 1966 with a treaty with Poland, the GDR signed treaties through the 1980s with Hungary, Algeria, Cuba, Mozambique, Vietnam, Mongolia, and China," offering occupational training or employment for foreign "contract workers."[12] These workers were relegated to unappealing shift work and low-skilled jobs, and the states involved further exploited the workers to relieve trade debts and improve production without investment. For example, in the bilateral "Treaty of Friendship and Cooperation," Mozambique would receive East German agricultural machinery, trucks, and training for its workers and the GDR would receive grain, coal, and several thousand contract workers.[13] By the mid-1970s, the focus on occupational training had waned, and the state increasingly viewed the workers in terms of their economic utility. East Germany limited contracts to three to five years, workers primarily lived in company-owned hostels or community housing, and the government strongly discouraged contact between these so-called Third World citizens and its own.[14] Contract workers lived throughout the GDR but were heavily concentrated in East Berlin and in the southern industrial cities of Chemnitz, Dresden, Leipzig, and Halle.[15] East Germany's foreign nationals lived mostly in isolation from mainstream society, creating a monocultural society.[16]

In contrast to Cahit's happy love story, which opened this chapter, historians have long noted xenophobia's prevalence in East Germany, which exploded into blatant violence after reunification in the 1990s. During the lifespan of the GDR, "socialist friendship among peoples" was the official party line, but acceptance of others was not always the norm.[17] The East German government played down xenophobic manifestations in its country or treated them as taboo. The media was also forbidden to report on them or even on the numbers of foreign workers living in the GDR while at the same time encouraged to scorn West Germany's guest worker program as capitalist exploitation.[18] According to a sociological study of anti-Semitism and xenophobia in East Germany, in the 1980s – when actual conditions and government propaganda differed the most – public opinion on former "friendly socialist countries" soured while sympathy for former "imperialist enemies" grew.[19] In 1975, the Socialist Unity Party's most important party organ – its official newspaper, Neues Deutschland, or "New Germany" – reported on West Germany's guest worker program two years after its official end with the intention of not just exposing the exploitation of workers in the West, but also pointing out the responsibility that receiving countries had to give them fair job options, job training, language training, humane living conditions, and much more.[20] Indeed Turkish guest workers with West Berlin residence permits skirted the line between constituting "imperialist enemies" with their consumer goods and belonging to the exploited working class.

In addition to political and social constraints, the Berlin Wall was a serious and dangerous border: between 1961 and 1989 at least 136 people were killed there.[21] This is the Berlin Wall story that is commonly told – the daring escape attempts from the East, the shoot-to-kill order, the tragic family divisions, and the state's escalating surveillance and countermeasures. Less well known, however, is that the borders were also less dramatically crossed, often daily. Indeed, the border was not entirely closed. After 13 August 1961, a series of treaties and agreements regulated the border, starting in 1963 with a border pass agreement between the West Berlin Senate and the GDR that allowed Christmas and New Year's visits.[22] That year 730,000 people put up with the long processing period and registered 1.2 million visits to East Berlin between 19 December 1963 and 5 January 1964.[23] The agreement continued until 1966, when negotiations broke down and the Christmas visits ended. The 1970 Four Powers Agreement and the subsequent Transit Agreement between the Federal Republic of Germany (FRG) and the GDR were two of the most significant in the period and regulated border crossings, visa requirements, and exchange rates.[24]

The Soviet Union, however, was not thrilled to see the two Germanys growing closer. The Soviet Communist Party's general secretary, Leonid Brezhnev, responded to the GDR's general secretary, Erich Honecker, directly: "Erich, let me tell you quite frankly, never forget this: the GDR cannot exist without us, without the Soviet Union, its power and strength. Without us there would be no GDR ... There must not be any process of rapprochement between the FRG and the GDR."[25] Nevertheless, both German states acted defiantly in their own interests and agreed on pacts to ease travel; to open new border crossings; and to improve road, rail, postal, and telephone connections between the two states. After years of division, starting 3 October 1972, West Berliners were allowed to visit the GDR multiple times a year for up to thirty days for "humanitarian, family, religious, cultural or tourism" reasons, resulting in 44 million trips before 1989.[26]

Humanitarian reasons were likely not the motivating factors for German-German border compromises and improved relations though. Since its inception, East Germany had wanted West Germany, among others, to recognize it as an independent state and accept the inviolability of its borders. In December 1972, West Germany and East Germany signed the "Basic Treaty," which resulted in just that: West Germany accepted East Germany and its borders in the name of "normal and neighborly relations," effectively ending East Germany's political isolation. The GDR's international recognition also reached its highpoint through the Basic Treaty with West Germany, including its acceptance into the United Nations and its signing of the 1975 Helsinki Accords, which were to improve relations between the Eastern Bloc and the Western Bloc, protect human rights, and promote peaceful negotiating. Indeed, the GDR did quite well in the 1970s in general – the state raised wages and pensions, added more holidays, built new housing, and froze the prices of basic foodstuffs. The border-crossing agreements, in other words, added another significant achievement to normalization and promotion of the East German state to its own citizens and to the world.

East Germany also stood to gain financially from its relaxed border controls. It collected transit, postal, and visa fees in addition to the exchange of currency required of visitors to the GDR – all paid in the hard foreign currency that Eastern Bloc countries desperately needed to operate in the world market.[27] Starting in 1973, Honecker allowed West German visitors into the GDR with this mandatory currency exchange and allowed West Germans to transfer funds to East German relatives. This hard currency could then be spent in government-run stores (*Intershops*) that sold select goods for Western currency.[28] Between 1975 and 1979, border-crossing income had increased to 1.56 billion West German marks, and it remained at this level for years.[29]

Not all border crossings or crossers were the same. Different crossing procedures applied to different groups: West Berliners specifically had different regulations governing their ability to travel to East Berlin than did West Germans from other cities. Unlike West Berliners, West Germans could continue to visit East Berlin with a visa that was good for one day.[30] Guest workers, estimated to form almost 10 per cent of the West Berlin population, were uniquely positioned within the divided city. On the one hand, because they were guest workers, their employment permits required that they have West German residency permits, and it was these permits that allowed them into West Berlin with greater ease than Eastern Bloc residents. On the other hand, because they were foreign nationals, their passports allowed them into East Berlin with greater ease than West Berliners had – as long as they crossed the border as foreign tourists and returned by midnight when their day visas expired.[31] In 1977, the count of border crossers by street and by train, including West Germans, West Berliners, and foreigners, was 18,084,000.[32] As a result, guest workers and other foreign nationals who did not have the same historical ties and political motivations as West Germans also became part of the everyday landscape in East Berlin.

Significantly, East Germans often considered Turkish nationals as Western, not just through their ready access to consumer goods but also because of their Western lifestyles. At the same time, many West Germans considered them inassimilable "Easterners." The East-West confusion here mirrors that of the Turkish republic itself: Turkey is a NATO and US ally but deemed by many to be at the heart of the "Orient," with all of the trappings of orientalism. And yet this small case study, featuring seemingly trivial social interactions – between Turkish men and East German women – reveals layers of meaning that recast traditional narratives of restrictive Cold War Berlin and guest worker experiences.[33] For this group, the Berlin Wall was easy to traverse and the people more welcoming to foreigners than the literature has allowed.

Despite both the relaxation of the border regulations and the political and financial gains of border crossing, East Germany remained deeply concerned with ideological infiltration from the West, in the form of packages, media, uncensored news, messages, and contact with Westerners themselves. The *Stasi* was known as the "shield and sword" of the party and took its mission very seriously. After the détente with West Germany, it expanded its surveillance system.[34] The number of *Stasi* employees doubled to 80,000 between 1970 and 1980.[35] In 1972, in the midst of the "humanitarian" treaties, Honecker actually ordered new land mines to be installed at the inner-German border.[36]

It is not surprising that border crossing and the ensuing international relationships sparked suspicion among East German authorities. After all, the East German state is well known for its close watch of its citizens. When the Berlin Wall fell in 1989, the *Stasi* employed 91,015 full-time employees and 173,000 informants, or roughly one in fifty East Germans between the ages of 18 and 80.[37] In short, it was a highly policed state. Indeed, the GDR took foreign visitors potential to corrupt and influence its population earnestly and set up *Arbeitsgruppe Ausländer* or "Working Group on Foreigners," specifically for foreigners in their territory who resided in West Berlin. The *Stasi*, like many in West Germany, found guest workers in its territory marginal yet threatening.

For many guest workers living in West Berlin, the various borders that defined their lives were quite fluid. In sharp contrast to the myriad negotiations, transnational bureaucracy, treaties, and visa applications (as discussed in chapter 2) that had preceded their residence in West Berlin, Berlin's own border proved easier for many to cross. Monthly, thousands of guest workers crossed from West Berlin to East Berlin for their social lives – for the evening or for a weekend – to go dancing, to eat out, and, for the largely male population, to meet women. Cahit met his future wife in East Berlin and was able, through marriage, to bring her to West Berlin.

Lovers

The theme of lovers explores the various types of intimate relationships between male Turkish guest workers from Berlin and East German women. Though the literature reveals that cross-border relationships were much more varied, the *Stasi* files on guest workers assumed that it was primarily heterosexual Turkish men who represented the guest worker population arriving from West Berlin. However, there was also conflation in the *Stasi* files among Turks, Arabs, and foreigners in general, hinting that it perhaps did not matter where one was from or who was officially part of the formal guest worker program. A diversity of relationships developed, with the potential grounds for these trysts including attraction, adventure, manipulation – for the East Germans – access to the West, including escaping to the West permanently. Not surprisingly, *Stasi* operatives followed border-crossing guest workers with both great interest and much concern, especially regarding the ensuing romantic and sexual relationships with their citizens. Their fears were broad-based, ranging from concern that these foreign men would negatively influence their citizens (especially their morality) and induce them into illegal activities to anxiety that they would assist citizens in leaving the GDR. More often than not, foreign border crossers were considered suspect because their intimate relationships with East German women often resulted in marriages and emigration out of East Berlin, a topic of perhaps the greatest concern. Emigration through marriage put a figurative hole in the border.

Indeed, the officially coined *eheähnliche Verhältnisse*, or "marriage-like relationships," between ethnic Turks and East Berlin women remained an official area of concern for decades. Concern over and the regulation of sex between those deemed to be "threatening outsiders" and "one's own women" is an age-old trope and was equally true in West and East Germany but still bears examination in this context. Communist prudishness was also nothing new. The East German state, like the Soviets before it (and similar to West Germany), took a repressive and conservative view of the body, sex, and relationships: abortions were difficult to obtain, prostitution and adultery socially condemned, homosexuality banned, and traditional nuclear families promoted.[38] According to historian Josie McLellan, promiscuity and erotica were also considered Western vices: "during the early Cold War, [the East German state] portrayed pinups, stripteases, and prostitution as typical of an Americanized, profit-oriented West German sexuality, contrasting them with the healthy sexuality of the East based in marriage and childbearing."[39]

In the eyes of the *Stasi*, political infiltration through the hard-to-police private realm was a real concern. Regardless of any moral code, intimate relationships can challenge belief systems successfully. According to one operative's report, "often marriage-like relationships … between Turks living in West Berlin and female citizens of the GDR arise," and a consequence was that some of these female citizens could be "pulled into the potential circles of the unlawful candidates for leaving the GDR."[40] By marrying a foreigner, an East German woman could apply for emigration out of the GDR. The operative in the report notes that in 1980, seventy female citizens applied to emigrate specifically through marriage with Turkish citizens.[41] Highlighting the ubiquity of the problem, an East Berlin customs officer who routinely searched Turks crossing the border apparently found Turkish men in possession of "hundreds of contact addresses and telephone numbers of GDR female citizens per year."[42] The *Stasi* recognized, just as many East Berlin women must have, that these foreign men provided a way out that was specific to East German women.

Not all relationships were of convenience or for personal gain, however. One man was reported to have attempted to go as far as to take up permanent residence in East Berlin because, according to the *Stasi* operative, he had developed an *intensive Liebesverbindung*, or "intense love relationship," with his East German girlfriend; the file also included pictures of them on picnics and in bed together.[43] Love-based relationships flourished, as evidenced by private photos of couples together, by requests to leave for Turkey to marry there, and by the children who were born to foreign fathers (see figure 7).

7 "Lovers." Stasi file photo of Turkish man with East German woman.
Source: BStU, MfS - HA II, Nr. 27442; Berlin, 7 August 1979.

In another case, a foreign man decided to divorce his West Berlin wife to marry an East Berlin woman instead.[44] One East Berlin woman applied to marry a West Berlin-living Turkish guest worker whom she had dated and received financial support from for *twelve* years since 1967.[45] The woman's daughter considered the Turkish man a father figure as he had been in her life consistently since she was six years old.[46] The mother wished to marry and move with her fiancé to Turkey but the GDR denied her request.[47] Despite the border, they had built a life and a family together. Significantly, these reports reveal an unmistakably high level of contact between the two groups that allowed relationships to develop over years.

On the whole, *Stasi* officials found the relationships between foreign men and East German women to be dubious and continued to comment on whether these relationships were "real" and on what types of contact they were based, often noting the promiscuity of the people involved. Those relationships deemed "real" were often couples who had been together for one or two years, seeing each other once or twice a week – in one case daily – or communicating through daily telephone contact. One woman had a "close relationship" with a "Turkish citizen from West Berlin" who, at the time of the report, arrived every Friday and stayed through Sunday for a year.[48] In another case, an officer noted, "Because the Turk arrives almost daily from West Berlin, one can assume that it is a case of a steady relationship."[49] In a more common case, a woman appealed to the state to let her emigrate to Turkey with her West Berlin-living fiancé, but the *Volkspolizei*, or "People's Police" (VP), refused her request because of doubts over the relationship's authenticity; it explained that she had *"laufend wechselnde Männerbekanntschaften,"* or "steadily changing relationships with men."[50] The police's impressions of her relationships' authenticity had major impacts for her.

The *Stasi*'s suspicion of the nature of these relationships was not unfounded. The case of two people, "Mesut" and "Corinna,"[51] shows the slippery politics of cross-border relationships. Mesut met Corinna, an East German dancer, when her troupe was on tour in Turkey in 1954.[52] In love with her, Mesut moved to Germany as a student in 1958, studying in Bavaria.[53] In 1963 he began to petition the East German state for permission to marry Corinna and have her join him in the West.[54] He wrote moving letters, pleading to be with his fiancée, writing that their "destiny and future together hang in the balance."[55] He appealed to the state's sense of morality, writing, "Surely it cannot be in the interest of a state to get involved in the deeply personal affairs of its citizens."[56] (This last statement, ironically, was noted by the *Stasi*.) Mesut also appealed to the state's international reputation, writing: "In my homeland, in which each citizen is entitled to every freedom, the GDR's negative stance toward its own citizens will not be understood. It is of upmost importance to not hinder the positive image of the GDR to my fellow citizens."[57] In the letter explaining the denial of his request, the East German authorities made two points. First, that Turkey did not recognize the state of East Germany and second, that without state representation in Turkey, his future wife would have no political protection there.[58] The geopolitics of the Turkish Republic's refusal to recognize East Germany is played out in this one man's request to be with his love.

In the meantime, his fiancée became pregnant with their child, leaving one to infer that they still had regular contact with one another, and she also lost her job, which implies that the East German state was punishing her for her wish to leave. Once again Mesut appealed to the international reputation of the East German state, writing, "The attraction of the socialist societal form on us developing countries is a certain factor."[59] He also took an emotional tone, saying it didn't make sense to give his bride false hope.[60] Mesut petitioned for help in the West German state as well, writing to the *Bundesnotaufnahmeverfahrens*, or Federal Emergency Department or BNV, for assistance. The BNV was designed to assist refugees and those fleeing the East German state and did so based on an 22 August 1950 law that stated that "Germans from other lands" who were in states of emergency would be accepted in the Federal Republic.[61] In 1967, the organization wrote back that what Mesut was asking for was extremely difficult to achieve.[62] Indeed, only those considered unable to work and the elderly were granted the right to leave the GDR, it noted.[63] After the construction of the Berlin Wall, it was nearly impossible.

Corinna applied for and was granted a travel visa to Turkey supposedly to search for her husband there, though she never travelled to Turkey. It is even odder that the state would grant this visa in the first place, demonstrating a curious labyrinth of both bureaucracy and reasoning. Corinna apparently somehow travelled from Vienna and then to Munich, legally, and on 28 June 1967 she had the residence permit for the family – her husband, herself, her daughter, and their son in Kreuzberg, West Berlin.[64] It took almost five years of wrangling for the couple to come together in West Berlin.

However, this story is no fairy tale. A statement in the file notes that a witness overheard Corinna saying that once she was in the West, she would leave Mesut.[65] While waiting for permission to move to West Berlin with Mesut, she had apparently fallen in love with a man she had met in a Pankow hospital in 1966.[66] The witness also testifies that Corinna and her family had been economically exploiting Mesut for years.[67] Was he naive? Was Corinna trying to improve her image with her family by denying being in love with this foreign man? In any case, the couple began a messy divorce in which custody of the son, as well as possession of a Turkish carpet, was hotly debated.

The *Stasi* concluded, however, that Mesut was the suspicious one, for having helped an East German citizen leave the country. It does not comment on Corinna's apparent exploitation of Mesut. While Mesut was not officially part of the guest worker program, the drama and complexity of the relationship's two-sided coin – loyalty and betrayal – suggest dynamics common to Mesut's countrymen who entered into similar relationships with East German women.

A Turkish man who was working unofficially for the *Stasi*, "Murat," reported on an East German woman whose address was regularly given as the required destination on the entry visa by men crossing into East Berlin for years until 1988. When asked about her relationship with foreign men, she curtly replied that she "just couldn't sleep with white men."[68] She was reported to have had a well-cared-for appearance and to dress primarily in Western clothing, obtained either from *Intershop* or from her "Western friends" – these friends were reported, ironically, to be primarily "Arabs" who drove Mercedes.[69] These border crossers' status as foreign, as "Eastern," and as cultural others apparently also played a role in how they were perceived. In short, even men who had not broken any rules were dubious because of their intimate relationships, which weren't necessarily illegal but nonetheless had great potential power to subvert the state.

A case in point is a 3 January 1989 report from an *Inoffizieller Mitarbeiter*, or "Unofficial Informer," (IM), "Ina," that noted that a woman who had contact with "Arabs" had filed for an exit visa to leave East Germany for West Berlin.[70] Ina reported that the woman in question had had extensive contact with "Turks and other foreigners," frequently meeting them in the popular Cafe Moskau or the disco Lindencorso.[71] The woman was suspected of prostitution and of taking advantage of her job at a travel agency on Alexanderplatz to provide customs declarations forms illegally. An earlier report notes that she was extremely interested in securing West German marks and would often use intimate relationships to do so. The *Stasi* watched her entire family, especially her parents, as a result of her actions.[72] (Her parents were found to have the correct political leanings and were deemed "red.") Since she lived with her parents, having men over was awkward. In the summer months her parents would stay at their weekend cottage, which allowed her to have male visitors at home. These were not cases of romance but rather financial transactions.

Monetary concerns had prompted Cahit to leave Turkey for West Germany as a guest worker in 1964: "The reason I came ... was for economic reasons, like everybody else ... My purpose was to earn some money and then return to Turkey again, but the situation changed and I understood that I couldn't return to Turkey."[73] Cahit initially worked at a metal company but cancelled his contract after just one year and transferred to a textile company. After two years there he began working for a newspaper, but he felt the newspaper would not survive because of its political leanings. At the end of 1969, he began working for the Berlin-based *Tagesspiegel*, or "Daily Mirror," and he stayed there for seventeen years. "I worked for seventeen years as the only foreigner, and we were like brothers there. But I [still] didn't establish a connection with them ... [because] I didn't want to have a lot of contact with them," he recounted. His first social contact with a German was in East Berlin. According to Cahit, he was the first Turkish man his wife had dated. "*Tarzanca*," a Turkish word for "Tarzan speak," is how Cahit describes his German when he met his future wife. She learned a little bit of Turkish and, after being married for two years, travelled with him to Turkey to meet his extended family, who loved her. Cahit, a Turkish national and West Berlin resident, provided a path to the West for an East German woman, as he crossed political, economic, and culturally constructed borders.

"It was easy to meet women [in East Berlin]," he bragged, "so the Turkish men showed up with gifts, gold rings."[74] Cahit reflects on his time in East Berlin as one of great virility. Starting in 1966, he and his friends went to East Berlin once a week to go dancing. In nightclubs in the East they felt desirable and masculine: "[Compared] to German men, in terms of sexual ability, [Turkish men] have more endurance and stamina, so [the East German women] preferred the Turks."[75] In this example, Cahit asserts his self-perceived masculinity over that of the men who had control over him. "I went to East Berlin once a week to go dancing, and after two years I moved to East Berlin because I had met an East German woman," he reported. Cahit met his wife while dancing at a club she frequented with a group of girlfriends, and after six or seven months, she and Cahit began dating. In other words, for six or seven months, Cahit lived in West Berlin and socialized in East Berlin, living his life across the divided city with apparent ease. Two years after he moved in with his East Berlin girlfriend, they had a baby boy. When his son was nine years old, they married in East Berlin. In 1980 he brought his family to West Berlin. He commented on his unusual transborder family, thusly: "I have been with my family for 27 years, and my son is now 25. This is a bit interesting, isn't it?" It is unclear how common Cahit's story was; another Turkish man who applied for permission to marry his East Berlin girlfriend and settle in East Berlin was denied permission to do so.[76] Cahit's marriage and subsequent emigration called into question the categories of "Westerner," "Easterner," "citizen," and "German," as well as concepts of loyalty, suspicion, and national membership.

Border Crossers

In a 1979 memo, years after regular border crossings had become common, a *Stasi* operative justified the need for broad-reaching surveillance of "Turks" crossing from West to East Berlin. He explained, "Monthly, around 8,000 Turks arrive in the capital of the GDR ... who have a multitude of contacts of an unexplained character to GDR citizens."[77] Interestingly, in contrast to their usual level of detail, the *Stasi* files used the term "Turk" without qualification, not always specifying whether the Turkish nationals were participating in the official guest worker program or living in West Germany for other reasons, such as to study at West German universities. This vital surveillance mission would protect citizens from "criminal and subversive dealings against the GDR or the socialist community," including drug smuggling, and, in general, look for solutions to the "Turkish problem."[78] The *Stasi* feared infiltration by right- and left-wing Turkish extremist organizations and emphasized the need to discover their plans and intentions.[79] In short, it was deemed a matter of national importance "to secure via official and unofficial sources ... an operational view of the Turkish concentration in [East Berlin]."[80] The *Stasi* report does not just focus on transgressors and "subversive dealings" but also demonstrates a more general concern over the growing Turkish concentration in East Berlin in general.

The *Stasi* operational plan explicitly stated that operatives were to observe Turkish men between the ages of twenty and thirty-five years. The *Stasi* notes are almost all about foreign men meeting with East

German women, adding a loaded gender dynamic. Considering the
dubious nature of intimacy and privacy in a police state, scholars have
since pointed out that it was the women of East Germany who were
uniquely positioned to understand how the state worked because of
their roles in the private and intimate realms.[81] Various power dynamics
politically charged these cross-border encounters with asymmetries of
wealth, allegiance, access, and freedom of movement. These men were
dangerous not just as foreigners but also as foreign men with an ability
to infiltrate a hard-to-police space. Cahit was just one of many men the
Stasi had its eyes on.

Unlike their lives in West Berlin, which were dominated by a low
status at work, poor living arrangements in company dormitories, and
a general suspicion and dislike of foreigners on the part of many West
Berliners, East Berlin provided a place for these men to socialize freely.
Cahit notes: "Moreover, we had heard that in the East there were a lot of
women, and there really were. So the Turks were always there. We were
young, so naturally it was normal that men needed women."[82] In the
end, Cahit changes his story a bit: it was less that East German women
preferred him and more that he had very little contact with West German women. Cahit recalled: "The Western [West German] women
didn't really want to have much to do with the Turkish men. To say
more, I didn't have any contact with West German women."[83] Cahit's
point about social exclusion in the West was genuine. For example, an
archived photo of the front window of a Gelsenkirchen disco, taken in
1974, shows a handwritten sign that reads, "*Für Ausländer Zutritt VER-
BOTEN,*" or "Entry for foreigners is FORBIDDEN."[84] The sign's capital-
ization makes for an aggressive tone, and the sign itself is reminiscent
of pre-war signs forbidding the entry of Jews. Informal discrimination
against guest workers in West Germany included refusal to rent to foreigners and exclusion from bars and clubs, and it escalated in the 1970s
as German unemployment rose for the first time in the post-war era.[85]

In contrast, multiple files mention Turkish men eagerly crossing to
dance for the evening with East Berlin girlfriends at the famous disco,
Lindencorso, on Unter den Linden Boulevard or at Cafe Moskau on
Karl-Marx-Allee.[86] The *Stasi* was less enthusiastic about the meetings,
and it began to track and investigate the East Berlin women who met
with foreign men. It was common for foreign crossers to provide a contact name and address, and often East Berlin women served this purpose, which placed many of the women under suspicion with the *Stasi* –
so much so that it often had notes in its files about these women's

suitability for "unofficial collaboration" with the *Stasi*.[87] Considering that historians now report that men dominated (between 80 and 90 per cent) the *Stasi* informant network, accessing potential female informants was noteworthy.[88] One woman was reported to have "frequently changing [foreign] male acquaintances," who would go home with her, have small parties there, and spend the night.[89] Three different couples in her building were reporting on her and her interactions with these foreign men.[90] They reported, for example, that a man from West Berlin visited with his Mercedes and renovated her whole apartment, apparently bringing his own tools and materials.[91] The woman with the many acquaintances later became engaged to a Bulgarian man, and when interviewed by the police about why Turkish men had given her address when they entered the GDR, she (dubiously) replied that a former female friend must have passed it on and that, furthermore, she was pleased the police were questioning her about it privately so that her fiancé would not learn about the Turkish men.[92] Apparently she had worked as a secretary for the *Stasi* and became alarmed when her relationship with a Turkish man had become known, so she implored him to provide various other addresses when he crossed the border; her file noted three different addresses. The report on her concludes, interestingly, with the point that she is "feminine and attractive" and a good potential candidate for "unofficial collaboration" with the *Stasi*.[93] Her assignment would be to work at Cafe Moskau. It appears that her associations with the West Berlin Turkish men might have resulted in her being pressured to work for the *Stasi*. It is unclear what appeal the foreign men, especially the Turks, had for her – entertainment or material concerns. However, it is clear that the associations impacted her standing with her neighbours and her state.

Turkish nationals like Cahit went to East Berlin for myriad reasons: exploration, adventure, and perhaps a feeling of greater social freedom. Cahit was not alone in feeling more welcome in East Berlin; others reported this as well. After the guest worker program officially ended in 1973, very little changed in the *Stasi*'s tracking of Turkish nationals in the GDR. Indeed, the files continue through 1989. Regardless of the stated reasons, such as suspicions of drug smuggling, illicit political activities, and the sale of illegal passports, it seems that many of the men the *Stasi* tracked were deemed risky solely because of their contact with East German women. A Turkish man from Varto, in eastern Anatolia, was tracked for his encounters with four different East German women in 1979, as noted in a report titled "Summary of a Turkish Citizen who has

Contact with multiple GDR female Citizens."[94] The man apparently was reported on in the name of "political filtering activities," a *Stasi* term for surveillance at the border train stations. Even under the guise of political suspicion, the contact with East German women always made it to the fore of the reports. When asked by an undercover agent about the differences between East and West Berlin, a Turkish man noted that a big difference was the widespread xenophobia common in West Berlin was not prevelant in East Berlin.[95] And he was not just trying to appease an East German friend: his answer was most likely sincere since he did not follow up with positive comments on the East German state, instead saying that it wasn't, in his opinion, "the real socialism."[96] According to a report three years later, this same Turkish national planned to marry his East German girlfriend and hoped to move to East Berlin to live with her. He reasoned that he didn't think that "as a Turk" he had good employment chances in West Berlin, expanding his comfort level in the East to the economic sphere.[97]

The same man also commented that former East Berliners who had moved to West Berlin were having difficulties socially and felt "as discriminated against as Turks," reinforcing his East-West comparison.[98] The report concludes with the foreign man apparently saying that in the East he has enjoyed "hospitality toward foreigners," even "as a Turk."[99] The undercover officer noted in his report that this man "has known no form of xenophobia in the GDR," and with an odd undertone, the officer also deemed him to be "intelligent" and "trustworthy," with "clean" and "orderly" clothing.[100] In other words, it was a point of pride for the *Stasi* that these foreign workers, whom the West German state economically exploited, apparently found more social and economic freedom in East Berlin.

The *Stasi* tracked another Turkish national ostensibly for his participation in an extreme right-wing political group, the ultranational Grey Wolves, yet his file concentrates mostly on his loose relationships with various East Berlin women.[101] The officers noted that he had been involved in the "terrorist group" in West Berlin as well as in Turkey, and as a result a detail was assigned to him from 22 October 1985 through 30 January 1986. However, files on his activities in East Berlin mainly report that he was out for a good time, not engaged in political organizing.

The man under suspicion, known in the file as "Number 279594" and also as "the Object," lived with his wife in West Berlin where he worked for the Ford Company.[102] He was a thin man of around twenty to twenty-five years, with an olive complexion, dark hair, a mustache, and "straight and separated" eyebrows.[103] His language was recorded as "*gebrochenes deutsch, ausländisch,*" or "broken German, foreign-speak."[104] During his frequent evenings out in East Berlin, he was in the company of women, including a woman given the cover name "Tunte."[105] Tunte was between eighteen and twenty-three years old, thin, blond, and blued-eyed, with full lips, a bit of a sunken chin that almost formed a double chin, and thin, plucked eyebrows lined with black pencil.[106]

A typical evening out for 279594 occurred on 22 November 1985 when he acted more like a typical womanizer than a political radical.[107] The *Stasi* tracked his every move, minute by minute, once he entered East Berlin at exactly 5:24 p.m. At exactly 6:01 p.m., 279594 greeted Tunte with a hug and went home with her. He was wearing a black leather jacket, black-grey speckled pants, and loafers. About ninety minutes later they emerged, with Tunte having changed her clothes from black pants to red pants and a black Adidas jacket. They first stopped at Cafe Moskau before continuing on to Lindencorso. The informant reports that the Object no longer showed any interest in Tunte once they arrived in Lindencorso, however, and instead sought out "other female companionship," leaving Tunte at a table so that he could pick up women at the bar and dance with them instead.[108] Around 11:55 p.m., apparently "other foreigners" who were the Object's acquaintances pointed out the late hour – the quickly approaching midnight deadline – and they all left at 12:01 a.m. for the Friedrichstraße border crossing, entering it at exactly 12:08 a.m.[109] More than a month later, this Turkish man had a similar evening out, arriving in East Berlin at 7:27 p.m. and then hanging out at Lindencorso to drink champagne with other "foreign men" while "openly searching for female companionship."[110] The report's clinical tone adds an air of judgment to the Object's free-spirited evening, leaving readers to wonder whether this man was really followed for his political activities or for his philandering.

Stories like that of the "the Object'" were not uncommon, and the acclaimed 2003 novel *Selam Berlin*, by Yadé Kara, has brought cross-border philandering into the public consciousness while it remains largely outside historical narratives.[111] The book, a coming-of-age novel narrated by a horny teenage boy, features a Turkish-German family at the time of German unification. Scholars think of the novel alternately as a post-unification novel, as a popular novel, as "self-consciously transnational," and as the first Turkish-German *Wenderoman*, or "German unification novel."[112] The narrator's father had become involved in a long-standing affair with an East German woman, Rosa, and the Wall's fall exposes his secret when she suddenly shows up in West Berlin. Petra Fachinger comments on the use of Berlin in the novel thusly: "Rather than using Berlin as a mere backdrop, Kara engages the city in several emerging literary discourses and paradigms: Berlin as a city in transition, as the 'other city,' as a 'play zone,' where a person can 'appropriate a range of identities without serious consequences.'"[113] The fictional account mirrors the historical realities: for many the city was indeed a "play zone" and area of escape, freedom, and social and sexual exploration.

These border crossings are significant from different vantage points: to East Berliners, these visitors not only were novel but also served as a conduit for hard-to-obtain goods. For their East German girlfriends, Cahit reported, the Turkish men brought gifts: "They were such idiots – bringing so many gifts."[114] As already noted, the introduction of the gifts also raises questions: what were East German women really after? In contrast to most narratives of ethnic Turkish guest workers – which feature uneducated, Anatolian or rural, and devotedly Muslim men – these border crossers were constructed as "Westerners," not just with their West Berlin residence permits but also through their ready access to Western material goods. In many cases, what concerned the *Stasi* the most was that these Turkish nationals served as representatives of West Berlin, of Western consumerism and political ideologies, and of the Turkish Republic's allegiance with the Western Bloc. Indeed, the history of material culture and consumerism in the Eastern Bloc is vast and draws on a wide range of sources; paradoxically, most socialist countries recognized both the spiritual alienation money creates and how poor material conditions contributed to their own demise.[115]

Transgressors

All of the categories in this chapter involve a level of transgression – literally and figuratively – but this final section focuses specifically on the point of view of the state and its deep suspicion of foreign nationals who entered its territory and broke its rules. As a group, the men discussed in the *Stasi*'s files are necessarily a skewed sample – they had violated a regulation or engaged in suspicious behaviour that had warranted the *Stasi*'s attention in the first place. Most of the Turkish nationals who ended up in the *Stasi* files missed the midnight deadline to cross back into West Berlin, or were caught with illegal goods, involved in political organizations considered suspect, or suspected of assisting with the illegal departure of an East German citizen. In short, they were suspicious as rule breakers, not necessarily singled out by their nationality, ethnicity, or religion.

In many of the cases against ethnic Turks, the GDR invoked moral codes. Morality was indeed a Cold War weapon. The East German struggle to define not only new legal codes but also new social ones made morality a part of the revolutionary rebuilding of society.[116] According to Jennifer Evans, "in East Germany, the struggle to define new social and legal maxims turned on the place that morality was to have in the revolutionary rebuilding of society."[117] For a case in point, in 1983, a Turkish man, Mr Halil, who had come to West Germany to work at the Ford factory, was arrested in East Berlin for carrying a pornographic film and a pornographic keychain in the lining of his coat.[118] Mr Halil said in his defence that a friend had given them to him two weeks prior, and that he had carried them in his coat ever since, having apparently forgotten that they were there. While possible, Mr Halil's explanation is not very believable; it is more likely that he was smuggling the pornographic goods into East Berlin to sell them for a profit and that he had been doing so once a week for thirteen years, from 1970 to 1983.[119] This case prompts the question of which aspect bothered the state more: the unwholesome nature or the underground economy. Despite its official morality, the East German state often used sex to sell its own ideas, most famously in its monthly *Das Magazin*.[120] *Das Magazin* specialized in racy stories and articles and was authorized to publish a nude photo in every issue; it was one of the only sources of publicly available pornography.[121] Maintaining the state monopoly on pornography was not easy, but keeping up the pretense of state morality remained a priority.

Many guest workers also sought to profit from their unique positions as border crossers. In a few cases, marriages between Turkish guest workers and East Berlin women reportedly occurred for money. Reports in the files note Turkish men charging between 10,000 and 12,000 marks (and in one case up to DM30,000) to facilitate the smuggling of people out of East Berlin and into West Berlin through marriage.[122] It is noteworthy as well that much of this information was gathered through the help of Turkish IMs (unofficial informers) reporting on their countrymen, calling into question loyalties on many levels. Indeed, the relationships between the *Stasi* and the West Berlin-residing guest workers defied simple definitions. One border guard reported with exasperation that a Turkish man been trying to befriend him and strike up a conversation

8 "People smugglers." Stasi file photograph of attempt to smuggle people in a car.

Source: BStU Zentralarchiv MfS – HA VI, Nr. 919.

with him whenever he crossed, wanting to know his address and offering him a pair of "real oriental slippers" from his homeland.[123] It is hard to tell whether the Turkish man sought to befriend the border guard for possible future benefit or simply out of cultural differences about appropriate familiarity. In another case, extensive photographs demonstrated how a Turkish man rebuilt the inside of his car to hide a woman behind the dashboard and console; they were discovered and arrested in December of 1973.[124] Another couple was discovered and arrested in 1979,[125] and in 1987 an attempt to smuggle out a man and child in the trunk of a Ford was also thwarted.[126]

Today the archived *Stasi* files are organized into four categories of people: the "affected," "third party," "collaborators," and "advantaged persons."[127] The archives avoid the loaded terms "victim" and "perpetrator." The "affected" category refers to those monitored, arrested, or controlled in some way and is the category containing much of the information on the border crossers in this chapter. However, the categories were not mutually exclusive. West Berlin-residing Turkish nationals were also "collaborators," challenging the view that they were only the *Stasi*'s subjects. Foreign men also spoke informally with *Stasi* officials and made it into their notes and files as well. Historian Gary Bruce has written that informal contacts, those the *Stasi* operatives contacted for information but with whom they did not formalize the relationship into IMs, were integral to *Stasi* work.[128] For example Turkish *Kontaktpersonen* (KP), or "contact persons," were common in the files, as was the case with "Panther," who reported on another West Berlin-residing Turk who had bragged to him about dating the tall blonde daughter of a manager of the border crossing at Friedrichstraße and, therefore, presumably knew when the "strictest" controls would be (the *Stasi* found the report dubious).[129] The fact that there were cases of guest workers functioning in a wide variety of roles for the *Stasi*, whether as informal contact persons or as official IMs, emphasizes how the East German state viewed these men: as useful, necessary, and competent.

Reliable figures on the numbers of IMs who were foreign nationals do not exist, but some information can be gleaned from the records. According to historian of East Germany Jens Gieseke, in 1988, for example, there were 1,553 West German citizens working as IMs. Gieseke reports that (non-German) foreign nationals served in even smaller numbers.[130] The total number of IMs remained between 170,000 and 180,000 from the mid-1970s onward.[131] Indeed, informants played such a large role in the everyday dealings of the *Stasi* that some historians have even debated whether the GDR could count as a "participatory dictatorship."[132] Motivations for working as an IM were often linked to fear and having been arrested, as in the case of Hidir Ciçek, who had come to West Germany from Istanbul in 1968 to work as a mechanic. Even in an internal *Stasi* poll (with potential bias) up to 45 per cent of IMs reported that "pressure and fear had played a role in their being recruited."[133] Indeed, many of the Turkish guest workers who became unofficial coworkers of the *Stasi* did so after having been arrested and "turned," though scholars remain divided on the roles consent and coercion played.[134] The recruitment and roles of Turkish contact persons and unofficial workers were diverse: one West Berlin-living Turk sought to help the *Stasi* because he thought it might aid his attempt to marry his East Berlin girlfriend, for example.[135]

The Turkish IMs were typically tasked with reporting on other Turks who had contacts and relationships with East Berliners. They were to investigate whether people were planning on leaving the GDR. In the case of Ciçek, after arrest he became an IM. Ciçek had often visited the East Berlin cafes Sofia and Pressecafe, where he got to know a woman from Königs Wusterhausen. After missing the midnight deadline for the third time, he was banned from entering the GDR with an *Einreisesperre*, or "entry ban." The entry ban (in addition to fines) was often given to Turkish nationals who missed the midnight deadline – including those who did so because of intoxication (in one case for being both drunk and barefoot),[136] those who spent the night illegally, and those who tried to smuggle unauthorized goods across the border (often scarves, perfume, and tobacco).[137] Desperate to return to East Berlin, Ciçek borrowed a friend's passport and forged the friend's name on the currency exchange form. His plan failed: he was arrested and sentenced to fourteen months in jail.[138]

During his incarceration, Ciçek reported on illegal drug smuggling, the illegal transport of an East Berlin woman out of the GDR over the Czech border, the illegal selling of Turkish passports, and that he had a "close relationship" with a woman from Königs Wusterhausen.[139] (It was also noted that he understood German and spoke "broken" German.)[140] At the time of his release to West Berlin, on 23 November 1971, Ciçek had apparently agreed to work as an IM under the code name "Tanju Abisch."[141] Ciçek apparently "wished to protect the GDR from harm" and wanted to "support the *Stasi*" in its mission.[142] The same memo also noted that he would have to be studied to see whether he could be trusted and counted on to provide truthful evidence.[143] During his tenure as an IM, he continued to live in West Berlin and was to report on ethnic Turks and other foreigners living there, especially those who started relationships with East Berlin women. In a 1971 memo about him, a *Stasi* operative notes that the GDR required "high quality unofficial work" to protect its borders because its opposition had a "global strategy" to "infiltrate the socialist states and undermine them from within."[144] In particular, Çiçek was to work to thwart "attacks on the border" that originated in West Berlin and draw on his contacts in West Berlin to learn of anyone seeking to help an East Berliner leave.

Coincidentally, the *Berliner Zeitung* (an East Berlin paper) reported on 9 July 1972 that Çiçek's place of employment planned to shut its plant by the end of the year, which the *Stasi* also included in its file on him. It is noted several times that Hidir had negative associations with the capitalist systems of both the FRG, the US, and Turkey, which was in the midst of its own social and political upheaval over the influence of socialist ideology. It is hard to tell why Çiçek initially risked arrest by trying to cross the border with a borrowed passport and what his true motivations for becoming an informant were: Was he so determined to get back to his East German girlfriend? Was he really dissatisfied enough with the capitalist systems in his life to turn to espionage work? Did the prospect of unemployment frighten him? Did he feel so threatened by his imprisonment in East Germany that he felt he had no alternative? We can only guess at definitive conclusions, but we can assume that Çiçek and many more like him had become quotidian parts of the suspicious, permeable border landscape of the divided city.

Some ethnic Turks flouted or tried to skirt the border laws of the East German state, often resulting in their arrest. If emigration through marriage was not possible, some Turkish nationals attempted to smuggle out their girlfriends illegally.[145] "Georg," a KP, reported that a Turkish national, who was no longer allowed into the GDR because of previously overstaying a visa, planned to smuggle out his East German girlfriend, her three children, and an unknown acquaintance (plus the acquaintance's wife and two children) who had lost his job as a result of applying to leave the GDR.[146] The extraordinary plan was to build a balloon to fly everyone out, and the East German citizen implored Georg to bring from West Berlin books on how to construct such a balloon.[147] It was of immediate significance to find out more about these acquaintances who had grand plans of escape, so a separate IM, "Mehmet," who was noted as being Turkish-Kurdish, was assigned to the case.[148]

West Berlin-residing Turks also intersected with the most significant political movements of the era. The family who had hoped to escape via balloon was a very interesting case. They were under suspicion in 1982 for their involvement in illegal trade union organizing at work and especially for their connections with the famous and historically significant Polish trade union Solidarity. Solidarity was the first trade union not controlled by the Communist Party in a Warsaw Pact country, and historians connect it with the social movement that helped end the Cold War. Political activism was common for this family, as it was reported that a sign in their window read, "We mourn Robert Havemann," the resistance leader and physical chemist who was arrested by the Gestapo, survived and flourished in the GDR after the war, and was placed under house arrest by the GDR in 1976 for his criticism of the state. He was still under house arrest when he died in 1982. The *Stasi* was also suspicious of the family because of their connections with "imperialist countries," their application to leave the GDR, and, interestingly, the fact that their daughter's boyfriend was a West Berlin-residing Turk. In fact, the files note that the family's "contact with foreigners" should be closely monitored. Significantly, three different Turkish nationals – the boyfriend in West Berlin and the informants Georg and Mehmet – were working on two different sides of the Cold War. In a highly significant historical moment of rising dissent – including the birth and growth of the Polish dissident movement and independent labour movements in the Eastern Bloc – three Turkish nationals' personal histories overlapped with larger themes and definitive Cold War events.

Conclusion

The relative ease with which West Berlin-residing Turkish nationals could maintain relationships with East Germans was fraught with political implications and irony. The surprising conclusion that this chapter's stories suggest is that – despite the *Stasi*'s attention in the East and distrust in West German society – these men were able to satisfy the most ordinary of human desires for connection, personal gain, and fulfilment and to operate in society in a remarkably diverse and contradictory range of ways. Unexpectedly, even though they lived on the margins of West Berlin and West German society, these men represented Western consumer culture for East Berliners: despite their limitations of language, employment status, and social standing, they represented the successes of Western capitalism. It is also ironic that behind the Iron Curtain they gained increased social liberty, demonstrated with their self-declared successes – evident in Cahit's bragging – with East German women.

Writ large, these examples highlight unique but important actions of minorities in Europe, show how integration can occur, and comment on Cold War interactions between the two Germanys. Border crossers both exemplify and complicate the Cold War climate – one of division, suspicion, and espionage. These stories also highlight constructions of gender in this period: Were East Berlin women informants? What role did controlling their morality and sex lives play in state decisions? Did they risk their standing with the state for relationships with foreign men? Were their relationships with foreign men a form of escapism or protest? Could their comment on the state and their opinion of its ideas be gauged from their choices in their personal lives?

Many of the foreign men who travelled to East Berlin invested in new lives and families there that spanned decades. In the *Stasi* files, they were, for the most part, a monolithic group of "foreigners" whose status was not decided by the guest worker program or relationships with West Germans. The workers in these peculiar cases had no intention of leaving when the program officially ended in 1973, or of having merely a temporary stay in Germany – West or East. Their personal relationships complement policy documents on immigration, citizenship, and labour laws in important ways by providing a view from the margins that complicates our understanding of Cold War history as a whole. Private relationships between Turkish citizens living in West Berlin and East German citizens continued well into the 1980s, demonstrating a participation and investment in a life – a personal one – in Germany.

5

Imperfect Solidarities

From 18 May to 28 May 1973, at the Duisburg-Huckingen steel mill, 380 of 700 workers went on strike over their increasingly poor working conditions, including speed-ups and dangerous tasks, such as working with burning-hot materials.[1] German workers organized the work stoppage and did not include their Turkish co-workers. Instead they accused the Turks of strike-breaking. However, Turkish workers could not remain passive about their working conditions either and joined the strike of their own volition. By the end of the strike, management attempted to fire the Turkish workers who had joined their striking West German co-workers. The *Betriebsrat*, or "workers council," was officially responsible for representing workers' interests (it ironically opposed the strike) and asked for the names of the striking Turkish workers. The Turkish workers all answered with the same name: "Atatürk," or "Father of the Turks," referring to the Turkish Republic's founder.[2] Though they were embodying the height of Turkish national pride, these workers had put themselves at great risk for solidarity with their West German colleagues. The temporary coalition produced results: all workers gained twenty-five to seventy cents more per hour and employees voted the entire existing workers council out of office.[3] In the end, everyone on strike was a de facto "German worker," meaning that, for some, they were no longer "guest workers," even if they would not have acknowledged this at the time.

This final chapter focuses on guest worker labour activism in West Germany in the 1970s with a closer look at a few key strikes. The intersection of ethnicity, class, and gender in a crucial moment in West German labour history highlights the important role immigrant female labourers played in resisting workplace inequality (sexism, wage differentials, and poor working housing). These strikes encouraged multi-ethnic and cross-gender solidarity among workers in early 1970s West Germany. In the strikes, foreign workers of different nationalities worked together and in interesting constellations, including with German workers, to build coalitions for successful labour organizing. In these case studies the term "Turk" stands in for a large, unqualified group of workers, especially in the eyes of employers, who were more likely to group foreign workers of different nationalities together. The main argument here, however, is that by the early 1970s and especially through labour activism, these foreign workers transitioned to *German workers*. In part 1 of this book, we saw how applicants transitioned into "guest workers" – a slippery category that represented both a group lacking agency and one agile enough to work around restrictions and even state borders as seen in the previous chapter. In this case study, identities expanded as the category working class (where class trumps ethnic difference) became more desirable and inclusive for many foreign workers. When the ultimate outcome of a successful labour strike was a benefit for German and foreign workers alike, management had no choice but to treat all workers as German workers, challenging the category "guest worker."

Most significant, striking foreign workers of all nationalities were no longer negotiating temporary problems; they were signalling that they were there to stay. In ways that parallel what foreign workers were achieving across the border in East Berlin in the same period, these workers engaged in life in West Germany in new and unexpected ways. While the previous chapter focused on primarily Turkish men's light-hearted adventures, escapism, and, for some, long-term investment in relationships across the Berlin border, the narrative now turns to the more serious fights for fair treatment and wage equality and the specific circumstances of being the lowest-paid workers of all: female foreign workers. Through their activism, guest workers altered their futures and demonstrated political consciousness and civic engagement. Their actions also highlighted the unsustainability of the guest worker program itself and their participation in it as they shifted from temporary workers to more permanent actors within German industry and society.

Foreign workers' notions of self-determination and newfound solidarity – with both other foreign workers and West German workers – challenged the power relations between workers and employers during negotiations of labour conditions and hinted at a longer commitment to life in West Germany. At the same time, foreign workers' labour activism was also a reason why West German employers began to lose interest in the guest worker program, contributing to the 1973 end to recruitment. Finally, guest worker activism can provide clues about the questions immigrant historians have long asked: When does an immigrant decide that home is no longer the place left behind? Or at what point do temporary "guest workers" become "immigrants"? When do they begin to invest in West Germany as a more permanent home? Or – from the other point of view – "why are you still here?"[4] After a brief introduction to the history of foreign workers' labour protests, this chapter will take a closer look at the wave of strikes at Pierburg Auto Parts Factory in Neuss, West Germany, which was notable not just for its great success but also for the fact that foreign women spearheaded it and succeeded once they achieved solidarity with their German co-workers.

A few representative strikes illuminate foreign workers', especially women's, activism and its impact in the early 1970s. The strikes at Pierburg reveal more than just an argument against the sexist "Light Wage Category II," which allowed the company to dodge equal pay for equal work. In choosing to strike, these foreign women also asserted a new identity – one forged through their intersecting experiences as women, foreigners, guest workers, and factory workers.[5] Ultimately, their labour activism benefited all workers at the factory and challenged the imposed category of guest worker, switching the emphasis from *guest* to *worker*. As such, these foreign workers stand at a crucial intersection of immigration history, labour history, and German citizenship debates.

Foreign Labour Activism in Germany

Since the early nineteenth century, foreign workers in Germany have used labour activism, legal and illegal, to negotiate definitions of belonging; of local, national, and class identity; and of solidarity. Historian John Kulczycki has argued that ethnic Polish miners in nineteenth-century Germany, though aware of cultural and linguistic differences, worked together with native German co-workers towards common working-class goals, with the main barrier to class solidarity being German workers' prejudice against them.[6] What connects the nineteenth-century movements with more contemporary protests is not only the role of migrants but also the civic participation inherent in labour activism. For nineteenth-century foreign miners, according to David F. Crew, "occupation ... provided the miner with an 'integrated' role in German society ... [that] combined economic, social, and legal functions," and it is this "occupational community" more than material deprivation that explains why workers strike.[7] In the case of post-war guest workers, occupational community cannot be assumed as a goal since many workers maintained a desire to eventually return "home." However, through labour activism, both supposedly temporary workers and their reluctant hosts often achieved occupational community, whether they meant to or not.

By the 1970s, foreign workers were well-integrated into the West German economy: by the early 1970s, the West German construction, steel, mining, and automobile industries had become largely dependent upon foreign labour.[8] In 1973, 35.7 per cent of all guest workers were employed in the iron and metals industry, 24.1 per cent in processing trades, and 16.6 per cent in construction.[9] In 1973, 11.9 per cent of all workers in West Germany were foreign; put differently, every ninth worker was foreign and, in manufacturing specifically, it was every sixth worker.[10] Yet despite the vital role they played, labour unions and smaller elected workers' councils often isolated foreign workers while employers exploited them.[11] German labour unions were initially critical of the guest worker program, fearing the program would depress wages and working conditions.[12] However, unions strategically ended their resistance to the program in order to be involved in the planning process – for example, in securing the same wages across the board – and to recruit foreign workers into their ranks.[13] By the end of the 1960s about 20 per cent of foreign workers were organized – a significant number considering that only 30 per cent of West German workers were organized.[14]

Guest workers participated in and initiated both legal and illegal labour activism from the beginning of the guest worker program.[15] On 30 April 1962, in the city of Essen, three hundred Turkish workers went on strike over underpaid *Kindergeld*, or child benefit payments. During the strike, workers sang the Turkish national anthem, and the police responded by shooting rubber bullets and deporting ten of the striking Turkish workers.[16] In the aftermath of the strike, which prompted much negative press in Turkey for the guest worker program, the Federal Labour Ministry complained that West German officials in Istanbul were falsely promising workers child benefit payments for children left behind in Turkey. "[The workers] cite that the Liaison Office reassured them that they would have the same rights as German workers and all other foreign workers," the BA explained; it warned the Liaison Office not to do anything that would "lead to misunderstandings."[17] In this way, the bureaucratic mismanagement and ineptness that imbued the application process and travel to Germany continued.

Turkish workers were indeed eligible for German child benefit payments but not for children left behind in Turkey, an arrangement that did not suit the transnational families that resulted from the guest worker arrangement. Those on strike in Essen appealed for help to West German labour unions, which replied in essence that though the striking workers were right, there was little unions could do to help. They also appealed unsuccessfully to the Turkish Consulate in West Germany.[18] Neither the West German unions nor the Turkish Consulate would represent these workers, placing them in a no-man's-land, which mirrored their lived reality as not truly welcome in West Germany and yet no longer under Turkish protection.

Foreign workers' problems stemmed from the fact that foreign workers were rarely considered in national discussions of "equal rights." Both employers and the West German government deducted money for taxes, pensions, social benefits, and rent from workers' paychecks, regardless of whether foreign workers planned to take part in the social services such payments supported. These benefits far exceeded what many workers would receive in their home countries and made labour immigration very desirable, but enthusiasm waned over time as workers received mixed messages. The patronizing orientation pamphlet *Hallo Mustafa!* explained that such deductions were simply a part of life and not meant to be understood by foreigners.[19] "You don't understand," the pamphlet chided, "and can't tell the difference between gross and net pay. Most of all you don't understand the deductions for social benefits and taxes ... [You] get the feeling that they are trying to take you for a ride with these complicated numbers and figures ... [Dear] Mustafa ... you all are much too suspicious."[20] However, Turks' suspicions were reasonable: the West German Liaison Office in Istanbul could not offer workers a clear idea of what their wages or benefits in West Germany would be – prompting the Turkish Federal Employment Ministry to request a set minimum wage, especially for female workers – and the information it did distribute was often misleading, erroneous, or misunderstood.[21] In light of how the guest worker program had functioned before the first day of work in West Germany, it is not at all surprising that many workers were suspicious of their paychecks.

Many guest workers were disappointed with their jobs because of a combination of negative aspects, including low wages, strenuous working conditions, the risk of workplace injury, and general underemployment.[22] Most significant, despite the length of their stay, guest workers had few chances of promotion over time.[23] "In the beginning our wages were very low. [But] everyone who wanted to go didn't care about the wages very much," reported a man from Bursa, Turkey, who came to West Germany in 1963. "The [West German] government didn't give this much importance ... I earned 3 DM per hour. A German worker doing something much simpler was earning about 6 to 7 DM per hour."[24]

However, the Turkish Employment Service did take notice of workers' poor wages abroad. The attaché for labour and social concerns of the Turkish Consulate informed the Liaison Office that a minimum wage of DM3 an hour for men and DM2.60 an hour for women was imperative and that the Turkish Employment Service would send workers only if these conditions were met.[25] The West German Association of Chocolate and Sweets, which employed many foreign women, replied that it found the request "astonishing," as it did not know of any wages above DM2.50 per hour in the category "unskilled and physical labour," which presumably was for female workers.[26] Furthermore, this wage of DM2.50 was for only a "certain part" of the unskilled category that "doubtful would be considered for female Turkish guest workers," it continued.[27] The Association of Chocolate and Sweets later reported that the minimum wage would be impossible to instate because it would be an "extremely unpleasant situation" to explain to those already working for DM2.27 that the newly arrived Turkish female workers were to earn DM2.50 an hour.[28] Turkish female workers could get a raise, the association reasoned, only when they could "handle the demands of a higher-paid wage category."[29] Despite Turkish officials' attempts to set a standard for their workers, West German employers remained resistant and continued to rely on sectoral collective bargaining instead.[30]

Foreign workers often had larger problems with their employers than their poor wages. Workers' housing, as discussed in chapter 3, was often a key point of exploitation of workers who had few alternatives but to live in company-supplied housing, with rent deducted from their paychecks. In a documentary film about the Pierburg strikes, one woman declared that the firm's housing represented "modern-day feudalism."[31] She paid DM60 a month to live four to a room with no running water and a manager who restricted all visitors, especially union representatives.[32] She emphasized during the 1973 Pierburg strikes that "foreign women haven't forgotten how they have been treated by the company." She responded by drawing up flyers that proclaimed, "Does feudalism still exist?" The flyers cited the West German Constitution's Article 13, which stated that one is guaranteed freedom within one's home, including the ability to receive guests. Another female employee at Pierburg apparently paid DM200 in rent for a damp cellar room that had previously been used to keep pigs."[33] Such horrific housing problems, which were specific to foreign workers, engendered unusual and fraught relationships between employer and employee.

Foreign workers also suffered from poor working conditions, such as *Akkordarbeit*, or the exasperating piecework system that many West German employers used. According to *Akkordarbeit*, wages could vary based on the number of days worked and on the completion of certain tasks.[34] A spinning factory's orientation booklet explained in Turkish: "As you know, nobody can work at the same speed and produce the same amount ... The *Akkord* system is simple. Whoever produces more gets paid more."[35] Elif explained to me the confusion and potential for errors in an *Akkord* paycheck thusly:

A day before [payday] we received a receipt listing how many hours we worked or how much we produced, because we worked on different machines and did different work, and [because] different work was worth different amounts ... three hours here, for example, three days, [then] a different machine. Every machine had different [a different] pay [scale], per hour and per piece ... Sometimes there were mistakes; sometimes it says you were on a different machine than you were. Then you go to the boss, and he checks it with his notes ... And then you go to the payment office, and they make corrections as well. [Then] you go get in line and wait because the department has a different opening hour.[36]

Piecework also depended upon collaboration with German co-workers, leading to aggravation and misunderstandings due not only to language problems but also to differing work speeds. There were even reports that West German workers complained Turkish workers were "spoiling the *Akkord*" by working too quickly.[37]

Guest workers had varying relationships with German co-workers. Elif reported that when she started working in West Berlin in 1964, the German women she worked with helped her learn her job and learn German.[38] Her co-workers wanted to be friends: "I had really good colleagues. They were the ones in the postwar generation, in the war times ... They were *Trümmerfrauen* ... and they wanted to become closer friends with me ... [They] were exploited too ... [and] had very low pensions ... [We] stayed in contact when they retired."[39] Elif's comment "They were exploited, too," signifies a sense of solidarity with her German co-workers, especially because they were women who had previously lived through a difficult time. Other workers also noted that in the initial years of the guest worker program they had good relations with their co-workers, citing problems with xenophobia later on in the 1980s and 1990s.[40]

However, despite signs of goodwill, guest workers had very different experiences at work than their German co-workers. Foreign workers were more likely to work on piecework and did shift work more frequently than their German co-workers.[41] As early as 1962, Turkish guest workers went on strike over the *Akkord* system. For example, Turkish guest workers at a West German mine in the Ruhr River region refused to work because they thought their pay was too little, and they insisted that they receive a steady paycheck instead of one that varied.[42]

Foreign workers, especially women, were ripe for labour organizing as the West German economy began to decline in the late 1960s and the guest worker system began to crack under the weight of long-standing problems. The particular hardships foreign workers faced, on and off the shop floor, coupled with their perceived temporary status, often hindered solidarity with German colleagues. Yet despite such vastly different experiences, within many strikes there were imperfect moments of solidarity, when German and foreign workers came together, motivated by either common issues or personal gain.

Economic Downturns and Worker Responses

A short-lived recession from 1966 to 1967 was the first point of stagnation in the post-war period to combine high unemployment and lower real wages. While the period of 1948 to 1966 was one of continued expansion in West Germany, the first half of 1967 saw the first decline (–2.3 per cent) in gross national product since 1948, signalling for many the insufficiency of existing business policies.[43] Correspondingly, this period witnessed the first significant wave of post-war labour activism, foreign and domestic, to spread across West Germany.[44] When the West German economy began to falter in 1966, employers reacted immediately by laying off around 1.3 million foreign workers.[45] Employers also responded by putting more than half of all enterprise investment into labour-saving technology, which increased mechanization and production speeds, worsening working conditions.[46] The 1966–7 recession also ended the conservative Christian Democratic Union party's (CDU) dominance in the government and ushered in a more social market philosophy; the CDU adopted the platform of a "social market economy" to win over workers would might vote for the SPD.[47] After the mid-1960s recession, the state's economic role expanded, especially with the 1967 Stability and Growth Law as well as a more general turn to Keynesian economics. However, these policies also proved unsustainable during the 1973 energy crisis, as West Germany was as heavily dependent on imported oil as other Western industrial nations were.

Workers also responded to the 1966–7 recession and its impact on workplace conditions, especially the speed-ups. In September 1969, 140,000 workers from sixty-nine companies within the steel, metal, textile, and mining industries made news throughout West Germany with their labour strikes.[48] Shortly thereafter, the 1973 OPEC oil embargo prompted further economic downturn and stagflation while workers' wages could not keep up with cost-of-living increases.[49] The West German "economic miracle" had relied on increasing productivity by hiring more workers to work in increasingly mechanized factories with faster machinery, such as conveyor belt production. At the same time, employers maintained low wages – wages that remained low especially in relation to profit margins, inflation, and the new speeds of production. In 1973, 275,240 workers, many of whom were foreign, from 335 firms went on strike.[50] The progressively insecure economic situation made workers' uprisings common.[51]

Foreign and West German workers had varying degrees of solidarity in labour organizing in the late 1960s and early 1970s. In some cases, West German and foreign workers did not support each other and yet both ultimately benefited, as was the case at the Hella Automobile Producer in Lippstadt, West Germany. On 16 July 1973, eight hundred German skilled workers received a fifteen-cent-per-hour raise while unskilled (mostly foreign) workers received no increase.[52] In response, the foreign workers went on strike, demanding fifty cents more per hour, which intimidated the workers' council at Hella. "They will kill us if we force them to work!" claimed the workers council's president, referring fearfully to the three thousand foreign workers from Spain, Greece, Italy, and Turkey who went on strike from July 17 to 19 July 1973.[53] On the third day of the strike, the press arrived and the tabloid *Bild* apparently reported, "Guest workers are beating their German colleagues."[54] As a result, the police came to "protect" those willing to work from the "violent" guest workers. While there were no punches thrown, the West German co-workers at Hella were also not willing to join the strike and only offered words of support, such as "you do good job!"[55] The foreign workers were, however, successful, and in the end all workers – including the West Germans – gained raises of between thirty and forty cents per hour. The foreign workers had risked more than their German co-workers could have: they might have lost their jobs and their housing, as well as the work and residency permits needed to stay in country.

In the majority of cases, foreign workers lent their solidarity to West German workers, but the reverse was less likely to occur.[56] One of the most famous strikes among foreign workers was prompted by vacation leave: the so-called "Turkish Strike" at the Cologne Ford factory from 24 to 30 August 1973.[57] The 3 September 1973 cover of *Der Spiegel* features Turkish men holding a sign demanding "*6 Wochen Urlaub*," or "6 Weeks of Vacation," eliminating any doubt that, at its core, this was a strike over foreign workers' issues. The image also highlights that this strike was all male, with a mustached Turkish man in the photograph's foreground. Because of the great distances foreign workers wished to travel, such as home to remote places in Turkey that could take up to five days to reach, they had different needs for vacation allotments than West German workers did, making it a common impetus for conflict.[58] Vacation time was a problem specific to foreign workers: for example, 1,600 Portuguese workers at the Osnabrück Karmann factory and 250 Spanish workers at the Wiesloch rapid printing press demanded new regulations about vacation time, including that they would be able to take their remaining vacation days all at once.[59]

In 1973, Ford management fired Turkish workers who had returned late from vacation, and 300 Turkish workers protested with a strike and sit in – against the wishes of their union.[60] Seeing an opportunity, German workers joined the Turkish workers' self-organized strike to request higher wages for themselves. When the Metal Workers Union and the company's workers' council joined in, the management agreed to pay for a small wage increase to offset inflation. The German workers and union members were satisfied, but management continued to ignore the Turkish workers, prompting outrage and an escalation of the strike. Turkish workers were 53.1 per cent of the workforce but only 12.7 per cent of the workers' council.[61] A large fight involving the police ensued, arrests were made, and the management fired many of the Turkish workers out of retribution, leading to their deportation.[62] For the Turkish workers, the main outcomes were widespread media

Table 1. Comparison of the average hourly wage of West German and Italian
workers at the Volkswagen plant in Wolfsburg, Germany, in the years 1963–1973

Year	West German male Wages (DM)	Italian guest worker male Wages (DM)
1963	3.95	3.35
1966	4.30	3.67
1970	4.63	3.98
1973	5.40	0.68

Source: Anne von Oswald "'Stippvisiten' in der 'Autostadt': Volkswagen,
Wolfsburg und die italienischen 'Gastarbeiter,'" in *Zuwanderung und
Integration in Niedersachsen seit dem Zweiten Weltkrieg*, ed. Klaus J. Bade
and Jochen Oltmer (Osnabrück: Rasch University Press, 2002), 234.

attention and a repeal of some of the layoffs – but at the expense of
"resentment of the foreigners' rabble-rousing."[63]

Foreign workers' grievances did not necessarily differentiate along
gender lines or nationalities: male and female foreign workers alike
had legitimate complaints about their pay scale's inequity. In a study
of Italian guest workers, historian Anne von Oswald found that West
German males' wages were higher than the Italian males', and that they
increased more quickly as well (see table 1). The situation was very
likely similar for Turkish and other foreign males' wages when compared to German men's wages.

And yet labour activism in the 1960s and early 1970s began to forge
new and even surprising alliances between West German and foreign co-
workers, even as the two groups continued to view each other as distinct.
On the other hand, moments of solidarity worked to dissipate, over time,
tensions between these groups, as they demonstrated to all sides that
guest workers were not necessarily temporary and that their lives in West
Germany were perhaps more permanent than even workers had planned
or were willing to acknowledge. In most of the early 1970s strikes, a precarious occupational community was achieved, in some cases, such as at
Hella in Lippstadt, through the result – raises for all – and in other cases,
as in Duisburg-Huckingen, through joint involvement.

That these two disparate groups came together through labour activism is not surprising considering that the workplace was the main source
of interaction. The Pierburg strikes, the subject of the next section, presents a case study that highlights both the tensions among different groups

and, at the same time, success through solidarity. Female foreign workers initiated wildcat strikes at Pierburg over discriminatory wages, but continued the strike to protest poor conditions (especially housing) and poor union representation. But by the end of the strike, all workers – male and female, foreign and German, skilled and unskilled – joined together in an increasingly common and successful coalition.

Post-war "Light Wage Categories" and the Pierburg Strikes

"The public is astonished by the determination of the foreign women," proclaimed a West German television reporter on 13 December 1973.[64] "And rightly so," she continued. "The foreign workers – women, no less – threatened to disrupt the entire West German automobile industry."[65] The 1971–3 wildcat strikes at the Pierburg Auto Parts Factory (near Düsseldorf) did indeed send shockwaves through the West German auto industry. The summer of 1973 saw a sharp increase in workers' activism more broadly, including a wave of "women's strikes." On 16 July, four thousand mostly female foreign workers went on strike at the Hellawerk Factory in Lippstadt, thirty female workers went on strike at the Opel factory in Herner, and seamstresses protested speedups in Cologne.[66] These strikes were part of a labour insurrection of men and women, foreign and German, that swept the country in the early 1970s as the post-war economic boom came to a crashing halt. Foreign guest workers, often the first to be laid off, bore the brunt of high inflation, rising prices, declining growth rates, widespread unemployment, and social discontent. For foreign workers, activism in the early 1970s had a larger significance than just securing better working conditions.

While scholars tend to pay more attention to the "Turkish Strike" at Ford, the Pierburg strikes in Neuss were arguably more significant, as they were spearheaded by foreign women, achieved full participation by all employees, and successfully challenged a federally mandated wage system. Foreign women do not make up a very large part of the literature on labour activism in post-war Europe. However, female foreign workers, often acting in solidarity with women of different national origins, were the primary instigators behind many battles over pay inequities for both foreign and German women. Female workers of various nationalities participated in the Pierburg strikes, and in this case gender provided the main source of solidarity. After an introduction to the history of the West German "light wage categories," this section turns to the Pierburg strikes that impacted both foreign and German women's wages.

The guest worker arrangement was designed to recruit single, prefer-ably male, workers for two-year stays in West Germany. However, this description rarely matched the applicant pool or employers' demands, especially demands for female workers for jobs deemed "women's work." Historian Monika Mattes notes that the dubious yet popular cliché of the male guest worker who later sends for his wife and children has yet to be seriously critiqued by scholars.[67] The increased demand for female labour occurred at the exact time that West German women were encouraged to leave the workforce to restore nuclear families in German society. As a result, West German factories relied heavily on foreign women to fill so-called women's positions.[68] By 1973, at the peak of the guest worker pro-gram, there were about 2.3 million foreign workers in West Germany and more than 52,000 of them were women.[69] By the time of the first Pierburg strike, there had been a long history of importing female foreign workers; it started slowly, dipped during the 1967 recession, and saw the largest surge beginning in 1968 (see table 2). In the early 1970s, workers from Tur-key, Greece, and Yugoslavia formed the majority of female foreign guest workers in West Germany, with Turkish women almost consistently com-posing the largest group starting in 1967 (see table 2).

West German "wage categories" differentiated and set the wages for "skilled" (often German men) and "unskilled" (often foreign and female) workers. The 1949 West German constitution guaranteed equal rights through a series of antidiscrimination guidelines in Article 3. In response, a 1955 Federal Labour Court declared the existing "women's wage" cat-egory unconstitutional. This ruling should have meant that women's sal-aries would increase by 25 per cent or more on average. Employers, who understandably wanted to keep wages down, invented a new category, the "light wage category," which had various levels – light wage category I, light wage category II, and light wage category III, light wage category IV, and light wage category V – meant to designate unskilled and "light work," to replace the now-illegal "women's wage category." From 1955 on, companies argued that women earned lower wages not because of their sex but because women had "less strength" and "lighter" work to do. When accused of renewed discrimination, employers countered that there were also men in the light wage categories. "Employers always get creative whenever it comes to the constitutional right of equal pay for equal work," reported the West German weekly *Stern* in 1973.[70]

Union leaders, most of whom were male, were generally unsup-portive of female workers' causes and did not protest the creation of the light wage categories. According to historian Ute Frevert, employ-ers and trade unions could agree on the new wage categories. For

Table 2. Female foreign guest workers in West Germany, 1961–1973

Year:	1961	1962	1963	1964	1965	1966	1967
Italy	2,942	1,608	545	517	729	520	157
Spain	6,280	8,615	9,013	8,078	8,050	7,508	1,436
Greece	5,879	11,852	13,681	11,155	14,310	14,035	1,471
Turkey	46	504	2,476	5,022	11,107	9,611	3,488
Portugal	–	–	–	5	232	1,188	334
Yugoslavia	–	–	–	–	–	–	–
TOTAL	15,147	22,579	25,715	24,777	34,428	33,505	6,886

Year:	1968	1969	1970	1971	1972	1973
Italy	212	224	111	55	32	14
Spain	4,646	6,816	6,924	5,689	4,632	4,226
Greece	10,740	21,328	19,931	2,092	5,629	1,776
Turkey	11,302	20,711	20,624	13,700	16,498	23,839
Portugal	1,118	2,313	3,298	3,627	3,489	5,550
Yugoslavia	–	14,754	19,908	17,252	12,432	16,461
TOTAL	28,088	66,146	70,810	52,484	42,992	52,070

Source: Monika Mattes, 'Gastarbeiterinnen' in der Bundesrepublik Deutschland: Anwerbepolitik, Migration und Geschlecht in den 50er bis 70er Jahren. (Frankfurt am Main: Campus, 2005), 39.

employers, the high court's ruling meant they would save money by avoiding wage increases, and for unions, higher wages for women might well have delayed the attainment of, according to Frevert, "more important trade union goals such as the implementation of the forty-hour week or the extension of paid holidays."[71] In collective bargaining agreements, officials designated unskilled and semi-skilled jobs according to the physical strength required, while in skilled and professional jobs the degree of "responsibility" was the criterion used for classification. According to economist Harry Shaffer's analysis of the ruling, the light wage categories were indeed created for female workers, even if this was unconstitutional: "encompassing 'light,' 'the lightest,' 'simple,' or 'the simplest' types of jobs, or … [those with] 'minimal physical exertion,' or 'minimal requirements,' these wage categories are presumably applicable to both male and female workers. In practice, work and wage categories are so defined that virtually all workers in the 'light wage categories' were women."[72]

Ultimately, "easy" and "simple" jobs were classified under wage categories I or II (the lowest wages), or at best under wage category III, while jobs that called for hard physical labour were generally classified under wage categories IV or V, which commanded considerably higher wages. In a kitchen furniture factory where both men and women worked on assembly lines to drill holes in doors, the women were in wage categories I and II, but the men were in wage categories III and IV, with the explanation that the men were drilling holes in "bigger and heavier doors."[73] In short, the new wage categories quickly came to differentiate men's from women's work. A 1970s government-sponsored study on the proper criteria for job evaluation recommended that only physical exertion be used for assessment, but it could do no more than provide suggested guidelines to the private sector.[74]

Female foreign workers in West Germany had long been performing heavy manual labour, a category largely gendered male; at the same time, employers paid foreign women according to the light wage categories, gendered female and often reserved for guest workers, regardless of their jobs' degree of physicality. For guest workers, the German Employment Offices in Turkey defied the spirit of the 1955 ruling and openly listed wages as: "Wage Category I (women)" and "Wage Category III (men)."[75] Protective legislation designed for female workers meant that *foreign* female workers were paid less but not that they were excluded, or actually "protected," from physically demanding jobs. It was this hypocrisy more than anything else that prompted the strikes at Pierburg in Neuss.

With the importation of guest workers, foreign women became the new "women workers" of West Germany. "Expanded employment of German females was economically a reasonable and feasible step, but it was undesirable from the standpoint of 'family policy,'" the industrial newspaper *Industriekurier* reported in a 1955 article explaining why guest workers were necessary.[76] Though this attitude of sending West German women home to rebuild nuclear families was primarily a product of the immediate post-war years (especially in contrast to East Germany), the real need for female workers remained unchanged, and West German companies increasingly sought foreign women to fill vacancies in "women's work."[77]

Like many West German industrial companies, Pierburg Auto Parts, which supplied carburetors to most of the West German automobile industry, relied heavily upon and profited from foreign female labour. Female foreign workers were drawn to the employment opportunities since the Pierburg factory in Neuss was one of the few factories in its area to hire women.[78] Pierburg also recruited the wives of men working in the surrounding area, in addition to foreign employees' wives, correctly guessing that working couples would put up with most any situation to be able to live and work together.[79] By 1973, Pierburg employed 3,600 workers, among them 2,100 foreign workers and 1,700 women (1,400 of them foreign) in the light wage categories."[80] About 70 per cent of the foreign workers were women, forming the majority of all female workers, all of whom were in the lower wage categories.[81] According to German sociologist Godula Kosack, who researched the strike in 1976, Pierburg employed 900 Greeks, 850 Turks, 380 Yugoslavs, 300 Spaniards, 200 Portuguese, 150 Italians, and 850 Germans.[82] Numbers like these show that Turkish women were a large part of the workforce, and necessarily a large part of those who stood to benefit from improved conditions and wages. Women in light wage category I earned 30 to 40 per cent less than their male colleagues. Pierburg's heavy reliance on female foreign workers made it ripe for a challenge to the discriminating light wage categories.

The first strike by foreign women at Pierburg, which took place in 1970, was initiated by 300 Yugoslavian women who were the first foreign workers Pierburg hired by contract in 1969. Pierburg housed them in three barracks on site, prompting, in the words of a workers' council member, an "uncanny sexual state of emergency" and the subsequent banning of male visitors.[83] These women apparently went on strike to protest the restrictions on their personal lives in addition to wage discrimination.[84] Unlike the traditional male and female roles, with romantic and sexual relationships, highlighted in the previous chapter, here we see female workers of various nationalities in a very different light. These female guest workers represented the political consciousness that foreign workers cultivated over time in addition to pursuing social lives and seeking escapism. The comments on the "sexual state of emergency" highlight that foreign women's freedom to socialize (and pursue a sex life) was severely restricted, especially when viewed in contrast to the seemingly limitless ability Turkish men in East Berlin had to cross literal and socially constructed borders, as seen in the previous chapter.

On 15 May 1970, foreign and German female Pierburg workers protested against light wage category I. Citing poor working conditions, unequal work distribution, and gender discrimination in raises, 800 foreign and German women signed a resolution requesting higher wages for all female employees.[85] Management did not respond until the next day when around 1,000 women were standing in protest on the factory grounds. Neither the union nor the all-male, all-German workers' council at Pierburg supported this initial strike. According to a 1970 newspaper report, Pierburg's management was not above threatening the striking women, especially the foreign ones.[86] Various department heads attempted to scare off the women with the threat of firing and deporting them: "If you don't want to work, then you'll go with the police to the airport!"[87] The risk of deportation was real, as their West German residence permits were contingent upon proof of employment and housing. Despite compromise attempts, intimidation attempts, and police intervention, the women (who numbered 1,400 in the end) persisted until they achieved the following: twenty cents more per hour for wage categories II to V, a bonus of DM20, and the use of a representative body to evaluate the wage categories of jobs.[88] After only a few days, management ended the strike by agreeing to eliminate wage categories I and II, but in reality wage category II remained.[89]

Three years later, on 7 June 1973, after becoming impatient about the promised wage reforms, 300 female workers at Pierburg conducted a "warning strike" and made the following demands:

(1) The Wage Category II (WC2) must be eliminated. All women of WC2 must be re-categorized to Wage Category III (WC3). (2) Those with seniority should earn more than newly-hired workers. (3) Because there are no clean work places in the firm, every employee is to receive a supplement for the dirty conditions. (4) Everyone (male and female) is to receive an additional 1DM per hour. (5) The women who are working on the special machines are to be regrouped in Wage Category V. 6) Workers must be paid for the wages lost during these proceedings [the strike]. (7) All of the women who perform heavy manual labor must finally be paid as much as men. (8) There cannot be any firings due to taking too many sick days. (9) Overtime may not be unfairly distributed. (10) Whenever one is sick and wants to go to a doctor, he or she should receive a half a day paid leave. (11) One day a month should be paid for housekeeping ["housewife's day"] … (12) Travel money must be increased. (13) Tomorrow everyone should be able to leave the factory two hours earlier to pick up his [sic] money.[90]

The elimination of wage category II and a DM1-per-hour raise for all workers were the main demands. In an attempt at solidarity, those on strike distributed flyers in workers' various languages – Spanish, Serbo-Croatian, Italian, Greek, and Turkish – proclaiming, "Two months ago, 200 of our workers mustered up the courage and went on strike for two days for higher wages."[91] It continued: "[The company said it] would not be coerced by terrorists, [and] that the majority of the employees were satisfied with their wages, since they were not striking along with them … Colleagues, why didn't you support us and strike with us? The demands are still valid: 1DM more an hour for everyone! Wage Category II must be eliminated!"[92] The organizers emphasized trans-ethnic solidarity against the management. After the union stepped in to negotiate, the strike ended on the second day. Management, however, maintained its goal of retaining the "cheap wage categories" at all costs, leaving most dissatisfied.

Pierburg did not take the strike seriously and planned to fire and replace the 300 workers with new, and therefore more insecure, foreign workers in the fall. The June "warning strike" ended with the promise of negotiations between management and the workers council, but new arrangements were not secured and the union did not follow up.[93] The foreign women who initially protested their wage category II found lit-tle support among their co-workers, in their workers' council, or in their union. The company's founder, professor Alfred Pierburg, called and spoke with the chair of the workers' council, Peter Leipziger, on 14 June 1973, and promised that there would be no firings, only paid suspen-sions of those the council fingered.[94] The workers' council incriminated the striking women by reporting them to the management (instead of representing their interests), and Pierburg deported six of the foreign women as a result.[95]

After such an unsatisfying result, it is little surprise that foreign women once again went on strike at Pierburg two months later, in August 1973, calling again for the elimination of wage category II. The union would not support the strike, and responded aggres-sively with an article in the union newsletter titled "Guest Workers Are Not Discriminated Against: The Pierburg Strike Is Illegal."[96] In a press release that was translated into Turkish, Greek, and Italian, the Metal Workers Union reported on 15 August that, "based on legal conditions in the Federal Republic, the Metal Workers Union cannot deem the work stoppage at the A. Pierburg Company legal."[97] How-ever, the press release continued, in order to dissipate the tensions, negotiations continued: "For some time the workers' council and the metal workers' union have been negotiating with the management for an equitable practice in the wage contracts. The hard work of the approximately 1,700 employees, especially the foreign women, is being unjustly characterized as 'physically light' (Wage Category II)."[98] The female foreign workers, however, lost patience with the negotiations and with the workers' council and carried out the strike on their own terms to great success. Significantly, the narrative of the Pierburg strikes is told by the striking workers themselves. A socialist industry and union publication collective, named "express," documented strikes across West Germany, focusing on fourteen different companies and published their finding in 1974 to make sure that the strikes entered the historical record. Despite the political agenda and often optimistic retelling of the strikes, this publication remains the main historical source of strikes.[99]

The August 1973 Strike over Light Wage Category II

On 13 August 1973, a Monday, as workers for the 6:00 a.m. shift began to arrive around 5:30 a.m., twenty female foreign workers distributed flyers, announcing that in an hour workers would go on strike for the elimination of wage category II and DM1 more per hour. By 5:50 a.m., between 200 and 250 (mostly foreign) male and female workers stood before the factory gates, declaring their support for the strike. At first the German foreman just observed; however, at 6:30 a.m. sharp, he demanded that they get to work. Shortly thereafter, the police arrived with patrol wagons and demanded that the factory gates be cleared of the striking workers. According to documentation published by strike leaders in 1974, the following melee occurred:

> One of the foremen fingers Elefteria Marmela – a Greek woman who along with her husband is a union member – as the organizer of the strike. As the police attempt to arrest Marmela, she resists and a scuffle ensues. Another Greek worker has a camera with him and snaps photos … The police respond by confiscating his camera. Another Greek man manages, however, to rip the camera out of his hand and throw it to another Greek worker. A new scuffle begins. Suddenly an officer grabs his pistol and screams, "Get Back!" A Greek woman steps up and yells, "So shoot me then! Or are you afraid?"[100]

The police tried to arrest Marmela, who resisted and was injured; she returned with a bandaged arm. In the end no one was arrested, but as the police wagons were pulling away, one officer apparently called back: "Dirty foreigners! I'll kill you!"[101] Three hours later, three Volkswagon buses filled with police officers arrived. This time the officers surrounded the protesters and arrested three Greeks, two women and one man, who were held for ten hours and interrogated. The police presence scared off many of those on strike, so at the beginning of the breakfast break, there were only 150 left on the picket line. The strikers cried, "*Al-le-raus!*" (or "Every One Out!"), in an attempt to secure solidarity with other workers. Their chants worked: by the end of the break, 600 additional workers (male and female) had joined the strike, completely stopping all production at Pierburg.[102]

The following day the entire early shift, about 350 people, stood in front of the factory gates. At 6:30 a.m. three buses filled with police arrived, and officers jumped out and immediately began battering the protesters. Many foreign women were injured and subsequently hospitalized.[103] The police again attacked Marmela, injuring her severely. The media, including television and radio reporters, arrived and began filming beatings and scuffles to be aired later. The German weekly *Stern* published a photograph of two policemen dragging a foreign woman away by her arm.[104] Once the cameras began recording, the police pulled back and there were no more arrests. By 11:40 a.m. the factory had closed. The striking workers had achieved almost total solidarity among the 2,000 foreign workers, male and female alike; likewise, the Metal Workers Union now stepped in to protest the violent police presence.

On the third day the strike began again with the morning shift blocking the factory gates in the early morning light. Several female foreign workers went into the factory, changed clothes, punched in, and then immediately returned to the strike. As a result, management, which was still refusing to negotiate, locked the main gates and in so doing locked the women out. According to eyewitnesses, the breakfast break again resulted in solidarity between those striking in front of the factory gates – who were calling "Every One Out!" – and those still inside.[105] One participant recalled that as workers greeted and hugged each other through the locked gate, they would break into tears and mutual hugs and the "will to strike remained unbroken."[106] In order to hinder their reunification, management apparently hung a chain about ten metres from the factory gate, but the workers repeatedly pulled it down; twelve female workers even stood on the chain so that it could not be pulled taut again.[107]

As the strike entered its fourth day, the women achieved the final turning point: they won the German skilled workers to their side. As the strike escalated, the strike committee presented the following demands: DM1 more for all workers, an end to wage category II, payment for all days on strike, and no firings.[108] These were conditions German and foreign workers alike could agree upon. The deciding moment was when the most highly skilled German workers of the factory, those from the tool shop, presented management with an ultimatum and stopped working at 9:00 a.m. sharp.[109] When the factory gates opened at 9:00 a.m., the solidarity between the German and foreign workers, which now united *all* workers against the management, was boisterously celebrated. Eyewitnesses offer a slightly more romantic version of the same event: the striking women handed each entering worker of the morning shift a red rose, to which was attached the statement, "We are expecting you at 9 o'clock."[110] The German-foreign solidarity "was a real blow to the management who had hoped to break the strike through the loyalty of the German workers," reported an eyewitness. "From that moment on the strike was won."[111] Telegrams from workers at other factories arrived to express support and solidarity.[112] An eyewitness reported: "Cash donations also arrived. Everyone stopped working. There were dances for joy as the German and foreign workers hugged each other. Foreign women fainted. The German workers … [who were] the skilled labor of the factory, gave an ultimatum to the management, at 10am you will have an agreement."[113] In the end, the solidarity among the workers – male and female, skilled and unskilled, foreign and native – changed the course of the strike, hastening the momentum the foreign women had already set in motion.

The following morning, the first results of the negotiations were made known: 12 cents more per hour, effective immediately, and, beginning 1 January 1974, 20 cents an hour more.[114] However, the results were disappointing, and a Turkish man called out, "If you stay at 12 cents, we will continue striking for twelve years!"[115] The negotiations continued, and at 1:00 p.m. the chairman of the local employers' association also stepped in to thwart the spread of workers' uprisings (strikes had begun breaking out in nearby areas, such as Lippstadt).[116] By 4:00 p.m. the decision was announced: Pierburg had eliminated light wage category II, guaranteed a raise of 30 cents more per hour, and promised a DM200 cost-of-living bonus.[117] Together these two raises equalled 53 to

65 cents more an hour. Those on strike accepted the terms and declared that they would be ready to return to work on Monday.[118] However, on Monday 150 foreign women continued to strike regarding payment for the days on strike. Management attempted to block them with trucks and shouted at them with megaphones. An office window was broken, and the police were called in. Again the German skilled workers stood up on behalf of the striking workers until management met their terms. Management issued a "warning" to those on strike.[119] But the real warning was to management, which learned through the course of the strike that the division of German versus foreign was becoming increasingly irrelevant, as the category of "worker" had expanded to include all.

The Strikes' Impact

In the early 1970s the Pierburg strikes could have served as the perfect case study. However, it was largely misunderstood or ignored by contemporary feminist and progressive sociologists at the time. The striking women at Pierburg did not necessarily view their actions in the same ways as their contemporaries, especially those drawing on negative stereotypes of Mediterranean women. A 1973 report on the strike told the story of Anna Satolias, a Greek woman who participated in the May 1970 strike, declaring at the end that it was a way for Mediterranean women to find emancipation. In the article, Satolias describes her dissatisfaction with her working conditions thusly:

> The work went from bad to worse, more production, more work, more workers, less working space. And the speed: faster and faster, the supervisor and the foreman shouting at us all the time – all that in the lowest wage category, which is called "light." First I joined the trade union – like my husband – then we women started making demands. We wanted the abolition of Wage Category I, because the work was and is heavy and not light – and because Category I is supposed to be only for beginners, although we had been working five or six years in this category. [120]

The article continues by pointing out that in the same year, Pierburg promoted Anna's husband, Nikiforus, to the position of tool-setter and placed him together with his wife and her colleagues in the machine room. "Perhaps," Anna said, "the firm thought we would be more docile then, because I would have to do what my husband said."[121] "Perhaps," Nikiforus responded, "the firm thought that as a tool-setter I would earn so much that I could let my wife stay at home – and there were even colleagues who said such things aloud."[122] Anna incredulously reported to the West German women's magazine *Jasmin*: "The firm might well have thought that he would leave his wife at home, and I would obey him."[123] Even though sociologist Kosack centres her 1973 discussion of the Pierburg strikes on the strong figure of Anna Satolias, her thesis is a nationalistic one that sees migration to Western Europe as a step towards emancipation for foreign women: "this is a term [equal rights] that she [Anna] has learned in Western Germany for the first time."[124]

In a troubling way, Kosack locates foreign women's exploitation in West Germany solely in their home cultures, which stand in mark contrast to West Germany: "[Migrant women] are virtually their husbands' servants. Their activities are limited to those typical in their home countries and indeed for all women in pre-capitalist societies – the kitchen, the children and the appropriate religious rituals."[125] The sociologist saw the strike as a sign of the rising tide of women's liberation movements and a raised consciousness, especially on the part of migrant women, who through their exploitation in West Germany had apparently come to realize a new feminist consciousness: "It is the extreme form of discrimination, which makes migrant women fight. They get much lower pay than male workers, have to suffer authoritarian behavior from the almost inevitably male foremen and, in addition, have a second day's work waiting for them at home – household and children – while their husbands consider it their right to relax after work. This obvious injustice mobilizes many migrant women against their previously unquestioned position as their husbands' servants."[126] However, to assume that migrant women were necessarily less progressive than West German women was a fallacy. It was not until 1956 that West German women were allowed to take jobs without their husbands' permission.[127] This interpretation failed to comprehend migrant women's unique circumstances, which compounded gender discrimination and the poor conditions guest workers (both male and female) had experienced for the last ten years in West Germany. Yet it was just such Mediterranean foreign women, not West German women, who first instigated successful protests against sexist wages in West Germany.

The Pierburg strikes also have important lessons about West German women's political consciousness and the West German feminist movement in the early 1970s. Although foreign women protested the light wage categories before West German women did, this fact was not always remembered. By 1973, West German women had not launched significant challenges to misuses of wage category II. One reporter wrote after the Pierburg strikes' conclusion that foreign women's heightened political consciousness impressed him, especially when compared with that of German women: "German female workers of this wage category [II] have neither at the Pierburg factories or elsewhere demonstrated that they were prepared to strike."[128] He continued with an even more stinging critique: "Among the German women of this wage category there is unfortunately missing, to a large extent, leadership-personalities." And yet despite the significance of the Pierburg strikes, it was all too easily forgotten in the larger narrative of the German women's movement. It was in 1978 that media reports on West German women's efforts to challenge wage categories first appeared, and, significantly, these reports did not reference the Pierburg strikes at all.[129] The Pierburg strikes quickly faded from view in the late 1970s and early 1980s. In these later reports, it is German industrial baker Irene Einemann who is credited as the first to challenge the sexist use of wage categories: "At long last, in the spring of 1978, Irene Einemann, a female baker's assistant in the North German city of Delmenhorst, filed suit demanding that her pay be brought up to the level of her male colleagues and won the case. Her wage was raised from the previous DM 6.86 per hour to DM 8.24 per hour, plus an additional supplement of DM 100 [that] her male counterparts were earning also, and the decision was made retroactive, with back pay due her as of January 1, 1976."[130] When reporting on Einemann, syndicated newspaper commentator Tatjana Pawlowski, five years after the Pierburg strikes, (falsely) credits Einemann as the first to stop "complaining" and actually protest her wage category: "Injustice cannot be overcome if justifiable criticism limits itself to complaining ... Who, until now, would have had the courage to oppose the long-established wage policies of many industrial enterprises?"[131] The courageous actions of the striking foreign women in 1973 at Pierburg seem to have been forgotten or lost among the broader West German population.

These lesser-known strikes provide important lessons about solidarity and the conditions that support it. First, certain homogenizing conditions – such as poor worker housing and discrimination – promoted cohesion among foreign workers, even merging national groups such as Turks and Greeks in new ways. Also, workplace sexism, wage differentials, and low representation among women created solidarity among foreign and native women that had not been seen before. Finally, the unity of all workers, despite the union's disinterest, provided the tipping point for the illegal Pierburg strikes, which challenged the traditional roles unions played in representing workers and negotiating on their behalf.

The impact of the Pierburg strikes and other strikes led by foreign workers in the early 1970s was not one-dimensional. Indeed, the Pierburg and Ford strikes were not truly "foreigners' strikes," as all of the strikes fundamentally altered working conditions, workers' solidarity, and the wage structure of the West German economy – by challenging the wage categories and the exploitation of foreign labour upon which it depended. Significantly, the strikes drew attention to the long-term effects of labour models that were meant to be "temporary fixes," including the guest worker program itself.

Conclusion: Our Fight Is Your Fight!

"That is no longer a strike. That is a movement!" Federal Chancellor Willy Brandt declared with consternation about the 1973 "Turkish Strike" at the Cologne Ford plant.[132] The Ford management apparently replied with resignation, "Over the years, we have discovered that foreigners came to us with a much too highly developed confidence."[133] Both Brandt's and the Ford management's comments effectively evoke the new image of guest workers in 1973 West Germany. After more than a decade of life and work in West Germany, they had indeed developed a political awareness that was effectively channeled into a successful labour movement. "The power that lay behind such a strike [at Pierburg] in the automobile parts supply industry demonstrates, for the first time, a real threat to West Germany's Fordist production model," journalist Martin Rapp commented in 2006.[134] However, the Pierburg strikes challenged more than just the West German economic and industrial model. In 1979, economist Martin Slater boldly reported that foreigners' successful labour activism – not just the recession of 1973 – directly affected the employers' decision to end the recruitment of temporary foreign labour: [Foreign] migrants, by the early 1970s, had increasingly come to be regarded as a ... political burden ... [Migrants] had come to be regarded as a social liability ... [due to their] own political transformation. By the early 1970s, the docile, hard-working migrant of the 1950s and 1960s had apparently *transformed into a radical member of the working class* ... Following close on the heels of protests and demonstrations by migrants over their housing conditions, these strikes were seen by governments as a sure sign that migrants were politically unreliable."[135] In other words, this economist is suggesting that workers' political consciousness and transformation into members of a larger, national working class helped end the exploitative labour recruitment program. While most historians agree that the end of labour recruitment was more multi-causal, labour militancy still had an impact.[136] The official end of the West German guest worker programs happened in 1973. However, the year 1973 is a false end to the program, which in many ways was never temporary and never really ended as this population continues to impact Germany today.

The narrative of the Pierburg strikes is neither a tale of victimization nor a triumph of good over evil. Rather, it tells the story of an evolution and slow integration of a supposedly temporary migrant population into a larger class and national consciousness. Foreign workers' activ-ism and collective bargaining, which occurred from the 1960s through 1973, provided an early sign of their commitment to West Germany as their home – a transition occurring earlier than scholars have pre-viously acknowledged.[137] Historians have long considered workers' decisions to stay in West Germany as occurring after the 1973 official recruitment stop. However, foreign workers, who had been saying for over a decade that they planned to return home, demonstrated through their activism a more permanent investment in West German society. Workers' protests, whether about housing or wages, indicated solidar-ity across nationalities as well as with West German co-workers. Dur-ing these strikes, foreign workers participated in German industry as "German workers" (consciously or not) and impacted German policy even if they were not officially included in the national polity, calling in to question later conservative claims about foreign workers' rights to German citizenship.

Foreign workers' dynamic roles in strikes and protests are not sur-prising considering that they were reacting to poor conditions not just at work but also in employer-managed housing, as well as drawing on memories of their deplorable train rides to West Germany and the long and tedious application process beforehand as outlined in the first two chapters of this book. However, material conditions alone cannot explain labour activism: there was also a more complicated social reality in guest workers' negotiations of their increasingly per-manent lives in West Germany.[138] Labour activism for foreign work-ers in the 1970s combined demands for economic, social, and in some cases legal parity in new ways – demands that signalled a claim on "occupational community" and a newfound sense of permanence in West German society for foreign workers. These strikes called into question who belonged to the category German citizen or German worker, long before foreign populations dominated public political debates.

Conclusion: Good Intentions and Contested Histories

In 2013, after a thirty-year embargo, a top-secret document of the British National Archives was released: the meeting minutes from a private discussion between Margaret Thatcher and Helmut Kohl on 28 October 1982. The newly elected Kohl wanted to keep the meeting a secret because he was presenting a plan he did not feel the German public was ready for – a radical plan to reduce the number of Turks in West Germany by half within four years. Kohl explained his rationale to Thatcher by saying that Turks "came from a very distinctive culture and did not integrate well" and therefore put West German society at risk. Kohl provided multiple examples, ranging from illegal employment to forced marriages, to demonstrate what he called "a clash of two different cultures."[1] As a point of comparison, he noted, "[West] Germany had no problems with the Portuguese, the Italians, even the Southeast Asians because these communities integrated well." Kohl's words were telling, as was the media response to the document's recent release. *Der Spiegel* ran the story of the top-secret meeting in 2013 as a big reveal, but the history of the two decades following the official end of guest worker recruitment in 1973 plainly demonstrates that the West German agenda to send the guests home was far from secret. At best, the West German government was indecisive about how to stop the migration it had begun. Indeed, how and when the guest worker program really ended remains debatable.

The West German Ministry of Labour in Nuremberg announced on 23 November 1973, that it could "no longer accept any foreigners" into West German territory.[2] Federal Labour Minister Walter Arendt, together with the Federal Cabinet, drew on the Federal Labour Promotion Act for the authority to halt guest worker recruitment. In 1973, both the oil shocks and labour unrest had made the maintenance of the guest worker program unattractive if not untenable. Before the recruitment stop, the Labour Ministry had taken measures to quell new foreign labour by raising the employer-paid recruitment fee from DM300 to DM1,000, but more drastic measures were needed. According to the *Süddeutsche Zeitung*, Arendt referred to the recruitment stop as precautionary and saw "no reason for serious concern."[3] Apprehension was not so easily subdued, however: West German employers and emigration countries both hoped the recruitment stop was temporary.[4] While the 23 November measure was indeed "precautionary," it stuck and ended formal recruitment.

The energy crisis and labour unrest were not the sole reasons for terminating the guest worker program though. With thoughts that anticipated Kohl's concerns, the Federal Labour Ministry also referenced an increasing number of attempts to "counteract the 'concentration' of foreigners in certain cities," implying that social and cultural concerns had prompted the recruitment stop even more so than economic ones.[5] To put these concerns in context, at the time of the announcement, Turks made up 23 per cent of all foreigners in West Germany, with the next highest population being Yugoslavians at 20 per cent.[6]

West Germany's conflicting ideas about and, at times, disdain for foreign populations were well known. In a 1973 study published by the Istanbul Institute of Economic Development, the authors, Duncan Miller and İhsan Çetin, reflected many Germans' concerns and referred to the period from 1972 to 1973 as one in which Turkish workers in West Germany experienced a "sudden metamorphosis from beauty to beast."[7] This "metamorphosis" alluded to foreign workers' transition to a "source of unforeseen industrial costs, a heavy drain on public services, and, as a seemingly permanent underclass, a threat to social and political stability."[8] More interesting, though, are the authors' revelations about the hidden problems of ending the guest worker program. According to the study, the German workforce had, in fact, been in a steady decline since 1960 and was projected to remain so through 1985, creating a labour shortage – a revelation incongruous with the recruitment stop.

Various West German labour initiatives sparked the indigenous labour decline, including increased vacation leave, shortened working hours, pensions for those younger than sixty years old, increased disability pension coverage, and the general Western European attitude of valuing leisure time and recuperation, such as enjoying the popular employer-funded *Kur* program, or "to take a cure." According to Miller and Çetin, only an influx of foreign workers could sustain the West German economy for the foreseeable future, as in 1972 when the West German workforce fell by 180,000 workers and 170,000 incoming foreign workers offset the loss.[9] The decline would continue, and "the German economically active population [would decrease] by another 1.2 to 1.85 million workers by 1985."[10] The crux of the authors' argument was that foreign workers continued not to supplant German workers but rather to make up for their shrinking numbers and, further, to support their Western European lifestyles and attitudes about work and workers. Foreign workers' benefits outweighed their costs. This conclusion was at best unrecognized and at worst unpopular and ignored.

Ending recruitment changed little, however. Scholars have long written that the end of the recruitment prompted many foreign workers to settle their families in West Germany because they feared that if they left West Germany in 1973, they might not be allowed to return from Turkey – a non-European community member.[11] The early 1970s also marked the years when many workers moved out of employer-supplied dormitories and into neighbourhoods together with family members who had joined them from Turkey.[12] By 1974 the Turkish Labour Placement Bureau [*İş ve İşçi Bulma Kurumu*] reported that 55 per cent of Turkish workers stayed abroad more than four years, up from just 17.2 per cent in 1968.[13] Ironically, at the time when workers were more likely to stay, larger economic forces, conservative responses, and increased resentment by the general public encouraged not just ending recruitment but also actively pursuing policies to send foreign populations home.

End of an Era

The end of the guest worker program occurred when much of Western Europe was dealing with both a financial crisis and the aftermath of migration prompted by what historian Tony Judt termed northwest Europe's "insatiable demand for labor" and postcolonial immigration to European metropoles.[14] The demographic events of the 1950s and 1960s came to a head in the 1970s and 1980s in a predictable way. As a result, demographics pressured states to develop stances on key issues, stances that would have lasting impacts in the subsequent decades. And yet, unlike other Western European countries, Germany did not develop a "regularization" program for illegal immigrants participating in the underground economy. Belgium, France, Greece, Italy,

Luxembourg, Portugal, Spain, the United Kingdom, and the United States all developed regularization programs in this period. Regularization (also referred to as amnesty, normalization, and legalization) remains a controversial term for states looking to deal with illegal or unauthorized immigration, as well as those mired in unclear citizenship and naturalization processes.[15] Social scientists Stephen Castles and Mark Miller characterize the period beginning in the 1970s as a quest for control in which key industrial democracies sustained efforts to contain and prevent illegal migration and the skirting of immigration regulations.[16] France's first socialist president, François Mitterrand, employed the Ministerial Order (and subsequent orders) between 1981 and 1982 to implement the regularization of immigrants who had been in the country before 1 January 1981, and who had either proof of stable employment or a work contract. France's attempts at regularization were short-lived: when faced with rising competition from the more right-wing National Front (FN), the government attempted to curry favour with the electorate by reverting to more conservative ideas, such as a repatriation scheme that compensated migrants for returning to their home countries.[17] After the 1986 election made Jacque Chirac prime minister under Mitterrand, more conservative laws came into effect, especially now that the FN had a seat in parliament. As a result, the zero-tolerance anti-immigration Pasqua laws of 1986 facilitated immigrant expulsions and deportations. In other words, across Western Europe, increasingly conservative governments dealt with both temporary workers and immigrants harshly in the 1980s, initiating the end of an era.

After the 1973–4 oil shocks slowed the world economy, many Western European countries radically altered not just industrial production but also national attitudes about foreign workers. The crisis was not temporary. Oil prices rose again from 1981 to 1982, and, accordingly, West Germany experienced economic recession from 1982 to 1983. A conservative political turn accompanied the early 1980s economic downturn, with the election of Ronald Reagan in the United States, Margaret Thatcher in the United Kingdom, and Helmut Kohl in West Germany – the result of a conservative coalition of the Christian Democratic Union (CDU), the Christian Social Union (CSU), and their allies the Free Democratic Party (FDP) in 1982.[18] According to historian Rita Chin, conservative rhetoric on the "foreigner question" played no small part in engendering this conservative political turn. Indeed, the CDU attacked the preceding, more liberal, Social Democratic Party's (SPD) "willful neglect" of foreign populations' drains on social infrastructure in the name of its failed "integrationist policy."[19] In short, the CDU gained support as the SPD's "foreigner" policies failed. Before the election, the conservative parties outlined proactive solutions such as rotation policies and, philosophically, transferred the work of integration solely to the immigrants, who were to "Germanize" on their own.[20] After recruitment ended in 1973, foreign populations were increasingly seen as problematic. This perspective seemed prescient of Kohl's 1982 comments, which singled out "Turks" as less easily integrated than say the Portuguese and Italians, and where most negative comments about foreigners were about the amorphous categories of "Turk" and "foreigner."

By 1973 Turkish workers formed the largest group of foreign nationals in the West German workforce and every ninth worker in the Federal Republic was a foreign national.[21] About 30 per cent of workers returned home each year in the 1960s, but in the 1970s lengths of stay began to rise steadily.[22] Chancellor Brandt, who preceded Helmut Schmidt and Kohl, in his January 1973 address, stated: "We should carefully consider where the absorptive ability of our society has been exhausted and where social common sense and responsibility dictate that the process be halted."[23] Furthermore, there was a large discrepancy in West Germany, as was common in many Western European countries at this time, between the number of employed foreign workers and the total number of foreign nationals. In November 1973, West Germany had 2.6 million employed foreign workers out of a total foreign population of 4 million. While the number of employed foreigners in West Germany fell to between 1.8 and 1.9 million in the late 1970s, the total foreign population remained unchanged at 4 million, with about 1 million from Turkey.[24] Foreign workers, who feared they might not be able to re-enter West Germany if they went home, brought their families to Western Europe regardless of their employment status. The foreign population in West Germany increased to 4.5 million by 1980.[25]

As the economic downturn intensified, governments stepped up efforts to coax foreigners into leaving on their own. Several Western European countries, including France, West Germany, Belgium, and the Netherlands, implemented "pay-to-go" programs, in which governments offered incentives – bonuses, paid travel expenses, the reimbursement of social security contributions, and unemployment compensation – for both employed and unemployed guest workers to return to their countries of origin.[26] On 28 November 1983, the same year that West German unemployment reached a post-war record of 2.3 million, West

Germany implemented its own pay-to-go program. The Federal Republic introduced a new law for the "Promotion of Readiness to Return," which included a monetary incentive of DM10,500 for unemployment benefits to foreign workers to encourage them to return to their countries of origin.[27] However, out of millions, only about 250,000 foreigners, mostly Turks, took advantage of the opportunity.[28] On the whole, these programs did not necessarily lead to a decrease in the total number of foreigners, especially in West Germany.

Monetary incentives from the West German government were not the only considerations for former guest workers; there was also the question of where to go. Events in Turkey also affected immigration and emigration decisions. Political unrest and ethnic conflict in Turkey influenced the rise of emigration to West Germany in the late 1970s and early 1980s. On 12 September 1980, General Kenan Evren headed a coup d'état, during which he enacted martial law, abolished the parliament, suspended the constitution, and banned all political parties and trade unions in Turkey. Two significant factors impacted outmigration from Turkey before the coup as well. First, the Turkish economy was in free fall with three-digit inflation, a chronic foreign trade deficit, and widespread unemployment. Second, unprecedented political violence between rival factions led to a death toll of around five thousand in the late 1970s. In sum, the Turkish Republic was not necessarily attractive to returning workers in the late 1970s. The events in Turkey also provide the larger context for the rising number of Turks in West Germany after the official recruitment halt, including a significant and increasing number of Turkish and Kurdish asylum seekers. Clearly, there were forces in Turkey that discouraged Turks from returning there, but as the case studies in this book have emphasized, these decisions were at their core ultimately personal and not necessarily driven by larger trends.

Guest Workers' Daily Negotiations

While it is important to acknowledge the national forces driving immigration and responses to it, the case studies in this book, by their very nature, provide nuanced insight into how actual people negotiated their lives within the evolving context. As previous chapters have argued, there can be no stock narrative of the guest worker experience, as there will always be individuals who defy it. This book has purposefully focused on the outliers, a small set of individuals who, upon reflection later in life, emphasized that they had thrived despite negative experiences. In spite of terrible living spaces, these ethnic Turkish workers created homes and manageable, even interesting and fulfilling, lives for themselves where possible, enjoying the escapism of a disco, a new relationship, or maybe living a double life across the border – a guest worker during the week and a carefree Casanova on the weekends. The first part of this book focused on how the category of "guest worker" was constructed in a way that conflicted with individual guest workers' understanding of their own identities – of lives and dreams frequently hidden from public view. The second part of the book revealed how at work and after work, through relationships both intimate and pragmatic, through formal or spontaneous moments of solidarity, these individuals transcended assumptions about their status as guests and as workers. Some Turkish workers formed unexpected alliances, personally and politically, as de facto German workers and, as such, achieved major national changes in the West German wage structure.

Though workers exerted influence where they could, nonetheless many endured horrible conditions. It is difficult not to ask why – despite negative experiences before departure, during travel, in their employer-supplied dormitories, in discriminatory West German society, and at work – these individuals ultimately decided to invest in West Germany.[29] Yet to ask the question "why in spite of exploitation did workers stay?" is to see guest workers' lives only as exploitation or only in terms of material conditions. It is also possible to recognize the ways workers invested in West Germany long before even they realized it. Even if workers had intended to stay temporarily when they arrived in West Germany, they already had a year-long relationship with West German authorities through the preparation stage and many had anticipated living in West Germany before that. Turkish guest workers further invested in new lives in West Germany when they took steps to create lives outside work. At some point workers transitioned from making a temporary situation seem tolerable to having something worth staying for, as was the case with personal relationships across borders as well as with striking workers. When she met with me, Elif did not hesitate to say: "Why should I leave? I like it here."[30]

The accounts in the second half of the book uncover moments of subversion, radical change, and uncanny alliances. For example, working with the *Stasi* to report on their countrymen challenged concepts of national loyalty, as did the intimate relationships many Turkish men pursued with East German women. In short, guest workers were individuals who took each condition and aspect of the program and transformed them, bending rules and defying norms, negotiating their lives on their own terms. These individuals fit uncomfortably if at all into any macronarrative of the guest worker program and disrupt, perhaps, more than explain. Measuring the success of the program is equally challenging.

Measuring Success

The Turkish government did not get what it expected from the guest worker program with West Germany. The Turkish economy did not see a significant post-war boom as other Western Bloc nations did, and the guest worker program did not achieve the goals the 1963 Turkish Five-Year Development Plan laid out. Republican Turkish labour historians have recently questioned the Western-centric ideas that modernity inevitably led to urbanization, industrialization, and secularization, especially through increased contact with the West. While the Ottoman Empire, both multi-ethnic and multireligious, influenced Europe, Africa, and Asia with its economy, politics, and culture, the Turkish Republic, by contrast, is a self-contained, secularly constructed nation state that looks to the West. Historians Touraj Atabaki and Gavin Brockett have recognized that the Turkish state's evolution is mirrored in its history: "Modernist historians, both in Turkey and beyond, contrived a historical narrative after 1923 [when the Republic was founded] that was predicated upon a representation of the Ottoman heritage as disreputable and shameful."[31] To turn away from the dominant idea that Turkey developed solely through state-imposed modernization and contact with the West, historians of republican Turkish labour history argue that Turkish workers were, as Donald Quataert has written, "agents in their own right and not pliable and hapless tools of the state."[32] There is no better case study for assessing the impact of republican Turkey's 1950s–1980s fraught modernization and westernization plans than the massive program designed to export Turkish citizens and then reintroduce them as Westernized labour to the Turkish economy. Guest workers like Elif and the many others included in this book were indeed agents in their own right, and each muddled the neat plans of both nation states, as well as their accepted national histories.

What did the bilateral agreements with Germany and other Western European nations provide for the Turkish Republic upon workers' return? For the many Turkish workers abroad, return "home" before retirement age was largely unappealing, especially for those who knew

Turkey could not offer skilled workers comparable favourable working conditions or wages.[33] Turkish social scientist Ali Gitmez reported in 1977 that most Turkish workers preferred to wait for retirement before returning to Turkey: "They choose to come back to Turkey ... [solely] to spend their years of pension 'in peace' and relative wealth ... [Such] migrants who will never again join the Turkish workforce may be considered a complete loss for Turkey."[34] Miller and Çetin concluded in 1974 that the bilateral agreements had a largely negative impact on the Turkish economy instead of assuaging economic pressures as had been hoped. They found that the emigration of workers from Turkey led to a high rate of labour turnover that crippled industrial expansion and caused more harm than good: "Many urban industrial employers especially in Istanbul are warning government officials that their labor force turnover rates have become intolerable and ... will soon be inimical to industrial expansion."[35] They continued by challenging the program's premise: "Employers faced with ... replacing experienced workers either must accept lower productivity and/or pay the cost of additional worker training. Indeed, for far too long it has been assumed that emigration is a costless 'windfall gain' to Turkey."[36] Seen from the economic point of view, the program was a detriment to the Turkish economy. Indeed, it was a solution policy makers wanted to believe in more than actually examine.

Turkey also lost the currency influx of wage remittance once workers returned to Turkey, or when family members moved to Germany permanently, as wages were then spent solely in Germany. According to Gitmez, though remittances represented a large influx of currency into the Turkish economy, their impact was less significant: "The remittances are usually unorganized and used in unproductive small commercial ventures. This is inevitable if the savings are not controlled and the areas of investment are not organized accordingly by the government."[37] The Turkish Republic's modernizing plans and dreams of Westernization and uplift through the guest worker program were not realized in the program's aftermath in the 1980s.

Many workers looked back on the Turkish authorities' handling of the Turkish guest worker emigration with resentment, stating that the Turkish state cared more about doing everything in its power to meet West German employers' and officials' needs than about its own citizens' wants and needs. "In general, the record of the Turkish policy of migration and of return migration has been one of almost complete neglect," Gitmez reported of government policies. He concluded that the Turkish government gave its all to "dispatch as many workers abroad as possible and to do everything to satisfy all requests from receiving countries in terms of number, qualification, age, health, etc."[38] However, when it came to devising a plan for their return, re-employment, reintegration, a productive use of their savings, and their general integration in the larger economy, the government was silent.[39] Clearly, returning workers needed to define success in their own terms.

Despite the state-level failures to process return migration in a positive way, some workers did return successful in their own eyes. Gitmez found that 81 per cent of those who returned to Turkey after working abroad reported that they had had a positive experience.[40] "I am living in the village from now on," reported a man who had gone to West Germany as a tourist and stayed for seven years. "I didn't get any harm from working in Germany. I couldn't have owned what I have now if I hadn't gone to Germany. If I had the chance to go once more, I would buy a house in the city and live there."[41] Another man reported that five hundred people from his village, including most of the young men, had left for West Germany, saying, "There, eating, drinking, and having fun is plenty."[42] Speaking of those who had returned from Germany to his village, the same man reported: "We built roads in the village, built a high-school, bought telephone [sic]. These were all because of Germany. We have a lot of tractors, all belonging to Germaners [the made-up word for those who had lived in Germany]."[43] However, other former guest workers reported returning out of frustration with their West Germany employment situations, including constantly moving from low-paid job to low-paid job until they had given up to return to Turkey.[44]

Many workers did not have homes in Turkey to go back to because they had sold their property to go to West Germany in the first place or because they no longer had strong social ties in Turkey. Some workers who returned had mixed feelings about it, as in the case of Murat, who told me in Istanbul that returning to Turkey was a huge mistake because he did not think he could earn enough to live there.[45] He said he also regretted leaving because he missed the social life he had once had in Germany, which included going to discos with German friends.[46]

The era of family unification, in which Turkish spouses and children settled in West Germany by joining their relatives there, brought many changes to those who chose to remain and retire in West Germany. Some brought their children to study in German schools and universities, while others sought to reconnect with religious and cultural traditions from home especially after bringing their wives and children to Germany. One man, Ahmet, was persuaded to come to Berlin in 1969 after seven years of listening to overwhelmingly positive reports on life in West Berlin.[47] An acquaintance reported earning DM3,500 a month in Berlin, an unbelievable amount. Ahmet sold off his store and possessions to move to Berlin, where he worked as a cleaner on an American military base. He got the job through a temporary employment agency that was exploiting foreign workers, offering no benefits along with a low salary of around DM700 a month. He sent money home from his personal savings to give the impression that he had not failed or made a poor choice. He eventually found the man who had told him he had been earning DM3,500 and accosted him. He discovered that the man was living in a dirty basement room. When he noticed that the man's walls were decorated with pictures of Atatürk and a Turkish flag, he ripped the man's flag off the wall, claiming that he did not deserve to have it, as he was a liar and deceiver. Ahmet also greatly resented the Turkish government and consulate in West Germany for, in his opinion, turning their backs on Turkish citizens abroad. To make matters worse, he also reported enduring years of xenophobia by Berliners.

Ahmet's story was, however, still one of great success. In 1973, the year of the recruitment stop, he resettled his entire family in Berlin. He apparently said to his children: "It's enough that one person in the family has had to have dirty, degrading work. You must study."[48] Ahmet proudly reported that one of his daughters was the first Turkish girl to attend a German *Gymnasium*, or a rigorous college preparatory high school. She went on to major in sociology and spoke German, French, and Russian. His son studied architecture. By 1980 he reported that he had earned back his initial output of savings from 1969. In 1995 he was retired in Germany but reported that the money was less significant to him than the social welfare benefits and that, despite xenophobia, he had more benefits in Germany than he would have had in Turkey. Ahmet's story is one of many personal histories that challenge the dominant narratives of minority life in 1970s through 1990s Western Europe. He might be a historic outlier, but his family ultimately benefited from his choices. He seized opportunities, negotiated his situation, and found the parts of the German system that were the most beneficial.

Settling permanently in West Berlin was the right choice for Elif too. In 1972 she was elected to the *Betriebsrat,* or workers' council, demonstrating that she was seen as a leader at work among her German and foreign colleagues. In 1995 she reported that she was financially independent because of both social welfare assistance and her work as a babysitter and in her own craft store.

Another man, Remzi, who was selected in1966 by BMW in Istanbul, arrived in Munich by train and lived in a BMW dorm, which he considered modern for the time. In 1974, a year after the end of the official recruitment, he reported that BMW opened a newer dorm. The guest worker program did not really end in 1973 for him – he continued to live and work at BMW through the 1970s. His main concern, however, was how difficult it had been for him to practice his religion until 1975, when BMW opened another new dorm that included a mosque. He also went on to be elected to the *Betriebsrat*. Remzi noted that he had not experienced much xenophobia in Munich until the early 1990s, when he was told while boarding a subway car that the Germans should board first. In 1991 he received a certificate from the Bavarian Labour Ministry, BMW, and the German Metalworkers' Union [IGM] commemorating his twenty-five years of work at BMW. Despite his positive experiences with BMW, however, he recalled that he had little to no contact with German co-workers or neighbours in all his years in Munich. The religious tolerance shown by BMW was not widespread in West Germany, and, decades later, debates of freedom of religion versus freedom from religion would come to a head in Western Europe. In sum, individual guest workers' achievements varied greatly, even if their contributions as a collective population were great. Unfortunately, negative press on and attitudes about foreigners after 1973 effaced the nuance of the preceding era as political responses to migration intensified.

Lasting Impacts on Germany

The guest worker program revealed many areas in which the new state of West Germany seemed unable to escape its past. Various actions – including enforcing biological borders with medical exams; holding on to Nazi-era terminology for train "transports"; repurposing temporary housing from Nazi-era *Fremdarbeiter*, or "foreign workers"; and having antiquated ideas of gender roles in private relationships and at work – inevitably evoked West Germany's dark past. Guest workers endured substandard conditions before, during, and after arrival in West Germany and reported exploitation at work, homesickness, and cramped living quarters. And yet for myriad reasons, which were personal, political, economic, and social, Turkish workers stayed, forever invested in their future despite signs that staying would prove to be a bad investment.

While this book has shed light on the intentions behind the program and the ensuing demographic shifts, assessing the legacy of the program is exceedingly difficult: it is often blamed for an aftermath of contemporary problems with minority communities in Germany, for which it created the context but not necessarily the subsequent course of events. Contemporary circumstances often overshadow the nuance of the program's participants. In the early 1980s, the focus on the role of Islam among Turks in Germany came to the fore. Along with family reunification, which caused many Turkish families to want to bring up their children as Muslims in West Germany, Turkey's banning of Islamist parties such as the National Salvation Party (*Millî Selâmet Partisi*, or MSP) contributed to a politicization of Islam and an increase in religiosity among Turkish migrants in Western Europe as banned parties set up among communities there. Different Islamic organizations vied for control over the Turkish diaspora in West Germany, including more radical groups that wished to see the Turkish Republic go from secular to Islamic. Take, for example, a 1982 rally that took place in West Germany: "The hands that reach for our head scarves will be broken" and "Muslim Turkey will be established!" read Turkish-language signs during a demonstration of almost fifteen thousand people protesting the headscarf ban in Turkish schools.[49] An Islamist, right-leaning, Turkish-language publication reported positively on the event: "Before the march, they recited the Koran and sung the [Turkish] National Anthem with excitement."[50] A local radio station accused the marchers of supporting the controversial Islamist Turkish politician Necmettin Erbakan.[51] However, this rally did not take place in Ankara or in Istanbul but in Bonn-Bad Godesberg, West Germany, and the conflicting Turkish-language press reports (the newspaper versus the radio) were both from Cologne. In brief, two rival positions on the role of Islam in the Turkish Republic were fighting in West Germany on a Saturday afternoon.

West Germany became the testing ground for radical Turkish political groups and their accompanying publications – including ones that had been banned in Turkey for challenging the secular government and were later banned in West Germany for being overtly anti-Semitic. Islamic-leaning Turkish political organizations attempted to spread their influence, while Germany and the Turkish Republic (with a new constitution after a fresh military coup in 1981) sought to control and moderate them and in so doing helped define new national stances on the interlinking elements of religion, migration, politics, and national image. West Germany in the late 1970s and early 1980s was home to close to one million ethnic Turks and as such represented a transnational public sphere in which Turkish politics were created and acted out – these politics reached from Turkey to Germany and back again via the migrating Turkish population. The migrant community with its large membership and deep pockets was a contested ground on which Turkish political organizations vied for power and influence.

Indeed, after the inception of the guest worker program in the 1960s, the role of Islam in ethnic Turks' daily lives in West Germany had both personal and political meaning. An Islamist identity could figure into self-definition in two ways: in West Germany, against the dominant Christian culture and in preservation of "Turkish culture"[52] and, conversely, in Turkey, against secular elites and in opposition to secularizing efforts. The needs of Muslim migrants to reconstitute the basic conditions necessary to practice their faith – for example, halal food services or places of worship – along with their search for a community in which they felt they belonged, motivated the creation in the 1960s of loosely connected Islamic communities in Europe that spread significantly in the 1980s and beyond.[53] Over the years, Germany's response to immigrant populations was to allow ethnic enclaves to persist in a strategy known as "parallel societies," a condition that Chancellor Merkel declared had utterly failed in her now famous speech from October 2010. The situation of increasingly politicized Islamic populations in West Germany was neither unique to West Germany nor the final chapter of the story of the guest worker program. Just as the guest worker program began as one of many migration movements sweeping across post-war Europe, Germany's situation was not unique and it was certainly not the necessary result of the guest worker program. Instead, political and social choices made by Western European policymakers played a much larger role in shaping the impact of demographic shifts than did the initial migrations that brought non-native populations in the first place. While the guest worker program did create the crucial conditions just by importing large numbers of Turks, it did not determine the outcomes.

On 7 January 2015, two radical Muslims, apparently funded by Al Qaeda, shot twelve people at the Parisian satirical magazine *Charlie Hebdo* in retaliation for what they deemed disrespectful portrayals of Islam. The same day, the United Kingdom's Prime Minister David Cameron and Germany's Chancellor Merkel issued a joint statement condemning the attack on *Charlie Hebdo*. Merkel noted: "All of us that live in Europe strongly condemn these attacks ... This is an attack against the values we hold dear, values by which we stand."[54] Two days later a separate attack occurred; this time, hostages (four of whom were killed) were taken at a Paris kosher deli. In Germany on the Monday before the first Paris attack, however, the newly formed anti-Islamic party Patriotic Europeans Against the Islamization of the West (*Patriotische Europäer gegen die Islamisierung des Abendlandes*, or Pegida) held its largest demonstration ever in Dresden. Pegida's central demands are a reduction in the number of foreigners entering Germany and tightened asylum laws in the country.[55]

On the Saturday after the attack in Paris, though, thirty-five thousand *anti*-Pegida protesters marched in Dresden pre-emptively. They began with a minute of silence for the victims of the terrorist attacks in France and then continued with a march for tolerance, one jointly organized by the Dresden city and Saxony state governments. Protesters carried a banner reading: "Wall of Friendship without Borders."[56] Despite the largest terrorist attack in recent French history occurring just days before, and even in a moment of renewed Franco-German support, the march for tolerance of Islam continued in the historic city. Anti-Pegida demonstrations were widespread and took place in Berlin, Cologne, and Stuttgart as well. How and whether contemporary problems should be linked to immigrant histories and migrations such as the guest worker program are complicated questions that deserve equally nuanced answers and investigations.

The events in January 2015 were just the beginning of a tumultuous year though. In May, Islamic State fighters seized territory in central Syria, and in June their control spread to north-eastern Syria as well. The civil war that began with the Arab Spring of 2011 culminated in a humanitarian crisis and an unprecedented wave of refugees and asylum seekers in Europe. In May 2015, media reports of 1.5 to 2 million Syrian refugees started to gain increasing attention as the refugees moved from Turkey and into the Balkan states.[57] (By the end of 2015, Germany alone had received a record 1.1 million migrants from outside the EU.)[58] On 31 August 2015, Merkel called for "European unity" in the face of a humanitarian crisis, reminding Europe of its open borders policy: "If Europe fails on the question of refugees, if this close link with universal civil rights is broken, then it won't be the Europe we wished for."[59] Lured in by Germany's economy and welcome, millions were risking their lives to reach Germany despite the EU regulation that they be processed in the first European country they reached.[60] Germany took on a "moral leadership" role through its efforts both to aid and welcome refugees and encouraged other European countries to do the same.

Significantly, Merkel saw a direct connection with Germany's guest worker history and prior experiences with asylum seekers. On 9 September 2015, she stated that Germany needed to learn from the mistakes it made with guest workers and do things differently in 2015 to focus on integration from the start: "Those who come to us as asylum seekers or as war refugees need our help so they can integrate quickly," Merkel told the German parliament.[61] A month later a *New York Times* article, answering a London reader's question about how to integrate the newcomers, responded: "Most politicians, planners and business people in Stuttgart and Berlin ... [thought it] crucial to integrate the new migrants ... providing not only language, education and job training but also access to the social and athletic clubs that bind many German communities." Significantly, the paper pointed out the striking difference between the contemporary policies and those from the guest worker period: "[Focusing on integration] did not happen in the 1970s and 1980s with Turkish guest workers in cities such as Berlin, where for various reasons communities avoided mixing for years, and the consequences are still obvious."[62]

The hopeful and welcoming tone changed after the 13 November 2015 coordinated terrorist attacks in Paris and the New Year's Eve attacks in Cologne. The honeymoon period was short-lived, and calls for stricter regulations began. Day after the Paris attacks, the news reports switched to headlines such as "Paris Attacks Shift Europe's Migrant Focus to Security," and once again, talk of integration evaporated.[63] Before the focus shifted, though, the immigrant crisis had prompted a new neologism in German *Willkommenskultur*, or the "culture of being welcoming," similar to the early days of the guest worker program. Germany was again pleased to improve its humanitarian record on the world stage and in light of its dark past, just as the policy makers discussed in the first two chapters of this book were. By December 2015, Merkel was again calling for "humanitarian" efforts and revisiting her comments from 2010 that *"multikulti"* or "multiculturalism" had been a "sham" that stood in for Germany actually adapting to the reality that their assimilation schemes were inefficient and that they were indeed a country of immigration. The New Year's Eve attacks on women in Cologne – during which one hundred women reported assaults, including sexual assaults, by men speaking foreign languages and apparently of North African and Arab backgrounds – soured the German public once again on the government's acceptance of refugees, as many of them were blamed for the attacks.[64] During the 2016 Cologne Carnival, despite increased police presence and low attendance, women again reported high numbers of sexual assaults; this time officials refused to release information about assailants' ethnicities.[65]

As this book is prepared for publication, it is hard to tell exactly what lessons were learned from the guest worker program. The idea that Germany never had sincere plans to deal with their guest workers is still prevalent, despite the findings in part one of this book that policy-makers made attempts at regulations that failed during implementation. The actions of individual guest workers – such as attempting to learn German to take charge of their situations through the means available – are also excluded from media reports that characterize the impact of the guest worker program by stating "today, certain districts are still predominantly populated by citizens of Turkish origins, many of whom do not speak German fluently."[66] While these claims are not necessarily false, they elide or ignore the more diverse range of behaviours and attitudes revealed in individuals' stories in this book.

Contested Histories

Too often immigrant groups are blamed for not integrating or assimilating by not taking on European values, or are seen as the root of social ills. West Germany's own culpability in creating social problems remains understudied. The facts of the guest worker program in the early 1960s will offer few answers to today's debates until we see them as providing a new understanding of the larger context, one in which a different future was entirely possible.

In any event, the impact of foreign workers' immigration on post-war Western Europe cannot be underestimated. The model of post-war labour migration, which occurred across Europe in the 1960s and 1970s, had similar effects regardless of the sending and receiving countries. In the 1970s and 1980s in West Germany, Austria, Switzerland, France, the United Kingdom, and the Netherlands, foreign nationals began to settle permanently with their families, forever changing the social fabric of Western Europe and calling into question ideas of "new" and "old" Europe. While historians have long concerned themselves with the rebuilding of the economy, architecture, and governments of Europe in the post-war period, a closer look at the ways in which European governments and societies rebuilt (or eschewed rebuilding) the social fabric of Europe has little been noticed. Yet in this same period, migrants forced Europeans to reconstruct questions of identity, culture, and citizenship, as well as the walls and borders that defined belonging in the West or the East, whether figuratively or literally. The stories of workers like Erol, Elif, and Cahit break down stock narratives not only about guest workers from Turkey but also about minorities and Muslims in Europe. Appreciating the textures of the immigrant experience, including the inherent will and ambition needed to move somewhere new, requires reframing historical debates about who guest workers were and where they belonged.

Notes

Introduction

1 Elif is a pseudonym. Dokumentationszentrum und Museum über die Migration in Deutschland e.V. (DOMiD, [Documentation Centre and Museum for Migration in Germany]) Interview 16, Berlin, 31 August 1995. Unless otherwise noted, all translations are my own. I also interviewed Elif in Berlin in 2003.

2 Aytaç Eryılmaz and Mathilde Jamin eds., *Fremde Heimat: Eine Geschichte der Einwanderung aus der Türkei / Yaban, Sılan olur: Türiye'den Almanya'ya Göçün Tarihi* [Foreign Homeland: A History of Immigration to Germany from Turkey] (Cologne: Klartext, 1998), 138.

3 For more on the Bloody Christmas of 1963, see Ulvi Keser, "Bloody Christmas of 1963 in Cyprus in the Light of American Documents," *Journal of Modern Turkish History Studies* 13, no. 26 (Spring 2013): 249–71.

4 Elif, interviewed by author, Berlin, 2003.

5 DOMiD Interview 16, Berlin, 31 August 1995.

6 Important early work empathetically exposed guest workers' miserable conditions, though such depictions have also effaced complex human experiences: see, among others, John Berger and Jenn Mohr, *A Seventh Man: Migrant Workers in Europe* (New York: Verso, 1975); Inga Steinen, *Leben zwischen zwei Welten: Türkische Frauen in Deutschland* (Berlin: Quadriga, 1994); Günter Wallraff, *Ganz Unten* (Köln: Kiepenheuer & Witsch, 1985); Rainer Werner Fassbinder, *Angst essen Seele auf* (Tango-Film, Munich,1974); Feo Aladağ, *Die Fremde* (ARTE, Independent Artists Filmproduktion, RBB, WDR, 2010).

7 For more recent scholarship on Turkish-German Literature, see B. Venkat Mani, *Cosmopolitical Claims: Turkish-German Literatures from Nadolny to*

Pamuk (Iowa City: University of Iowa Press, 2007); for more on Turkish-German cinema see, Deniz Göktürk, "Mobilität und Stillstand im Weltkino digital," in *Kultur als Ereignis:* Fatih Akıns Film Auf der anderen Seite als transkulturelle Narration, ed. Özkan Ezli (Bielefeld: Transcript, 2010), 15–45; David Gramling "On the Other Side of Monolingualism: Fatih Akın's Linguistic Turn," *The German Quarterly* 83 no. 3 (2010): 353–72; Berna Gueneli, "Challenging European Borders: Fatih Akin's Filmic Visions of Europe" (PhD diss., University of Texas at Austin, 2011).

8 Elif, Berlin, 2003.

9 Hanna Schlisser, "'Normalization' as Project: Some Thoughts on Gender Relations in West Germany during the 1950s," in *Miracle Years: A Cultural History of West Germany, 1949-1968*, ed. Hanna Schissler (Princeton, NJ: Princeton University Press, 2001), 359–75.

10 The idea of the "Zero Hour" is debatable as for many, such as the majority of German women and displaced persons who remained in camps sometimes until 1955, faced situations little different from wartime. Robert G. Moeller, *Protecting Motherhood: Women and the Family in the Politics of Postwar West Germany* (Berkeley: University of California Press, 1993), 11; Sibylle Meyer and Eva Schultz, *Wie wir das alles geschafft haben: Alleinstehende Frauen berichten über ihr Leben nach 1945* (Munich: Beck, 1985), 92; for displaced persons in post-war Germany, see Atina Grossman, *Jews, Germans, and Allies: Close Encounters in Occupied Germany* (Princeton, NJ: Princeton University Press, 2007).

11 For useful examples and discussions of the "long post-war," see Tony Judt, *Postwar: A History of Europe since 1945* (London and New York: Penguin, 2005); Karen Hagemann and Sonya Michel, eds., *Gender and the Long Postwar: The United States and the Two Germanys, 1945–1989* (Baltimore: Johns Hopkins University Press, 2014).

12 Tony Judt, *Postwar*, 2.

13 Elizabeth Heineman, "The Hour of the Woman: Memories of Germany's 'Crisis Years' and West German National Identity," *American Historical Review* 101, no. 2, (April 1996): 354–95.

14 Historians have concluded that the German social discourse of the time held that the image of the *Trümmerfrauen* was to be admired, but also to be quickly overcome. Petra Goedde, "From Villains to Victims: Fraternization and the Feminization of Germany, 1945–1947," *Diplomatic History* 23 (1999): 1–20; Elizabeth Heineman, *What Difference Does a Husband Make? Women and Marital Status in Nazi and Postwar Germany* (Berkeley: University of California Press, 1999); Maria Höhn, "Frau im Haus, Girl im Spiegel: Discourse on Women in the Interregnum Period of

1945–1949 and the Question of German Identity," *Central European History* 26 no. 1 (1993): 57–90.

15 Monika Mattes, *'Gastarbeiterinnen' in der Bundesrepublik: Anwerbepolitik, Migration und Geschlecht in den 50er bis 70er Jahren* (Frankfurt: Campus, 2005).

16 Mattes, *Gastarbeiterinnen*; Schissler, "'Normalization'"; Robert G. Moeller, *Protecting Motherhood*, and Mark E. Spicka, *Selling the Economic Miracle: Economic Reconstruction and Politics in West Germany, 1949–1957* (New York and Oxford: Berghahn Books, 2007). Spicka's analysis of political rhetoric in the late 1940s associated "normalcy" with recovering the Federal Republic from the taint of the Nazi past and from wartime and post-war hardships such as hunger and male unemployment, 66–9.

17 Rebecca Boehling notes, "The model of the 'male-breadwinner family' found more political and cultural support than ever before, reflecting a desire for 'normalcy' in response to defeat, military occupation, and growing Cold War tensions … [However, this was not] the whole postwar story. Some women questioned men's inherent ability to lead either families or society as a whole." Rebecca Boehling, "Gender Roles in Ruins: German Women and Local Politics under American Occupation, 1945–1955," in *Gender and the Long Postwar: The United States and the Two Germanys, 1945-1989*, ed. Karen Hagemann and Sonya Michel (Baltimore: John Hopkins University Press, 2014), 51–72, here 52.

18 Spicka, *Selling*, 73.

19 Boehling, "Gender Roles," 52; Heineman, *What Difference.*

20 Donna Harsch provides an excellent overview of the evolution of socialist though on nuclear families from early Marxists, orthodox Stalinists to SED in East Germany in "Women, Family, and 'Postwar': The Gendering of the GDR's Welfare Dictatorship" in *Gender and the Long Postwar*, 253–73, here 258–61. In the case of East Germany, Harsch uses gender relations to demonstrate that the SED evolved to see women's usefulness to the state not defined by production, but instead as reproducers, producers, and consumers with particular interest in the "unforeseen consequences of women's family-based decisions," 254.

21 Monika Mattes, *Gastarbeiterinnen*; Karen Schönwälder, "West German Society and Foreigners in the 1960s," in *Coping with the Nazi Past: West German Debates on Nazism and Generational Conflict, 1955–1975*, ed. Philipp Gassert and Alan Steinweis (New York: Berghahn, 2006), 113–27, here 115–16.

22 Yasemin Nuhoğlu Soysal, *Limits of Citizenship: Migrants and Postnational Membership in Europe* (Chicago: University of Chicago Press, 1995); Ruud Koopmans and Paul Statham, "Challenging the Liberal Nation-State?

Postnationalism, Multiculturalism, and the Collective Claims Making of Migrants and Ethnic Minorities in Britain and Germany" *American Journal of Sociology* 105 no. 3 (1999): 652–96; Irene Bloemraad, "Who claims dual citizenship? The Limits of Postnationalism, the Possibilities of Transnationalism, and the Persistence of Traditional Citizenship" *International Migration Review* 38 (2004): 389–426.

23 Irene Bloemraad, Anna Korteweg, and Gökçe Yurdakul, "Citizenship and Immigration: Multiculturalism, Assimilation, and Challenges to the Nation-State" *Annual Review of Sociology* 34 (2008): 153–79.

24 Karen Schönwälder, "West German Society," 115.

25 Ulrich Herbert and Karin Hunn, "Guest Workers and Policy on Guest Workers in the Federal Republic: From the Beginning of Recruitment in 1955 until Its Halt in 1973," in *The Miracle Years: A Cultural History of West Germany, 1949–1968*, ed. Hanna Schissler (Princeton, NJ: Princeton University Press, 2001), 187–218; Rita Chin, Heide Fehrenbach, Geoff Eley, and Atina Grossmann eds., *After the Nazi Racial State: Difference and Democracy in Germany and Europe* (Ann Arbor: University of Michigan Press, 2009).

26 Duinger Steinzeugwerk Mühle & Co an den Herrn Präsidenten der Bundesanstalt für Arbeitsvermittlung Nürnberg, 20 July 1973, BArch B 119/ 4031.

27 Ibid.

28 Ahmet Akgündüz, "Guest Worker Migration in Post-war Europe (1946–1974): An Analytical Appraisal," in *An Introduction to International Migration Studies*, ed. Marco Martiniello and Jan Rath (Chicago: University of Chicago Press, 2012), 182.

29 Panikos Panayi, "Exploitation, Criminality, Resistance: The Everyday Life of Foreign Workers and Prisoners of War in the German Town of Osnabrück, 1939–49," *Journal of Contemporary History* 40, no. 3 (July 2005): 483–502; Ahmet Akgündüz, "Guest Worker Migration," 183.

30 Klaus J. Bade, *Migration Past, Migration Future: Germany and the United States* (New York: Berghahn Books, 1997) 68–71; see also Veysal Oezcan, "Germany: Immigration in Transition" Migration Policy Institute, 1 July 2004, accessed 23 February 2016, http://www.migrationpolicy.org/article/germany-immigration-transition.

31 Frederick Taylor writes that the Berlin wall resulted in the guest worker agreement between Turkey and West Germany: "Robbed of the previous supply of new labor for its booming industries by the sealing off of the East, in October 1961 West Germany took the radical and far reaching step of signing a treaty with Muslim Turkey, allowing for Turkish 'guest

workers' to fill vacant jobs." *The Berlin Wall: A World Divided, 1961–1989* (New York: Harper Collins, 2006), 345.

32 Atina Grossmann writes that in the immediate post-war period, all of war-torn Europe became "a moving stream of humanity" in which 20 people were on the move. In addition to 7 million displaced persons, some 8 million ethnic Germans also arrived in West Germany from Soviet-dominated territories in the late 1940s. Atina Grossmann, *Jews, Germans, and Allies*, 131–82. Between 1947 and 1954, 1 million North Africans entered France; between 1962 and 1965 alone, 111,000 migrants entered France; between 1956 and 1961, 115,000 immigrants entered Britain; and, an estimated 5.5 million to 8.5 million people of European origin returned to Europe from colonial posts. For more on postcolonial immigration see "Postimperial Europe, 1947–1980," in *Europe in the Contemporary World: 1900 to the Present*, ed. Bonnie G. Smith (New York: Bedford St Martin's, 2007), 498–553; "Decolonization and Immigration in Britain and France" and "Post-war European Society: A Consumer Society and Welfare State," in *Europe since 1945: A Concise History*, ed. J. Robert Wegs and Robert Ladrech (New York: Palgrave MacMillan, 1996, 2006), 98–9, 139–72.

33 Akgündüz, "Guest Worker Migration," 184.

34 Judt, *Postwar*, 334.

35 Karin Hunn, *Nächstes Jahr kehren wir zurück … 'Die Geschichte der türkischen, Gastarbeiter' in der Bundesrepublik* (Gottingen: Wallstein, 2005), 35–6.

36 "Bericht des Westfälisch-Lippischen Landwirtschaftsverbandes e.V., Kreisverband Soest" an BAVAV, 10 November 1956, BArch, B 119/ 3070.

37 Hanna Schlisser, ed., *The Miracle Years: A Cultural History of West Germany, 1949–1968* (Princeton, NJ: Princeton University Press, 2001).

38 Judt, *Postwar*, 354.

39 Judt, *Postwar*, 324–55.

40 Herbert points out that it was the devastation of the transportation network that crippled the West German economy in 1945 and 1946 not the destruction of industrial plants; industrial capacity had been expanded during the war and left intact. Herbert, *A History of Foreign Labor in Germany*, 194–5; Judt points out that Nazi investments in the war economy of the 1930s paid off in the 1950s when German economic infrastructure that had survived the war was put to use, *Postwar*, 355.

41 Mark E. Spicka, "The Korean Crisis, the Social Market Economy, and Public Opinion," in *Selling*, 94–107. Spica, like Abelshauser before him, points out that the Korean Crisis was a formative event in post-war West German economic history, and not just in the increase in production but

also in prompting the creation of the National Bank, an increase in wages, the liberalization of trade, and in the German citizen's perception of their economy, especially once inflation set in; while other historians have debated the specific political economic causes and impacts of the crisis, it was nevertheless a significant event for labour migration. See Werner Abelshauser, "The First Post-Liberal Nation: Stages in Development of Modern Corporatism in Germany," *European History Quarterly* 14 (1984): 285–317; Volker Berghahn and Paul J. Friedrich, *Otto A. Friedrich, Ein politischer Unternehmer: Sein Leben und seine Zeit, 1902–1975* (Frankfurt: Campus, 1993).

42 Judt, *Postwar*, 303–4.

43 Ibid., 304.

44 Ahmet Akgündüz, "Guest Worker Migration in Post-war Europe (1946–1974): An Analytical Appraisal," in *An Introduction to International Migration Studies*, ed. Marco Martiniello and Jan Rath (Chicago: University of Chicago Press, 2012).

45 Ibid.

46 Akgündüz, "Guest Worker Migration," 184.

47 Ahmet Akgündüz, *Labour Migration from Turkey to Western Europe, 1960–1974: A Multidisciplinary Analysis* (Burlington, VT: Ashgate, 2008), 101.

48 Hunn, *Nächstes Jahr*, 31–2.

49 Ibid., 32.

50 Akgündüz, "Guest Worker Migration," 192.

51 The 1960 military coup was partially linked to Menderes's attempts to improve relations with the Soviet Union, making the coup a recommitment to Westernization. See Bulent Gokay, *Soviet Eastern Policy and Turkey, 1920–1991: Soviet Foreign Policy, Turkey and Communism* (New York: Routledge, 2006), 87.

52 Akgündüz, "Guest Worker Migration," 190.

53 Hunn, *Nächstes Jahr*, 32.

54 Akgunduz, "Guest Worker Migration," 192.

55 Ibid.

56 Akgündüz, "Guest Worker Migration," 187.

57 Sen and Goldberg argue that the benefits system also fiscally supported West Germany because the majority of the Turkish population, for example 83 per cent in 1973, was legally employed and contributing to West Germany's social insurance system – a system from which others have argued they were not able to receive the full benefits; see Andreas Goldberg and Faruk Sen, *Türken als Unternehmer: Eine Gesamtdarstellung und Ergebnisse neuere Untersuchungen* (Opladen: Leske and Budrich, 1996).

See also, Triadafilos Triadafilopolous and Karen Schönwälder, "How the Federal Republic Became an Immigration Country: Norms Politics and the Failure of West Germany's Guest Worker System" *German Politics and Society* 24, no. 3 (2006): 1–19; Sandra M. Bucerius, *Unwanted: Muslim Immigrants, Dignity, and Drug Dealing* (Oxford: Oxford University Press, 2014), 24–5.

58 Akgündüz, "Guest Worker Migration," 193.

59 For a complete history of the drafting of the bilateral plans, see Hunn, "Deutsch-türkische Anwerbevereinbarung" in *Nächstes Jahr*, 29–70; Karen Schönwälder, *Einwanderung und ethnische Pluralität. Politische Entscheidungen und öffentliche Debatten in Großbritannien und der Bundesrepublik von den 1950er bis zu den 1970er Jahren* (Essen: Klartext 2001); Aytaç Eryılmaz and Mathilde Jamin, eds., *Fremde Heimat, Eine Geschichte der Einwanderung aus der Türkei / Yaban, Sılan olur. Türkiye'den Almanya'ya Göçün Tarihi* (Essen: Klartext, 1998).

60 The Brookings Institute study of the 1960–1 Turkish Revolution concluded that the roots of the revolution lay in Atatürk's initial reforms for the Republic – issues of secularism and of rapid social change: "In 1960 it was widely felt in Turkey and abroad that the government … had strayed far from the path of the Atatürk revolution, and it was to return Turkey to democratic, secular politics that the armed forces took power on May 27, 1960." Walter F. Weiker, *The Turkish Revolution 1960–1961: Aspects of Military Politics* (Washington, DC: The Brookings Institution, 1963), 2.

61 In the words of the Young Turks, "we followed the path traced by Europe" quoted in Bernard Lewis, *The Emergence of Modern Turkey* (London: New Oxford University Press, 1961), 199.

62 Erik-Jan Zürcher, "How Europeans adopted Anatolia and Created Turkey" *European Review* 13 (2005): 379–94.

63 Fatma Müge Göçek, "Why is there Still a 'Sèvres Syndrome'? An Analysis of Turkey's Uneasy Association with the West" in *The Transformation of Turkey: Redefining State and Society from the Ottoman Empire to the Modern Era* (New York: I.B. Tauris, 2011), 98–184.

64 Brian J.K. Miller, "Reshaping the Turkish Nation-State: Migrant Communities in Western Europe and Return Migration, 1960–1985," (PhD diss., University of Iowa, May 2015); Nermin Abadan-Unat, *Turks in Europe: From Guest Worker to Transnational Citizen* (New York: Berghahn Books, 2011).

65 The OECD reported that in 1965 Turkey had received seventy dollars in remittances from workers abroad: "An unforeseen and costless source of

foreign exchange developed over the last few years, through migration of Turkish workers to foreign countries … Over the longer-run perhaps as important as the foreign exchange earnings will be the technical and general know-how the Turkish thus acquire," "Turkey: 1965–1966," *Economic Surveys by the OECD* (1966): 45.

66 Nermin Abadan-Unat, *Turks in Europe: From Guest Worker to Transnational Citizen* (New York: Berghahn Books, 2011), xxi.

67 Abadan-Unat, *Politics of Immigration Policy*, 310.

68 Henryk M. Broder, "Integrationsdebatte: Die Parallelgesellschaft, sie lebe hoch!" *Spiegel Online*, 21October 2010, accessed 25 February 2016, http://www.spiegel.de/kultur/gesellschaft/integrationsdebatte-die -parallelgesellschaft-sie-lebe-hoch-a-723895.html; Werner Schiffauer, *Parallelgesellschaften: Wie viel Wertekonsens braucht unsere Gesellschaft? Für eine kluge Politik der Differenz* (Bielefeld: Transcript, 2008).

69 "Merkel says German multicultural society has failed," *BBC News*, 17 October 2010, accessed 5 March 2016, http://www.bbc.com/news/ world-europe-11559451.

70 "Erdoğan Urges Turks not to Assimilate: 'You are Part of Germany, But Also Part of Our Great Turkey,'" *Spiegel Online International*, 28 February 2011, accessed 20 February 2015, http://www.spiegel.de/international/ europe/erdogan-urges-turks-not-to-assimilate-you-are-part-of-germany -but-also-part-of-our-great-turkey-a-748070.html.

71 Anthropologist Jenny White points out that particularly after German reunification in 1990, the term *Ausländer* became increasingly synonymous with "Turks" and even expanded after reunification to also include *Aussiedler*, or political refugees from Eastern Europe. See Jenny B. White, "Turks in the New Germany" *American Anthropologist* 99 no. 4 (1997): 754–69, here 762; Ruth Mandel, "'Fortress Europe' and the Foreigners within: Germany's Turks," in *The Anthropology of Europe: Identity and Boundaries in Conflict*, ed. Victoria A. Goddard, Joseph R. Llobera, and Cris Shore (Oxford: Berg, 1994), 113–25; Rita Chin, *The Guest Worker Question in Postwar Germany* (New York: Cambridge University Press, 2007), 14–15.

72 The Turkish community in Germany, especially in Berlin, is far from unified; ethnic, religious, and political cleavages have carried over from Turkey. Jenny White, "Belonging to a Place: Turks in Unified Berlin," *City and Society*, 1996; White, "Turks in the New Germany" *American Anthropologist* 99 no. 4 (1997): 754–69, where White writes, "The 2 million Turks in Germany are a disparate community [who] identify not only with Turkishness but also or even primarily with their social class, with

a particular regional or non-Turkish ethnic origin, or with a transnational creole 'third culture.'"

73 In 1992 alone, more than five thousand attacks against foreigner were reported in the newly reunified Germany, see Jenny White, "Turks in the New Germany"; see also Andreas Goldberg "Status and Problems of the Turkish Community in Germany" (Essen: Zentrum für Türkeistudien und Integrationsforschung, 1996).

74 Frederick D. Weil, "Ethnic Intolerance, Extremism, and Democratic Attitudes in Germany since Unification," in *Antisemitism and Xenophobia in Germany after Unification*, ed. Hermann Kurthen and Rainer Erb (Oxford: Oxford University Press, 1997), 111.

75 Göktürk et al., 13.

76 Foreign journalists accused the German police of "subtle racism," saying that they were taking xenophobic violence too lightly; see "Police Under Fire in German Unrest," *The New York Times*, 27 December 1992, accessed 20 February 2015, http://www.nytimes .com/1992/12/27/world/police-under-fire-in-german-unrest.html. Some have repeated this conflation of ethnic groups unwittingly or worse, pointedly, such as Thilo Sarrazin in his controversial book in which he claimed that "Turks, Arabs, and Africans" have failed to integrate and add little to the German economy and society, unlike more valuable minorities such as Jews. Thilo Sarrazin, *Deutschland Schafft Sich Ab: Wie wir unser Land aufs Spiel setzen* (Munich: Deutsche Verlags-Anstalt, Random House, 2010); see also Michael Meng, *Shattered Spaces: Encountering Jewish Ruins in Postwar Germany and Poland* (Cambridge, MA: Harvard University Press, 2011), 264.

77 Joyce Mushaben, *The Changing Faces of Citizenship: Integration and Mobilization Among Ethnic Minorities in Germany* (New York: Berghahn Books, 2008), 14.

78 Ibid.

79 For recent studies on ethnic diversity among those from Turkey see: Alexander Clarkson, *Fragmented Fatherland: Immigration and Cold War Conflict in the Federal Republic of Germany 1945–1980* (New York: Berghahn, 2013); Ruth Mandel, *Cosmopolitan Anxieties: Turkish Challenges to Citizenship and Belonging in Germany* (Durham: Duke University Press, 2008); Joyce Mushaben, *The Changing Faces of Citizenship*; Martin Sökefeld, *Struggling for Recognition: The Alevi Movement in Germany and in Transnational Space* (New York: Berghahn Books, 2008).

80 Michael Kuhlmann and Alwin Meyer, *Ayşe und Devrim: Wo gehören wir hin?* (Göttingen: Lamu Taschenbuch, 1983); Rita Rosen, "Ausländische

Frauen: Ignoriert, im Stich gelassen, unterdrückt" *Informationsdienst zur Ausländerarbeit* 4 (1980): 20–7.

81 Andrea Baumgartner-Karabak and Gisela Landesberger, *Die verkauften Bräute: Türkische Frauen zwischen Kreuzberg und Anatolien* (Reinbek bei Hamburg: Rowohlt Taschenbuch, 1978); Christine Huth-Hildebrant and Jürgen Micksch, *Ausländische Frauen: Interviews, Analysen und Anregungen für die Praxis* (Frankfurt am Main: Otto Lembeck Verlag, 1982); Gaby Franger, *Wir Haben Es Uns Anders Vorgestellt: Türkische Frauen in der Bundesrepublik* (Frankfurt am Main: Fischer, 1984); Füruzan, *Frau ohne Schleier: Türkische Erzählungen* (Vienna: Europa Verlag, 1976); Giacomo Maturi, *Arbeitsplatz Deutschland: Wie Man Südlandische Gastarbeiter verstehen lernt* (Mainz: Krausskopf Verlag, 1964); Sigrid Meske, *Situations Analyse türkische Frauen in der BRD* (Fulda: Express ed, 1983); Rita Rosen and Gerd Stüwe, *Ausländische Mädchen in der Bundesrepublik* (Opladen: LeskeVerlag, 1985); Rita Rosen, *Muss Kommen, aber nix von Herzen: Zur Lebensituation von Migratinnen unter besonderer Berücksichtigung der Biographien türkischer Frauen* (Opladen: Leske and Budrick, 1986); Rita Rosen, "On the situation of Foreign Women Living in the Federal Republic of Germany: An Outline of the Problem" *International Migration* 19 (1981): 108–13; Rita Rosen, *Sie müssen bestimmen, wo sie lang gehen wollen. Zur Sozialpädagogischen Arbeit mit ausländischen Frauen und Mädchen* (Frankfurt/Main: ISS Materialien, 1984); Werner Schiffauer, *Die Migranten Aus Subay: Türken in Deutschland: Eine Ethnographie* (Stuttgart: Ernst Klett Verlag für Wissen und Bildung, 1991); Pia Weische-Alexa, *Sozial-Kulturelle Probleme junger Türkinnen in der Bundesrepublik Deutschland mit einer Studie zum Freizeitverhalten türkischerMädchen in Köln* (Pia Weische-Alexa, Manderscheider Str. 29, 5000 Köln 41).

82 In the film, the main character, Shirin, is arranged to be married as a child, migrates to West Germany where she is raped and fired by her German boss, and turns to prostitution out of desperation. *Shirins Hochzeit*, directed by Helma Sanders-Brahms (Cologne, West Germany: Westdeutscher Rundfunk, Arbeitsgemainschaft Kino, 1975) 35mm.

83 Günter Wallraft, *Ganz Unten* (Köln: Kiepenheuer and Witsch, 1985).

84 "Bei türkischen Medien werde das Bild des unterdrücken Migranten immer wieder unterstrichen – anders also bei „Köln Radyosu" [The Turkish media repeatedly underscored the image of the oppressed migrant counter to [the preceding Turkish-language radio program] Cologne Radio.] „ Erste Sendung der ARD für ‚Gastarbeiter' startet," 21 October 2011, accessed 2 March 2016, http://www1.wdr.de/stichtag6058.html.

85 B. Venkat Mani, *Cosmopolitical Claims: Turkish-German Literatures from Nadolny to Pamuk* (Iowa City: Iowa University Press, 2007), 3.
86 Ibid.
87 Klaus Bade, *Ausländer, Aussiedler, Asyl in der Bundesrepublik Deutschland* (Bonn: Bundeszentrale für politische Bildung, 1992); Ulrich Herbert, *A History of Foreign Labor in Germany: Seasonal Workers, Forced Laborers, Guest Workers*, trans. William Templer (Ann Arbor: Michigan University Press, 1993); Hanns Thomä-Veske, *Islam und Integration: Zur Bedeutung des Islam im Prozeß der Integration türkischer Arbeiterfamilien in die Gesellschaft der Bundesrepublik* (Hamburg: Rissen, 1981); Rita Rosen "Ausländische Frauen: Ignoriert, im Stich Gelassen, Unterdrückt" *Informationsdienst zur Ausländerarbeit* 4 (1980): 20–7; Gökçe Yurdakul, *From Guest Workers into Muslims: The Transformation of Turkish Immigrant Associations in Germany* (Newcastle upon Tyne: Cambridge Scholars, 2009).
88 Karen Schönwälder and Triadafilos Triadafilopoulos, "How the Federal Became an Immigration Country: Norms, Politics and the Failure of West Germany's Guest Worker System," *German Politics and Society* 24 no. 3 (2006): 1–19.
89 Göktürk et al., *Germany in Transit*.
90 Brittany Lehman, "Education and Immigration: Federal Debates and Policies in West Germany, 1963–1989" (master's thesis, University of North Carolina, 2010).
91 Ruth Mandel has noted that the German right and left align in their resistance to headscarves, with the right using the scarf as "proof of the fundamental 'nonintegrateability' of the Turks" and the feminist left seeing the scarf as a symbol of "innate Turkish practices of sexism, backward and primitive patriarchal domination of women, and repression," *Cosmopolitan Anxieties*, 305.
92 Deniz Göktürk et al., *Germany in Transit*.
93 Ulrich Herbert writes that Germany's Nazi experience affected West German cultural responses to foreigners, especially because the guest worker programs began just ten years after the end of the Second World War. See Ulrich Herbert, *A History of Foreign Labor in Germany*.
94 There is a rich literature on race, specifically of those of African descent, in West Germany, see Heide Fehrenbach, *Race after Hitler: Black Occupation Children in Postwar Germany and America* (Princeton, NJ: Princeton University Press, 2005); Tina Campt and Michelle Maria Wright eds., in "Reading the Black German Experience," special issue, *Callaloo* 26 no. 2 (Spring 2003); Maria Höhn, *GIs and Fräuleins: German-American Encounter in 1950s West Germany* (Chapel Hill: University of North Carolina Press,

2002); May Opitz, Katharina Oguntoye, and Dagmar Schultz, eds., *Showing Our Colors: Afro-German Women Speak Out*, trans. Anne V. Adams (Amherst: University of Massachusetts Press, 1986); Panikos Panayi, *Ethnic Minorities in Nineteenth and Twentieth Century Germany* (New York: Longman, 2000).

95 See, for example, Klaus J. Bade, *Auswanderer, Wanderarbeiter, Gastarbeiter: Bevölkerung, Arbeitsmarkt und Wanderung in Deutschland seit der Mitte des 19. Jahrhunderts*. 2 vols. *Referate und Diskussionsbeiträge des Internationalen Wissenschaftlichen Symposiums "Vom Auswanderungsland zum Einwanderungsland?" an der Akademie für Politische Bildung Tutzing 1982* (Ostfilder: Scripta Mercaturae, 1984); Klaus Bade, *Population, Labour, and Migration in Nineteenth- and Twentieth-Century Germany* (New York: Berg, 1987); Klaus Bade, *Deutsche im Ausland – Fremde in Deutschland: Migration in Geschichte und Gegenwart* (München: Beck, 1993); Ulrich Herbert, *History of Foreign Labor*.

96 Herbert, *History of Foreign Labor*, 1.

97 Christopher A. Molnar, "Imagining Yugoslavs: Migration and the Cold War in Postwar West Germany," *Central European History* 47 (2014): 138–69.

98 For studies on Muslim minorities in Europe see, Valerie Amiraux, "Restructuring Political Islam: Transnational Belonging and Muslims in France and Germany," in *Transnational Political Islam: Religion, Ideology, and Power*, ed. Azza Kara (Sterling, VA: Pluto, 2004); Katherine Pratt Ewig, "Legislating Religious Freedom: Muslim Challenges to the Relationship between 'Church' and 'State' in Germany and France," *Daedalus: Journal of the American Academy of Arts and Sciences* 129, no. 4 (Fall 2000): 31–54; Sigrid Nökel, *Die Töchter der Gastarbeiter und der Islam: zur Soziologie alltagsweltlicher Anerkennungspolitiken. Ein Fallstudie* (Bielefeld: Transcript, 2002); Hanns Thomä-Venske, *Islam und Integration: Zur Bedeutung des Islam im Prozeß der Integration türkischer Arbeiterfamilien in die Gesellschaft der Bundesrepublik* (Hamburg: Rissen, 1981); Werner Schiffauer, *Die Gottesmänner: Türkische Islamisten in Deutschland* (Frankfurt am Main: Suhrkamp, 2000); Wolfgang Ritsch, *Die Rolle des Islams für die Koranschulerziehung in der Bundesrepublik Deutschland* (Cologne: Rahl-Rugenstein, 1987); "West Germany," in *Muslims in Western Europe*, ed. Jorgen S. Nielsen (Edinburgh: Edinburgh University Press, 1992), 23–38; James Helicke, "Turks in Germany: Muslim Identity: 'Between' States," in *Muslim Minorities in the West: Visible and Invisible*, ed. Yvonne Yazbeck Haddad and Jane I. Smith (New York: Altamira, 2002), 175–94; Jeroen Doomernik, "The Institutionalization of Turkish Islam in Germany and the

Netherlands: A Comparison," *Ethnic and Racial Studies* 18, no. 1 (1995, Jan): 46–63.

99 Joyce Mushaben, *The Changing Faces of Citizenship*, 151.

100 Ibid.

101 Ruth Mandel, "Reimagining Islams in Berlin" in *Cosmopolitan Anxieties*, 248–93; Rita Chin, "The Politics of Sexual Democracy in the New Europe," (conference paper given at "Mobilizing Difference: Gender, Islam and the Production of Contemporary Europeanness," University of Illinois at Urbana-Champaign, 13–14 September 2013).

102 The murder of Dutch filmmaker Theo van Gogh is an excellent example of a media storm against Muslims as a group after the radical action of a single person. Ian Buruma, *Murder in Amsterdam: Liberal Europe, Islam, and the Limits of Tolerance* (New York: Penguin Press, 2006).

103 In discussions of Turkey's potential European Union membership, some German historians have pointed out that Turks could not be "European" due to deeply engrained cultural differences, introducing an ethnocultural definition of the otherness of Muslims within a Christian-defined Europe. In response, Mehmet Mıhrı Özdoğan writes, "Historians, who are actually known for being liberal, such as Hans-Ulrich Wehler, and also Heinrich August Winkler and Jürgen Kocka, base their arguments on supposed unbridgeable cultural differences between Muslim lands and Christian Europe … The quintessence of their argument is: if one is not a European one cannot become one," in Mehmet Mıhrı Özdoğan, "Zum EU-Beitritt der Türkei: Grenze der Erweiterung oder Grenze der Vernunft?" *Werkstattgeschichte* 37 (2004): 93–9; see also Jürgen Kocka, "Wo liegst du, Europe," *Die Zeit*, 2 December 2002; Hans-Ulrich Wehler, "Das Türkenproblem," *Die Zeit*, 12 September 2002; Heinrich August Winkler, "Grenzen der Erweiterung: Die Türkei ist kein Teil des 'Projekt Europe,'" *Internationale Politik* 2 (2002): 59–66; Heinrich August Winkler, "Europa am Scheideweg," *Frankfurter Allgemeine Zeitung*, 12 November 2003; Dirk Schumann, "Is the EU Complete Without Turkey? Opportunities and Challenges for Europe's Identity and the Foreign and Security Policy of the European Union and the United States," *GHI Bulletin* 34 (2004): 190–2; The World Press Organization reported on Turkey's EU prospects thusly, "Some said that even if part of Turkey is in Europe, this does not cancel the reality that Turkey lacks European roots in its culture and traditions," in "The International Press on Turkey's European Union Membership Bid, Comment and analysis from London, Dubai, Beirut, Frankfurt, and Istanbul," 8 October 2004, accessed 3 March 2016, http://www.worldpress.org/Europe/1951.cfm.

104 Joyce Mushaben, *The Changing Faces of Citizenship*, 151.
105 Initially historians of foreign labour in Germany did not consider the perspective of the workers or use Turkish or other non-German sources to explore migration history. These important pioneering works consider guest workers within studies of either foreign labour in Germany or migration in or out of Germany since the nineteenth century instead of considering the specificity of the post-war period. See for example, Ulrich Herbert, *History of Foreign Labor*; Klaus Bade, *Deutsche im Ausland*.
106 Early social science studies offer important initial investigations, statistics, and logistical data of guest worker immigration to West Germany, see Nermin Abadan-Unat, ed., *Turkish Workers in Europe, 1960–1975: A Socio-Economic Reappraisal* (Leiden: E. J Brill, 1975); Stephen Castles and Godula Kosack, *Immigrant Workers and Class Structure in Western Europe* (London: Oxford University Press, 1973); Ali S. Gitmez, *Dışgöç Öyküsü: araştırma-deneme* [Immigration Story: A Research Report] (Ankara: Maya Matbaacılık, 1979).
107 "Elif," Berlin, 2003.
108 Ibid.

1. The Invitation

1 "1964 yılının 10 bininci işçisi Almanyaya gitti," ["In the year 1964 the 10 Thousandth Worker Left for Germany] *Cumhuriyet*, 17 March 1964.
2 Elizabeth D. Heineman, *What Difference Does a Husband Make? Women and Marital Status in Nazi and Postwar Germany* (Berkeley: California University Press, 2003).
3 "Almanya'ya on bininci işçi gitti," [Ten Thousandth Worker Arrives in Germany] *Dünya*, 17 March 1964. At this point there were currently two million more women than men in West Germany.
4 "1964 yılının 10 bininci işçisi Almanya'ya gitti," [1964's Ten Thousandth Worker Arrives in Germany] *Cumhuriyet*, 17 March 1964; see also "76 Günde 10,400 İşçi Gitti," [10,400 Workers Depart within in 76 Days] *Milliyet*, 17 March 1964.
5 Abadan-Unat, *Turks in Europe*, 63.
6 "1964 yılının 10 bininci işçisi Almanya'ya gitti," *Cumhuriyet*, 17 March 1964; see also "76 Günde 10,4000 İşçi Gitti," *Milliyet*, 17 March 1964.
7 Mathilde Jamin, "Fremde Heimat: Zur Geschichte der Arbeitsmigration aus der Türkei," in *50 Jahre Bundesrepublik 50 Jahre Einwanderung: Nachkriegsgeschichte als Migrationsgeschichte*, ed. Jan Motte, Rainer Ohliger, and Anne von Oswald (Frankfurt: Campus, 1999), 145–64, here 153.

8 For a comprehensive history of the "Economic Miracle" in Western Europe, including the Marshall plan, see Werner Abelshauser, *Deutsche Wirtschaftsgeschichte seit 1945* (Munich: Beck, 2004); Tony Judt, *Postwar*, 95–7, 125, 324–55; Spicka, *Selling*.

9 For more on the will inherent in migration, see Dirk Hoerder, *Cultures in Contact: World Migrations in the Second Millennium* (Durham: Duke University Press, 2002), xxi.

10 Giacomo Maturi, "Die zweite Phase der Ausländerbeschäftigung in der Bundesrepublik" (Heidelberg: Heidelberger Verlagsanstalt und Druckerei GmbH, undated) DOMiD Archive 424 SD, 2.

11 Ibid, 3.

12 Dr Giacomo Maturi, Willi Baumgartner, Stefan Bobolis, Konstantin Kustas, Vittorio Bedolli, Guillermo Arrillage, and Sümer Göksuyer, eds., *Hallo Mustafa! Günther Türk arkadaşı ile konuşuyor* [Hello Mustafa! Günter speaks with his Turkish friends], illustrations Richard Haschberger (Heidelberg: Dr Curt Haefner Verlag, 1966), 10.

13 "siz Türkler sıcak kanlı," ["you Turks are hot blooded"] *Hallo Mustafa!*, 10.

14 For contemporary comparisons and studies of urban and village life in Turkey, see Nuri Eren, *Turkey Today and Tomorrow: An Experiment in Westernization* (New York: Frederick Praeger, 1963); John Kolars, *Tradition, Season, and Change in a Turkish Village* NAS-NRC Foreign Field Research Program Report No. 15 (Chicago: University of Chicago Press, 1963); Walter F. Weiker, *The Turkish Revolution 1960–1961: Aspects of Military Politics* (Washington, DC: Brookings Institution, 1963); Joe Pierce, *Life in a Turkish Village* (New York: Holt, Rinehart, Winston, 1964); Robert E. Ward and Dankwart A. Rustow, eds., *Political Modernization in Japan and Turkey* (Princeton, NJ: Princeton University Press, 1964); Denis Hills, *My Travels in Turkey* (London: George Allen & Unwin, 1964); Paul Stirling, *Turkish Village* (London: Weidenfeld and Nicolson, 1965); sociologists from the United States and from England conducted these studies providing a useful look at how Turkish life was perceived from the outside in the 1960s.

15 Abadan-Unat, Nermin, ed., *Turkish Workers in Europe, 1960–1975: A Socio-Economic Reappraisal* (Leiden: E.J. Brill, 1976), 9.

16 Previous studies emphasis that Turkish women did not play a significant role in guest worker migration because they did not come in large numbers until after 1973. Karin Hunn and Ulrich Herbert write, "The history of guest workers in the 1960s is a history of men," in "Guest Workers and Policy on Guest Workers in the Federal Republic" in *Miracle Years*, 199; see also Karin Hunn, *Nächstes Jahr*; however, women guest workers did play significant roles, see Monika Mattes, *Gastarbeiterinnen*.

17 Abadan-Unat, *Politics*, 331.
18 For more information on asylum seekers in West and East Germany
   see, Klaus J. Bade and Jochen Oltmer, "Migration im Kalten Krieg" and
   "Einwandererbevölkerung und neue Zuwanderungen im vereinigten
   Deutschland seit 1990" in *Normalfall Migration* (Bonn: Bundeszentrale für
   politische Bildung, 2004), 52–132.
19 An excellent example of this is the now infamous *Spiegel* cover, "Gettos
   in Deutschland: Eine Million Türken," and accompanying story, "Die
   Türken kommen –rette sich, wer kann," which reports on legal and illegal
   immigration and on foreign workers from Yugoslavia, Italy, and Turkey
   all in one article; this article emphasizes a threatening trend of a loss of
   German culture, a comparison with New York's Harlem neighborhood,
   and worse an impending integration crisis in cities such as Berlin, Munich,
   and Frankfurt. "[vor lauter Ausländer] die Integrationskraft der Stadt
   allmählich an ihre Grenze gelangt," *Der Spiegel* no. 31 (30 July 1973): 24–34.
20 Akgündüz, *An Introduction*, 193.
21 "Murat," DOMiD Interview 14, Berlin, 30 August 1995, trans. Pinar
   Gibbon.
22 "Aygül," DOMiD Interview 8, Frankfurt am Main, 22 May 1995. She ended
   up joining her parents in West Germany a few years later.
23 Ibid., 79–99. There were also a significant number of Turkish workers
   who went to West Germany via the so-called "second path" (unofficial
   channels) and "third path," such as entering the country as a tourist.
   Statistics on unofficial travel are hard to calculate, though there are
   plenty of references to them in both West German official notes as well
   as in interview with former workers who openly admit coming to West
   Germany as tourists and then looking for work after arrival. Some
   were only able to work "under the table." Serhat Karakayli provides
   an excellent study of the second path and non-citizens' negotiations
   of bureaucracy in *Gespenster der Migration: Zur Genealogie illegaler
   Einwanderung in der Bundesrepublik Deutschland* (Bielefeld: Transcript, 2008).
   See also Serhat Karakayali and Enrica Rigo "Mapping the European Space
   of Circulation" in *The Deportation Regime: Sovereignty, Space, and the Freedom
   of Movement*, ed. Nicholas de Genova and Nathalie Peutz (Durham: Duke
   University Press, 2010), 123–46.
24 Karin Hunn, *Nächstes Jahr*, 79.
25 İş ve işçi bulma Kurumu Genel Müdürlüğü Yayınları [Labor Office
   Directorate Publication], *İşçi Olarak Almanya'ya Nasıl Gidiler? Federal
   Almanya'da Yaşama Şartları* [How Does One Go to Germany to Work?
   Living Conditions in the Federal Republic], no. 28 (Ankara: Mars

Matbaası, 1963), [National Library Ankara]; the same guidelines for the application procedure are also outlined in "Bericht: Dienstreise vom 14.29, October 1961," BArch B 119 / 3077 I.

26 "Hallo Mustafa: Gesprächen des deutschen Arbeitnehmers mit seinem italienischen, spanischen, griechischen und türkischen Kollegen in vier separaten Sprachausgaben" ["Hello Mustafa: The German Worker's Conversation with his Italian, Spanish, Greek and Turkish Colleagues in Four Separate Foreign-Language Editions"] (Heidelberg: Dr Curt-Haefner Verlag, 1966). The fine print on the Turkish version notes that all translations of the booklet have identical contents. It is striking that one booklet was designed for all workers, treating this vast population of foreign workers as a unified group.

27 "Hallo Mustafa: Gesprächen," 4, emphasis mine. Translation by the author of the German edition.

28 Ibid.

29 Ibid., 6.

30 Ibid., emphasis mine.

31 Barbara Sonnenberger, "Verwaltete Arbeitskraft: die Anwerbung von 'Gastarbeiter' in den 1950er und 1960er Jahren," in *Migration Steuern und Verwalten*, ed. Jochen Oltmer, IMIS Schriften 12 (Göttingen: Hubert & Co, 2003), 145–76, here, 160; see also Jamin, "Die deutsch-türkischen Anwerbevereinbarung von 1961 und 1964," in Aytaç Eryılmaz and Mathilde Jamin, eds., *Fremde Heimat*, 69–82, here 82.

32 Jamin, *Fremde Heimat*, 82. See also Karen Schönwälder, *Einwanderung und ethnische Pluralität: Politische Entscheidungen und öffentliche Debatten in Großbritannien und der Bundesrepublik von den 1950er bis zu den 1970er Jahren* (Essen: Klartext, 2001), 215–16; 618; Bucerius, *Unwanted*, 24.

33 *Hallo Mustafa!*, 5.

34 "1919 yılında Milletler Cemiyet'in kontrolü altında milletlerarası bir idareye tabi tutulmuş olan Saar Havası 1935 yılında yapılan bir plebisit neticesinde tekrar Almanya'ya iltihak eder." The year 1935 is perhaps better known as the year of the introduction of the Nuremburg Laws, which sought to give legal validity to racial discrimination and introduced categories of full and partial citizenship. This same year also saw clear breaches of the Treaty of Versailles by Germany, including a rearmament program, introduction of conscription, and the existence of a German air force. Needless to say, this single, one-sentence description of the interwar period and rise of Hitler was lacking in a troubling way. Helmut Artz, *Almanya'yı Tanımak istermisiniz?* [Would you like to get to know Germany?] (Wiesbaden: Wiesbadener Graphischer Betriebe, 1965).

35 *İşçi*, 8–9.
36 Ibid., 6.
37 Ibid., 9.
38 Ibid.
39 Ibid., 4.
40 "Hasan," DOMiD Interview 12, Berlin, 22 June 1995.
41 "Adil," DOMiD Interview 28, Essen, 22 June 1995.
42 "Mehmet," DOMiD Interview 17, Hamburg, 27 June 1995.
43 Dr Keintzel, "Bericht über Erkundung der Anwerbemöglichkeiten von türkischen Bergleuten für den deutschen Steinkohlenbergbau in der Türkei. Dienstreise vom 14–29. October 1961" BArch B 119/ 3077 I, 9.
44 "Mehmet," DOMiD Interview 23, 9 October 1995, Schweinfurt.
45 *İşçi*, 7.
46 Ibid., 8.
47 "Bericht: Dienstreise vom 14–29 October 1961" BArch B 119/ 3077 I, 4.
48 "Adil," DOMiD Interview 28, Essen, 22 June 1995.
49 *İşçi*, 15.
50 Ibid., 30–1.
51 In his study, Aker writes that workers in Germany earned four times as much as they did in Turkey, Ahmet Aker, "A Study of Turkish Labour Migration to Germany," *Institute of Foreign Policy Research: The Johns Hopkins University Bologna Center School of Advanced International Studies*, no. 10 (July 1974): 1–32, here 28.
52 Nermin Abadan, *Batı Almanya'daki Türk İşçiler ve Sorunları* [Turkish Workers in West Germany and Their Problems] (Ankara: T.C. Başbakanlık Devlet Plânlama Teşkilâtı, 1964), 57.
53 Ibid.
54 1 October 1968 BArch B 119 / 3073.
55 *İşçi*, 5.
56 Ibid., 9.
57 "Erol," DOMiD Interview 22, Munich, 12 October 1995.
58 A committee of BA officials would determine an applicant's departure position by taking into consideration West German employers'' wishes, the candidate's age, education, skill level, physical build and even "personal appearance and attitude," *İşçi*, 96.
59 *İşçi*, 14, emphasis mine.
60 Nürnberg, Weicken, "Tätigkeit der Deutschen Verbindungsstelle in der Türkei und der Deutschen Kommission in Griechenland," 17 May 1968 BArch, B 119/ 3074, notes problems with nominated appointments, pointing out that requested relatives are not always "ready for departure;

4,700 applicants were reported to be nominated applicants between 18 October and 22 November 1969, BArch B 119/ 4031.

61 Landesarbeitsamt Baden-Württemberg an BAVAV, 23 January 1963, BArch B 119/ 3071; in this case the State Employment Office in Stuttgart is petitioning the Federal Office on her behalf for a work visa.

62 İşçi, 8.

63 Jamin, 50 Jahre, 158.

64 Werner Schiffauer, Die Migranten aus Subay: Türken in Deutschland Eine Ethnografie (Stuttgart: Ernst Klett Verlag für Wissen und Bildung, GmbH, 1991), 30.

65 DOMiD Interview 16, Berlin, 15 August 1995.

66 Ibid.

67 BAVAV Türkei, Der Direktor, Istanbul, An BAVAV, Nürnberg, 12 August 1970 BArch B119/ 4031.

68 DOMiD Interviews 18 and 19, "Almanya'ya yalnız gelen bir anne ve kızı," ["A Mother and Daughter Go to Germany"] Herne, 1995.

69 BAVAV Deutsch Verbindungsstelle in der Türkei and BAVAV Nürnberg, "Anwerbung und Vermittlung türkischer Arbeitskräften ach der Bundesrepublik Deutschland; hier: Wochenbericht für die Zeit 29.8.1964-4.9.1964," 4 September 1964 BArch B 119/ 4035.

70 Karin Hunn writes that some Anatolian women were "forced" or at least highly encouraged by their families or spouses to sign up to be guest workers in Nächstest Jahr; see also Jamin, 50 Jahre; DOMiD Interviews 18 and 19, "Mother and Daughter."

71 "Erol," DOMiD interview 22, Munich, 12 October 1995.

72 "Mehmet," DOMiD interview 23, Schweinfurt, 9 October 1995.

73 Ibid.

74 Hallo Mustafa!, 25.

75 Hallo Mustafa!, 25.

76 Jamin, "Fremde Heimat," in 50 Jahre, 153.

77 An BAVAV Nürnberg, 30 October 1962, BArch B 119/ 3071 II.

78 Ibid.

79 Ibid.

80 Abadan, Batı Almanya'daki Türk İşçiler [Turkish workers in West Germany], 58.

81 Ibid.

82 BA Der Präsident, an Firma Klaus Esser KG, Düsseldorf, 24 August 1970, BArch B 119/ 3041.

83 DOMiD Interview 20, "Remzi," Munich, 10 October 1995.

84 DOMiD Interview 22, "Erol," Munich, 12 October 1995.

85 Bundesvereinigung der Deutschen Arbeitgeberverbände Köln October 1969, BArch B 119/ 4036 I.
86 "Bericht: Dienstreise vom 14– 29 October 1961" BArch B 119/ 3077 I, 3.
87 Ibid., 4.
88 Ibid., 5, "Als ich darum bat, in diesem Verteilungsplan Einblick zu nehmen, mußte ich zu meinem Entsetzen feststellen, daß die Zentralstelle in Istambul [sic] die Aufträge des deutschen Bergbaus auf insgesamt 17 türkische Arbeitsämter über die ganze Türkei verteilt hatte."
89 Bundesvereinigung der Deutschen Arbeitgeberverbände Köln October 1969, BArch B 119/ 4036 I.
90 Ibid.

2. In Transit

Parts of this chapter first appeared in *German History* 30, no. 4 (2012): 550–73 and is published here with permission.

1 "Notbremse im Hellas-Istanbul Express," *Salzburger Nachrichten*, no.17, 28 June 1969, BArch B 119/ 4030. *Salzburger Nachrichten* is known as a centre-right, Christian liberal paper.
2 Ibid.
3 Ibid.
4 Ibid.
5 Ibid.
6 West German and German Rail officials continued to use terms like "transport" to refer to guest worker transportation, even though, for some, the term had a negative and historically loaded connotation, because it was the same term used to describe trains travelling to concentration and extermination camps. For recent scholarship on the use of train transportation during the Holocaust see, Simone Gigliotti, *The Train Journey* (New York: Berghahn Books, 2009); Todd Samuel Presner, *Mobile Modernity: Germans, Jews, Trains* (New York: Columbia University Press, 2007). For a look at the intersections between mechanized technology, corporate power, and modernized space see, Barbara Young Welke, *Recasting American Liberty: Gender, Race, Law, and the Railroad Revolution, 1865–1920* (New York: Cambridge University Press, 2001).
7 Guest worker transportation received much press coverage: a BBC film crew even travelled with Turkish workers from Istanbul to West Germany to make a documentary. The filmmakers noted, "to be able to travel with the Turkish workers on their train was one of the most important factors

in the success of the film. Only then could we really observe first-hand
the realities of the men leaving their country for a new job and life
in Germany ... We were highly impressed with the handling of vast
numbers of potential and actual workers ... The film will be shown
here in October," Sue Pugh to Herr Karl Maibaum, BBC TV, London,
Bundesanstalt für Arbeit, Nürnberg, 7 June 1973 BArch, B119/ 4029;
see also, Deutsche Botschaft, Ankara, an das Auswärtiges Amt, Bonn,
"Stellungnahme der türkischen Presse zu dem Ausgang der Gespräche
der deutschen-türkischen Gemischten Kommission," which mentions the
growing amount of Turkish press coverage Turkish "guest workers" in
Germany were especially receiving, because apparently, in comparison to
Italy and Spain, this program caused the first large emigration of ethnic
Turks out of the country, 16 May 1968 BArch B119/ 3074.
8 Ahmet Aker, "A Study of Turkish Labour Migration to Germany."
9 Historians of guest workers in West Germany often begin with a train
station motif. See, Klaus J. Bade and Jochen Oltmer eds., *Zuwanderung
und Integration in Niedersachsen Zeit dem Zweiten Weltkrieg* (Osnabrück:
Universitätsverlag Rasch, 2002); Rita Chin, *The "Guest Worker" Question
in Postwar Germany* (New York: Cambridge University Press, 2007); Karin
Hunn, *"Nächstes Jahr kehren wir zurück ... " Die Geschichte der türkischen
"Gastarbeiter" in der Bundesrepublik* (Göttingen: Wallstein Verlag, 2005).
See also the film *Almanya: Willkommen in Deutschland* [*Almanya: Welcome
to Germany*], which shows a Turkish guest worker deciding to go to
West Germany, boarding the back of a pickup truck in Turkey, and
then stepping into a West German train station after arrival, Yasemin
Şamdereli, dir., (Roxy, Infa, Concord, 2011), DVD.
10 Karen Schönwälder writes that West Germans could feel "nationalistic"
and "superior" by recruiting thousands of foreign workers, "as evidence
of their own economic superiority, of their role as a leading civic force
in Europe and even as political educators," "West German Society," 115.
For the historical legacy of train travel as part of modernity see, Steven
Kern, *The Culture of Time and Space, 1880–1918* (Cambridge, MA: Harvard
University Press, 1986); Angela Woollacott, "'All This Is the Empire, I told
Myself': Australian Women's Voyages 'Home' and the Articulation of
Colonial Whiteness," *American Historical Review* 102, no. 4 (October 1997):
1003–29.
11 Proponents of "new labour history" have argued for a move away from
the "shop floor" in order to understand the development of working-
class experience. David Brody, "The Old Labor History and the New: In
Search of the American Working Class" in *Labor History* 20 (Winter 1979):

111–26; in this classic essay, Brody asks labour historians to look beyond the workplace to capture the American working-class experience. See also *In Labor's Cause: Main Themes on the History of the American Worker* (New York: Oxford University Press, 1993); see E.P. Thompson, *The Making of the English Working Class* (Vintage, 1963), which argues that class is a cultural formation. While "new labour history" is no longer "new," its application to Turkish guest worker remains novel. For a look at new labour history and the reinforcement of racial stereotypes, see David R. Roediger, *The Wages of Whiteness: Race and the Making of the American Working Class* (New York: Verso, 1999).

12 This is largely cited to be the first transport of Turkish guest workers to West Germany organized by the German Liaison Office, however, unlike later group trips, it was organized by the Fäustel Travel Agency in Istanbul, BAVAV Holjewilken Nürnberg, 14 October 1961, BArch B 119/4035.

13 BAVAV Holjewilken Nürnberg, 14 October 1961, BArch B 119/4035. The term "escort" is a translation of the term *Transportbegleiter*. Though the file does not mention if Mr Ibrahim was paid, it is likely that he was also a travelling guest worker, who took on the task of escort for a nominal fee and was chosen for German language ability.

14 Jamin, "Fremde Heimat," in *50 Jahre Bundesrepublik*; see also Jamin, "Die deutsche Anwerbung, Organisation und Größenordnung," in *Fremde Heimat*, 207–31. Workers were also able to apply to arrive in West Germany privately, and some firms also organized flights for workers; for information on flights see BAVAV Nürnberg, 19 May 1965, BArch B 119/4031; see also BAVAV Türkei, 31 January 1972, BArch B 119/4029.

15 Münir Egeli, *Almanya'ya Gidiyorum* [I am going to Germany] (Bonn: İnkılap ve Aka, 1962), 28. The pamphlet also lists departure days and times for air routes to West Germany, though until 1970, train travel was far more common.

16 *İşçi*, 16.

17 In her study of the conditions and problems of Turkish workers in West Germany, Abadan-Unat noted that 58 per cent of those she interviewed said that they did not read instructional materials before departure or after arrival. It is not clear from this statement if workers actually received the materials or if they were choosing to ignore them. Abadan-Unat, *Studie Über die Lage und Die Probleme der Türkischen Gastarbeiter in der Bundesrepublik Deutschland: Kurze Zusammenfassung*, (Türkische Republik Ministerpräsidum Staatssekretariat für Wirtschaftsplanung, Ankara, 1964, 6 October 1964, BArch, B 119/3073).

18 For example, an arrival packet in Southern Bavaria contained exactly 1,111.4 calories. Landesarbeitsamt Südbayern, "Verpflegung der ausländischen Arbeiter in der Weiterleitungsstelle," 1963 BArch B 119/ 4032.

19 BAVAV Nürnberg, "Bericht des VAm Krusch über die Dienstreise nach Belgrad zwecks Beobachtung eines Sonderzug-Transportes Istanbul-München," 11 November 1963, BArch B 119/4035; Istanbul, BAVAV Türkei an BAVAV Nürnberg, "Reiseproviant," 13 December 1964, BArch B 119 / 4035. This memo noted that one firm was so eager to secure the deal with the employment bureau that they reportedly offered gold watches to officials and their wives.

20 "Der Nähr- und Sättigungswert der Lebensmittel kann als ausreichend bezeichnet werden. Mit Ausnahme der Wurst keine Beanstandungen in hygienischer und qualitativer Hinsicht." Istanbul 13 December 1964, Bundesanstalt für Arbeitsvermittlung und Arbeitslosenversicherung, Deutsche Verbindungsstelle in der Türkei, An den Herrn Präsidenten der Bundesanstalt für Arbeitsvermittlung und Arbeitslosenversicherung; Betr: Transportangelegenheiten; hier: Reiseproviant; BArch B 119/ 4035.

21 BAVAV Nürnberg Holjewilken, "Anwerbung und Vermittlung türkischer Arbeitskräfte; hier Eintreffen der 1. Und 2. Sammelfahrt mit türkischen Arbeitskräften in München-Hbf," 14 October 1961, BArch B 119/ 4035.

22 Ibid.

23 Ibid.

24 In interviews, former workers reported packing food for the trip that including the Turkish garlic-flavored sausage, *sucuk,* see Documentation Center and Museum of Migration in Germany (DOMiD) Interview 16, Berlin, 31 August 1995; DOMiD Interview 62, "Metin," place redacted, April 1995, trans. Pinar Gibbon; DOMiD Interview 39, "Yalcın," Nuremberg, 19 October 1995; see also "Ungenehmigte Einfuhr von Fleisch- und Wurstwaren durch ausländische Arbeitnehmer," BArch B 119/ 4029. Apparently the Minister for Nutrition, Farming, and Forestry wrote the employment bureau in Nuremberg to remind them that "the introduction of forbidden meat products" from Turkey and Greece should be stopped.

25 "Betref: Transporte neuangeworbener griechischer und türkischer Arbeiter nach Deutschland," 15 March 1967, BArch B119/ 4029.

26 "Betr: Besuch der Weiterleitungsstelle im Hauptbahnhof München am 14 January 1963," 24 January 1963, BArch B 119/ 4032.

27 "Notbremsa im Hellas-Istanbul-Expreß," *Salzburger Nachrichten* BArch B 119/ 4030.

28 BAVAV Nürnberg, an Herrn Präs. Landesarbeitsamtes Südbayern, München, 16 January 1962; Deutsches Zollamt Salzburg an BAVAV Nürnberg, 23 November 1967, BArch B 119/ 4031.

29 BAVAV Türkei an BAVAV Nürnberg, Betr: Transportangelegenheiten, hier, Das zu reichlich mitgeführte Gepäck türk. Arbeitnehmer, Die Nutzung von Sitzplätzen zur Gepäckbeförderung, Die Verschmutzung der Sonderzüge, 15 May 1964, BArch B 119/ 4035.

30 Ibid.

31 Ibid.

32 Ibid.

33 Ibid. German Rail officials mention that they would have to have a guarantee from Turkish Rail that they would be exempt from certain fees in order to arrange transportation. However, there are only vague references to what these fees are for and what amount they are. Weicken, Nürnberg, April 1962, BArch B 119/ 4035.

34 Weicken, Nürnberg, April 1962, BArch B 119/ 4035.

35 "Verbesserung im Balkan-Verkehr erst 1966? Die ausländischen Bahnverwaltungen können keine weiteren Züge übernehmen," *Frankfurter Allgemeine Zeitung (FAZ)* 1 October 1965, BArch B 119/ 4031; see also *FAZ* 29 September 1966.

36 Ibid. See also BAVAV Türkei an BAVAV Nürnberg, 3 January 1962, BArch B 119/ 4035; Deutsche Bundesbahn Oberbetriebsleitung Süd, Stuttgart, an Generaldirektion der Österreichischen Bundesbahnen, Wien, Gemeinschaft der Jugoslawischen Eisenbahnen, Belgrad, Transportministerium Abteilung für internationale Angelegenheiten Sofija, Direction Générale des Chemins de fer de l'Etat hellénique Direction de l'Exploitation, Athènes, Direction générale d'Exploitation des Chemins de fer d'état de la République turque, Ankara, Direction de la 7e Région Exploitation TCDD Istanbul, 12 December 1963, BArch B 119/ 4035.

37 BAVAV Türkei an BAVAV Nürnberg, Betr: Anwerbung und Vermittlung türkischer Arbeitnehmer, hier, Wochenbericht, 6 September 1963, BArch B 119/ 4035.

38 "Notbremse im Hellas-Istanbul-Expreß," BAVAV Türkei, Istanbul, 13 July 1964, an BAVAV Nürnberg, BArch B 119/ 4031.

39 BAVAV Türkei an BAVAV Nürnberg, 12 September 1961, BArch B 119/ 4035; see also, BAVAV Türkei an BAVAV Nürnberg 6 September 1963, "Anwerbung und Vermittlung türkischer Arbeitnehmer, hier, Wochenbericht," BArch B 119/ 4035.

40 " Notbremse im Hellas-Istanbul-Expreß," BAVAV Türkei, Istanbul, 13 July 1964, an BAVAV Nürnberg, BArch B 119/ 4031.

41 "Prügelszenen um reservierte Plätze: Bundesbahn ist ratlos: Gastarbeiter blockieren Urlauberzüge" *Rheinische Post* No. 188, 14 August 1965, BArch B 119/ 4031.

42 Ref. Weicken, "Bericht des VAm Krusch über die Dienstreise nach Belgrad zwecks Beobachtung eines Sonderzug-Transportes Istanbul-München," BArch B 119 / 4035.

43 Ref Ia6, Weicken, Nürnberg, April 1962, BArch B 119 / 4035.

44 Landesarbeitsamt Südbayern an BAVAV Nürnberg, 11 December 1961, BArch B 119/ 4035; BAVAV Nürnberg, Weicken, March 1962, BArch B 119/ 4035.

45 Landesarbeitsamt Südbayern an BAVAV Nürnberg, 11 December 1961, BArch B 119/ 4035; officials mention paying the cost of seat reservations, however, it is unclear if they did so for every departing train; see BAVAV Türkei an BAVAV Nürnberg, 12 August 1963, BArch B 119/ 4035 and BAVAV Türkei, an BAVAV Nürnberg, 23 August 1963, BArch B 119/ 4035. Another memo mentions that it was not possible to reserve seats for non-German trains: "Platzkarten können nicht ausgegeben werden (kein Platzkartenverfahren mit Jugoslawien, Griechenland und der Türkei. Für eine ordnungsgemäße Durchführung der Transporte (für alle Kräfte sind Plätze in einem Wagen vorhanden) müssen Wagen der Deutschen Bundesbahn eingesetzt werden," Ref Weicken, Nürnberg, April 1962, BArch B 119/ 4035.

46 BAVAV Türkei an BAVAV Nürnberg 1 April 1964, BArch B119/ 4035.

47 BAVAV Nürnberg, 13 April 1964, BArch B 119/ 4035; see Also, Bundesvereinigung der Deutschen Arbeitgeberverbände, Köln, an die Mitglieder des Ausschusses "Ausländische Arbeitskräfte," 30 October 1969, BArch B 119/ 4036 I, which notes that working with Yugoslavian rail caused particular problems.

48 "Die beiden Leerzüge sind pünktlich eingetroffen. Sie führten allerdings einmal 14 und das andere Mal nur 12 Wagen mit. Infolge Verspätung des fahrplanmäßigen Yugoslavienexpress konnten die Sonderzüge erst um 21 [Uhr] bereitgestellt werden." BAVAV Deutsche Verbindungsstelle in der Türkei, An den Herrn Präsidenten der BAVAV Nürnberg, 24 July 1964; Betr: Anwerbung und Vermittlung türkischer Arbeitskräfte nach der Bundesrepublik Deutschland, hier Wochenbericht für die Zeit vom 17–23 July 1964; BAVAV Türkei an BAVAV Nürnberg, "Betr: Transportangelegenheiten," 1 April 1964, BArch B119/ 4035.

49 Bundesvereinigung der Deutschen Arbeitgeberverbände, Köln, "Tätigkeit der Deutschen Anwerbekommissionen in Istanbul, Athen und Belgrad," 30 October 1969, BArch B 119/ 4036 I.

50 BAVAV an Deutschen Bundesbahn, "Transportangelegenheiten
     ausländischer Arbeitnehmer," 19 January 1970, BArch B 119/4031; see
     also Ref. Weicken, Holkewilken Nürnberg, March 1962, BArch B 119/
     4035.
51 Landsarbeitsamt Südbayern an BAVAV Nürnberg 11 December 1961,
     BArch B 119/ 4035; see also Ref. Weicken, Holkewilken Nürnberg, March
     1962, BArch B 119/ 4035.
52 "Während der Fahrt durch Jugoslawien verlangte die jugoslawische
     Bahnpolizei an einer Haltestelle die Mitnahme von zwei Jugoslawen in
     dem Sonderzug bis nach Zagreb. Das jugoslawische Zugbegleitpersonal
     weigerte sich und suchte Unterstützung bei der Transportleitung. Die
     Polizei bestand darauf, die zwei Personen mitfahren zu lassen; Sitzplätze
     wurden nicht in Anspruch genommen." Ref. Weicken, Nürnberg,
     11November 1963, BArch B 119/ 4035.
53 Ref. Weicken, Nürnberg, 11 November 1963, BArch B 119/ 4035,
     "Die Eisenbahnverwaltungen der Durchfahrtsländer [sind] nicht
     unschuldig."
54 Ref. Weicken, Nürnberg, 11 November 1963, "Bericht des VAm Krusch
     über die Dienstreise nach Belgrad zwecks Beobachtung eines Sonderzug-
     Transportes Istanbul-München," BArch B 119/ 4035.
55 BAVAV Türkei an BAVAV Nürnberg, 12 April 1962, BArch BA 119/ 4035.
56 BAVAV Türkei 12 April 1962, an BAVAV Nürnberg BArch BA 119/ 4035;
     see also BAVAV Türkei an BAVAV Nürnberg, 11 October 1963, which
     notes that around two thousand people were awaiting departure from
     Istanbul, BArch B 119/ 4035.
57 The German Liaison Office in Istanbul requested that special
     consideration be taken of the backed-up situation in Turkey because it
     could "affect the West German economy": "Die Verbindungsstelle bittet
     daher im Hinblick auf die besonders gelagerten Verhältnisse in der
     Türkei, die Transporte von hier im Interesse der deutschen Wirtschaft
     so abfertigen zu können, wie sie anfallen." BAVAV Türkei an BAVAV
     Nürnberg, 12 April 1962, BArch BA 119/ 4035.
58 Weicken, Nürnberg, 13 April 1962, BArch B 119/ 4035; see also BAVAV,
     Nürnberg, "Übernachtung und Verpflegung von Transportteilnehmern in
     der Weiterleitungsstelle – Bahnhofsbunker – München," 11 March 1963,
     BArch B119/ 4032.
59 Ref. Weicken, "Vermittlung qualifizierter türkischer Arbeitnehmer nach
     der Bundesrepublik Deutschland, Nürnberg," notes that Saturday and
     Sunday arrivals mean that Turkish workers have to spend the night in the
     Munich train station, 13 April 1962, BArch B 119/ 4035.

60 BAVAV, Nürnberg, "Anwerbung und Vermittlung ausländischer Arbeitnehmer nach der Bundesrepublik Deutschland; hier: Übernachtung und Verpflegung von Transportteilnehmern in der Weiterleitungsstelle – Bahnhofsbunker –München," 11 March 1963, BArch B119/ 4032.

61 DOMiD Interview 39, "Yalcın," Nuremburg, 19 October 1995.

62 DOMiD Interview 16, Berlin, 31 August 1995.

63 BAVAV Türkei an BAVAV Nürnberg, "Betr: Transportangelegenheiten" 1 April 1964, BArch B119/ 4035.

64 Some workers sold their land to come to West Germany, some workers reported owning up to three hundred acres of land in Turkey before departure, see Ali Gitmez, *Göçmen İşçilerin Dönüşü: Return Migration of Turkish Workers to Three Selected Regions* (Ankara: Orta Doğu Teknik Üniversitesi Idari Ilimler Fakültesi, 1977), 73, 85, 93; BAVAV Türkei an BAVAV Nürnberg 12 April 1962.

65 Nürnberg 13 April1964, BArch B 119/ 4035; see also BAVAV Türkei an BAVAV Nürnberg 4 September 1964, BArch B 119/ 4035, where an official notes that 246 workers who could not depart were given 30 Turkish lira apiece for room and board for three nights, costing the BAVAV an additional 7,380 Turkish lira.

66 BAVAV Türkei an BAVAV Nürnberg, 19 February 1964, BArch B 119/ 4035.

67 Ibid.

68 BAVAV Türkei an den Herrn Präsident BAVAV Nürnberg, 15 May 1964, BA B 119/ 4035, emphasis mine.

69 On the inaugural trip, ten-litre bottles were issued, presumably to share, starting in 1963, two-litre bottles were issued to workers together with their travel provisions, BAVAV Türkei, an BAVAV Nürnberg, 16 August 1963, BArch B 119 / 4035; BAVAV Nürnberg 24 May 1965, BArch B 119/ 4031; Landesarbeitsamt Südbayern, Der Präsident, An der Herrn Präsidenten Der Bundesanstalt für Arbeit Nürnberg, 9 April 1970, BArch B119 4031.

70 Abteilung I, Nürnberg, "Betr: Durchführung der Ausländertransporte," 24 May 1965 BArch B 119/ 4031.

71 "Verbesserung im Balkan-Verkehr erst 1966? Die ausländischen Bahnverwaltungen können keine weiteren Züge übernehmen," *FAZ*, 1 October 1965, BArch B 119/ 4031; see also a report from *FAZ* on 29 September 1966; BAVAV Türkei an den Herrn Präsident BAVAV Nürnberg, 15 May 1964, BArch B 119/ 4035.

72 "BAVAV Türkei, Istanbul, an BAVAV Nürnberg, 13 July 1964, BArch B 119/ 403; BAVAV Nürnberg an BAVAV Türkei, Griechenland, Spanien, Landesarbeitsamt Südbayern, 4 August 1964, BArch B 119/ 4031.

73 BAVAV Türkei, Istanbul, an BAVAV Nürnberg, 13 July 1964, BArch B 119/4031.

74 Weicken, BAVAV Nürnberg 11 November 1963, BArch B 119/4035.

75 OBL Süd 15 January 1964, BArch B 119/4035; BAVAV Türkei, Istanbul, an BAVAV Nürnberg 13 July 1964, BArch B 119/4031; BAVAV Nürnberg, an BAVAV Türkei, Griechenland, Spanien, Landesarbeitsamt Südbayern, Landesarbeitsamt Nordrhein-Westfallen, 4 August 1964, BArch B 119/4031; BAVAV Nürnberg, 24 May 1964, BArch B 119/4031; BAVAV Nürnberg, An Deutsche Bundesbahn Oberbetriebsleitung Süd, 18 January 1966, BArch B 119/4031; BA Nürnberg, an Oeftering, Präs. Deutschen Bundesbahn, 19 Januar 1970, BArch B119/4031; Landesarbeitsamt Hessen, an BA Nürnberg, 6 March 1970, BArch B 119/4031; Landesarbeitsamt Südbayern, An BA Nürnberg, 9 April 1970, BArch B 119/4031.

76 BAVAV Türkei an BAVAV Nürnberg, 28 January 1966, BArch B 119/4035; BAVAV Nürnberg, an BAVAV Türkei, 20 July 1964, BArch B 119/4029; Landesarbeitsamt Südbayern, "Merkblatt für Reiseleiter und-begleiter von Sammelreisen türkischer Arbeitnehmer von Istanbul nach München," November 1973, BArch B 119/4032 – this instructional sheet recommends that travel escorts receive immunizations eight days before departure from Istanbul. BAVAV official, Weicken, noted that it would be a good idea for escorts to walk the aisles and remind passengers with the megaphone to be clean. Weicken, Nürnberg, 11 November 1963, BArch B 119/4035; see also BAVAV Nürnberg an Landesarbeitsamtes Südbayern, BAVAV Türkei, 17 October 1966, BArch B 119/4029; BAVAV Griechenland an BAVAV Nürnberg, 8 November 1966, BArch B 119/4029; BAVAV Griechenland an BAVAV Nürnberg, "Transportangelegenheiten griechischer und türkischer Arbeitnehmer, 8 November 1966, BArch B 119/4029.

77 BAVAV Nürnberg, "Bitte Sofort Lesen, Wichtige Hinweise für die Fahrt in die Bundesrepublik Deutschland," undated, BArch B 119/4029.

78 Ibid.

79 Ibid.

80 Ibid.

81 Ibid.

82 Ibid. The escort noted that the train was marked in such a way that anyone could see what its purpose was and that Yugoslavia had such limited train service that everyone wanted to use it.

83 Ibid. German rail blamed the unsanitary conditions on the trains not only on the duration of the trip but also on guest workers' "south-eastern-

European mentality," see Deutsche Bundesbahn Bundesbahndirektion München, an BAVAV Nürnberg, 13 November 1973, BArch B 119/ 4029.

84 BAVAV Nürnberg an BAVAV Türkei 4 August 1964, BArch B 119/ 4031.

85 BAVAV Nürnberg an die Deutsche Bundesbahn Oberbetriebsleitung Süd, 6 November 1964, BArch B 119/ 4029.

86 BAVAV Nürnberg, an die Deutsche Bundesbahn Oberbetriebsleitung Süd, 18 January 1966, BArch B 119/ 4031; see also, BAVAV Nürnberg, an Präsident und Vorsitzer des Vorstandes der Deutschen Bundesbahn, 19 January 1970, BArch B 119/ 4031.

87 Deutsche Bundesbahn, Frankfurt, an BA Nürnberg. "Arbeitersonderzüge vom Balkan – Süddeutschland," 23 November 1964, BArch B 119/ 4031.

88 Ibid.

89 BAVAV Türkei an den Herrn Präsident BAVAV Nürnberg; 15 May 1964, BA B 119/ 4035.

90 Deutsche Bundesbahn Bundesbahndirektion München an BA Nürnberg, 10 September 1964, BArch B 119 /4029; these sentiments are repeated for years, Deutsche Bundesbahn Bundesbahndirektion München, BA Nürnberg, Landesarbeitsamt Bayern, 1 December 1964, BArch B 119/ 4029; Deutsche Bundesbahn Bundesbahndirektion München, an BA Nürnberg, 12 May 1965, BArch B 119/ 4029; Eichner, BA Nürnberg, November 1969, BArch B 119/ 4029; Deutsche Bundesbahn Bundesbahndirektion München an BAVAV Nürnberg, 19 November 1969, BArch B 119 / 4029.

91 BAVAV Nürnberg, 13 September 1964, BA B 119/ 4029.

92 BA Nürnberg, "Reinigung von Sonderzügen in München," BArch B 119/ 4029.

93 Ibid.

94 Karen Schönwälder explores the West German public's reaction to the recruitment of "guest workers" as one that ranged from economic necessity to pride over West German economic superiority in relation to applicant countries, see "West German Society," 113–27.

95 Duinger Steinzeugwerk Mühle & Co an den Herrn Präsidenten der Bundesanstalt für Arbeitsvermittlung Nürnberg, 20 July 1973, BArch B 119/ 4031.

96 Notiz zur Besprechung am 15 November 1963, bei der OFD in München, "Unterbringung der Weiterleitungsstelle für ausländische Arbeitnehmer in Münch Hbf," BArch B 119/ 4032.

97 Ibid. Karen Schönwälder has noted than even if West German employers did not consider the larger implications of foreign labour in post-war Germany "ordinary Germans" did; see "West German Society," 113–27.

98 Mathilde Jamin, *Fremde Heimat*, 142–3.
99 DOMiD Interview 15, "Cahit," Berlin, 30 August 1995.
100 DOMiD Intervew 22, "Erol," Munich, 12 October 1995.
101 29 January 1964, BAVAV Präsident an Landesarbeitsämter, Südbayern, Nordrhein-Westfalen, BArch B 119 / 4029.
102 "Heimreisende italienischer Fremdarbeiter an Weihnachten 1963" BA B119/4031; "Transportlisten für Fremdarbeiter" 1969 BA B 110/4031; "Sammeltransporte von Fremdarbeitern" 1963 BA B 119/4033; see Rita Chin, *The Guest Worker Question*, 8–9; Karin Hunn *,Nächstes Jahr*, 59–60; Monika Mattes, *Gastarbeiterinnen'*, 16.
103 Gewerkschaft Holz und Kunststoff an BA, "Verwendung sogenannter "Transportlisten" bei der Einreise ausländischer Arbeitnehmer in die Bundesrepublik" 18 December 1972, BArch B 119/ 4029; it was in the early 1970s that unions started working on behalf of foreign workers in West German for improved conditions. This request was a part of a larger movement of concern over guest worker conditions in West Germany in the early 1970s.
104 Gewerkschaft Holz und Kunststoff, an Bundesanstalt für Arbeit Herrn Minta, Betrifft: Verwendung sogenannter "Transportlisten" bei der Einreise ausländischer Arbeitnehmer in die Bundesrepublik"; 18 December 1972, BA B 119/ 4029.
105 BA der Präsident Nürnberg an die Landesarbeitsämter und die Auslandsdienststellen 24 October 1972, BArch B119/ 4029.
106 Übersicht über die Anwerbung und Vermittlung ausländischer Arbeitnehmer nach der Bundesrepublik Deutschland, Nürnberg, 22 December 1970, BArch B 119 4031.
107 Aker, 1; Istanbul University published a study that reported 1.25 million people were on the waiting list in 1974; see Duncan Miller and İshan Çetin, *Migrant Workers, Wages, and Labor Markets: Emigrant Turkish Workers in the Federal Republic* (Istanbul University Faculty of Economics, Institute of Economic Development, 1974), 4, IISG.
108 Miller and Çetin, *Migrant Workers*, 4.
109 Ibid.
110 Ahmet Aker, "A Study of Turkish Labour Migration to Germany"; this study, conducted from 1970–1 was based on a random sample of 590 Turkish workers who were one week from their departure date and had already finished all of the required paperwork.
111 Ibid., 4.
112 Ibid., 19.

113 Ibid., 7.
114 "In der türkischen Öffentlichkeit wird in letzter Zeit häufiger die
    Lage der türkischen Arbeiter in der Bundesrepublik neben wenigen
    positive Stellungnahmen zunehmend kritisiert. Hierbei wird besonders
    auf die Verhältnisse in Nordrhein-Westfalen verwiesen. In diesem
    Zusammenhang wird die Entsendung eines Sozialattachés an die
    türkische Botschaft in Bonn von einigen Zeitungen empfohlen," Schmidt,
    Auswärtiges Amt, Bonn, an den Herrn Bundesminister des Innern, Herrn
    Bundesminister für Arbeit und Sozialordnung, Bonn, 30 March 1962,
    BArch B 119/ 3071 II.
115 Aker, "A Study of Turkish Labour Migration to Germany," 27.
116 A more recent wave of literature has provided a rich field of scholarship
    that adds nuance to guest workers' experiences in West Germany;
    see Katherine Pratt Ewing, *Stolen Honor: Stigmatizing Muslim Men in
    Berlin* (Stanford: Stanford University Press, 2008); Damani J. Partridge,
    *Hypersexuality and Headscarves: Race, Sex and Citizenship in the New
    Germany* (Bloomington: Indiana University Press, 2012); Serhat
    Karakayali, *Gespenster der Migration: Zur Genealogie illegaler Einwanderung
    in der Bundesrepublik Deutschland* (Bielefeld: Transcript, 2008); Rauf
    Ceylan, *Die Turkensiedlung* (Leipzig: Engelsdorfer, 2015); Manuela
    Bojadzjiev, *Die windige Internationale: Rassismus und Kämpfe die Migration*
    (Münster: Westfälisches Dampfboot, 2008).
117 Orals histories were not usually included in the classic histories of "guest
    worker" migration to West Germany. See Ulrich Herbert, *A History of
    Foreign Labor in Germany, 1880–1980: Seasonal Workers, Forced Laborers,
    Guest Workers* (Ann Arbor: University of Michigan Press, 1990); Klaus
    Bade, *Migration in European History*, trans. Allison Brown (Malden, MA:
    Blackwell, 2003).
118 "Cahit," DOMiD Interview 15, Berlin, 30 August 1995.
119 "Erol," DOMiD Interview 22, Munich, 12 October 1995.
120 Ibid.
121 Ibid.
122 "Metin," DOMiD Interview 62, "Metin," location redacted, April 1995.
123 Ibid.
124 Ibid.
125 Jefferson Cowie, *Capital Moves: RCA"s Seventy-Year Quest for Cheap Labor*
    (Ithaca, NY: Cornell University Press, 1999), 198.
126 "Notbremse im Hellas-Istanbul Express," *Salzburger Nachrichten*, 17,
    28 June 1969, BArch B 119/ 4030.

3. Finding Homes

1 Ursula Mehrländer, "Wohnverhältinisse Ausländischer Arbeitnehmer in der Bundesrepublik Deutschland," Contribution to the International Conference on Migrant Workers, 12–14 December 1974, Arbeitsgruppe Internationales Institut für vergleichend Gesellschaftsforschung (DOMiD doc 434), 14.
2 Mehrländer, 14.
3 Ibid.
4 Abadan-Unat found in her 1964 study that 85 per cent of workers lived in "Heims," or employer-managed dormitories for foreign workers. Nermin Abadan-Unat, *Batı Almaya'daki Türk İşçileri ve Sorunları* [Turkish Workers in West Germany and Their Problems] (Ankara: Başbakanlık Devlet Planlama Teşkilâtı [State Planning Organization], 1964), 103.
5 Here "interviews" refers to the DOMiD interview collection as well as my own.
6 Aytaç Eryılmaz and Mathlide Jamin eds., *Fremde Heimat/ Yaban, Sılan olur: Eine Geschichte der Einwanderung aus der Türkei/ Türkiye'den Almanya'ya Göçün Tarihi* (Essen: Klartext, 1998), 52–3.
7 Ernst Zieris, *Betriebsunterkünfte für Ausländische Arbeitnehmer und ihre Familien* (Opladen: North Rhein Westphalia Labor Ministry for Labor, Health, and Social Welfare, 1973), 11, quoted in *Fremde Heimat*, 171.
8 Mehrländer, "Wohnverhältnisse," 16.
9 Ibid., 23.
10 "Unterkunft, " *Fremde Heimat*, 52.
11 "Ein kleines Herrenvolk sieht sich in Gefahr: man hat Arbeitskräfte gerufen, und es kommen Menschen," Max Frische, Überfremdung (1965), in *Gesammelte Werke* Bd. I–VII (Franfurt am Main, 1976–86, Bd V, p. 374, quoted in Mathilde Jamin, "Fremde Heimat: Zur Geschichte der Arbeitsmigration aus der Türkei," in *50 Jahre Bundesrepublik 50 Jahre Einwanderung: Nachkriegsgeschichte als Migrationsgeschichte*, ed. Jan Motte, Rainer Ohliger, and Anne von Oswald, 163.
12 "ama şunu da unutmamalısın ki, Almanya bundan 20 sene evvel bir harabeden başka bir şey değildi, *Hallo Mustafa!*, 24.
13 Ibid.
14 Schönwälder "West German Society," 115–16.
15 Ibid.
16 Lynn Abrams, *Worker's Culture in Imperial Germany: Leisure and Recreation in the Rhineland and Westphalia* (New York: Routledge, 1992).
17 Herbert, *A History of Foreign Labor in Germany*; Anne von Oswald and Barbara Schmidt, "'Nach Schichtende sind sie immer in ihr Lager

zurückgekehrt' Leben in, Gastarbeiter' Unterkünften in den sechziger und siebziger Jahren," in *50 Jahre Bundesrepublik*, ed. Motte et al., 184–214.

18 Herbert, *A History of Foreign Labor in Germany*, 199.

19 Tony Judt, *Postwar*, 16; Jeffry M. Diefendorf, *In the Wake of the War: The Reconstruction of German Cities after World War II* (New York: Oxford University Press, 1993), 16.

20 Herbert, *A History of Foreign Labor in Germany*, 193.

21 Ibid.

22 DOMiD Interviews 18 and 19, "Almanya'ya yalnız gelen bir anne ve kızı," Herne, 1995.

23 "Elif," Berlin, 2003.

24 Heidi Fehrenbach, *Race after Hitler: Black Occupation Children in Postwar Germany and America* (Princeton, NJ: Princeton University Press, 2005).

25 "Elif," Berlin 2003.

26 Emine Sevgi Özdamar, *Die Brücke vom Goldenen Horn* (Cologne: Kiepenheuer and Witsch, 2000), 16.

27 Ibid., 19.

28 Metin Uyaner und Sami Özkara, "Arbeiterwohnheime für die Migranten im Ruhrgebiet: Eine historische Darstellung der 60er und 70er Jahre" Untersuchung 2 (Essen: DOMiD, June 1996).

29 Von Oswald and Schmidt, "'Nach Schichtende,'" 186.

30 For rare photos and descriptions of dormitory life, see Aytaç Eryılmaz, "Das Leben im Wohnheim" in *Fremde Heimat*, 171–91.

31 Metin Uyaner und Sami Özkara, "Arbeiterwohnheime für die Migranten."

32 *Industriekurier*, 6 October 1960, quoted in Metin Uyaner and Sami Özkara "Arbeiterwohnheime für die Migranten im Ruhrgebiet: Ein historische Darstellung der 60er und 70er Jahre" Untersuchung 2 (Essen: DOMiD, June 1996), 24.

33 "Unterkunft," in *Fremde Heimat*, eds. Eryılmaz and Jamin, 52.

34 Ernst Zieris, "Integration ausländischer Arbeitnehmer," quoted in Metin Uyaner und Sami Özkara, "Arbeiterwohnheime für die Migranten," 25.

35 "Gebetsräume für unsere türkischen Heimbewohner wurden bereitgestellt. Ebenso wurden Sondertoiletten für diese Arbeitergruppen," Bergwerksgesellschaft Walsum 3 November 1965, AfsB- IGBE-Archive 19094 A (Org) 18 Mappe 3.

36 Ibid., 195.

37 DOMiD Interview 15, "Cahit," Berlin, 30 August 1995.

38 Ibid.

39 *Hallo Mustafa!*, 30.

40 Ibid.

41 Ibid., 30–1.

42 Karen Schönwälder, "West German Society," 113–127, here 115.

43 Mete Atsu, AfsB A (org) 18, Mappe 3: "also eine Unterkunft, die man heute unterentwickelten Ländern ohne weiteres zutraut, aber nicht der Bundesrepublik. Kollegen bestätigten mir, daß es eine sehr gute Unterkunft für die Nachkriegszeit sei – mehr nicht."

44 DOMiD Archive Image; Eryılmaz and Jamin, *Fremde Heimat*, 187.

45 DOMiD Interview 22 "Erol," Munich, 12 October 1995; for comments on lack of sleep in the dormitories see also the report on "Bergmannsheim Westfalen I by Mete Atsu compiled for the German Federal Trade Union AfsB-IGBE-Archiv 19094 A (org) 18 Mappe 3.

46 "Viele der Ursachen für die kritische Stimmung liegen zweifellos in der Überbelegung. Und daran wird sich wohl kaum etwas ändern; denn in den nächsten Wochen werden weitere 60 Arbeiter erwartet, die zusätzlich in diesem Heim unterzubringen sind," Deutscher Gewerkschaftsbund Bundesvorstand an die Vorstände der Gewerkschaften und Industriegewerkschaften und an die Mitglieder des Arbeitskreises, 22 July 1971, AfsB – IGBE-Archiv A (org) 18, Mappe 3.

47 Deutscher Gewerkschaftsbund Bundesvorstand, an die Vorstände der Gewerkschaften und Industriegewerkschaften und an die Mitglieder des Arbeitskreises 'Ausländischer Arbeitnehmer': Bericht über die Situation der türkischen Arbeitnehmer in Betrieben und Beziehungen zu den Gewerkschaften, Mete Atsu, 22 Juli 1971, AfsB-IGBE-Archiv 19094, A (Org) 19, Mappe 3.

48 Ibid.

49 Ibid.

50 Ibid.

51 DOMiD interview 39, "Yalcın," Nuremburg, 19 October 1995.

52 Ibid.

53 "Heimordnung für das Wohnheim der Firma Wieland, Singen 1971," Donated by Frigitte Teotonia-Müller, DOMiD-Archiv.

54 Ibid.

55 Ibid.

56 DOMiD Interview 22, "Erol," Munich, 12 October 1995.

57 DOMiD Interview 39, "Yalcın," Nuremberg, 19 October 1995.

58 Ibid.

59 Notiz über die Besprechung im Türkenwohnheim der Schachtanlage Emscher-Lippe, Datteln (Dümmerheim), 13 Juli 1970, AfsB-IGBE-Archiv 19094 A (Org) 18 Mappe.

60 Emine Sevgi Özdamar, *Die Brücke vom Goldenen Horn*, 28.
61 *Bergmannsheim Westfalen I Rapportbuch*: 12,13,14,15, 16, 20, 26 and 27 October 1970, DOMiD.
62 *Rapportbuch*, 8 October 1970.
63 *Rapportbuch*, 19 November 1970.
64 *Rapportbuch*, 23 November 1970.
65 *Rapportbuch*, 2–7 December, 1970.
66 *Rapportbuch*, 2, 4, 7 December 1970.
67 *Rapportbuch*, 24 February 1971.
68 *Rapportbuch*, 17 February 1971.
69 DOMiD 88 (1–15) SD.
70 Ibid.
71 "Opel-Arbeiter über die Zustände im Wohnheim, Bochum, 1977, Wohnheim Probleme: 30.1.77" DOMiD.
72 From the exhibition at the Cologne Art Collective: Migration: "Monitor: Kritik an Wohnverhältnissen in Gastarbeiterlager der Baufirma Holzmann AG, Frankfurt – Rödelheim 4.1. 1971) Description: Stellungnahme von Dr Georg K. einer Mitarbeiter der Holzmann AG, zu den Vorwürfen wegen des Schlechter Lagerzustandes. Eine Delegation von Kirchenvertreten unterstützten den Protest der Bewohner," provided by Westdeutscher Rundfunk. Part of the "Transit" exhibition, Cologne, 2005.
73 Mieter für jedes Bett: Gutes Geschäft mit Sammelunterkünften für die Gastarbeiter?" Tolf Elbertzhagen, *Kölner Stadt-Anzeiger* Sat–Sun 20–21 October 1962, no. 245 p 13 (AfsB IGBE-Archiv File 11227).
74 DOMiD Interview 22, "Erol," Munich, 12 October 1995.
75 *Rapportbuch*, 7 February 1971; emphasis added.
76 *Rapportbuch*, 11 and 19 November 1970. The fine for having a visitor was five marks.
77 DOMiD Interview 16, Berlin, 31 August 1995; "Elif," Berlin 2003. Elif has also organized a social club in Berlin for retired female migrants called *"Aile Baçesi"* or Family Garden," where former dormitory roommates among others meet to drink tea, dance, sing, and visit. Other social organizations also exist in Cologne and in Berlin, such as the "Second Spring" group.
78 DOMiD Interview 22, "Erol," Munich, 12 October 1995.
79 Between 1960 and 1973, the number of female foreign workers in West Germany increased from 43,000 to 706,000 and, in percentages, from 15 per cent to 30 per cent; see Monika Mattes, "Zum Verhältnis von Migration und Geschlecht: Anwerbung und Beschäftigung von

'Gastarbeiterinnen' in der Bundesrepublik 1960–1973," in *50 Jahre*, ed. Motte et al., 285.

80 Inga Steinen, *Leben zwischen zwei Welten*; Huth-Hildebrant and Micksch, *Ausländische Frauen*; Gaby Franger, *Wir haben es uns anders vorgestellt*; Sigrid Nökel, *Die Töchter der Gastarbeiter und der Islam*; Pia Weische-Alexa, *Sozial-Kulturelle Probleme Junger Türkinnen*; Rita Rosen and Gerd Stüwe, "Young Turkish girls can't walk on the street. They cannot go to the movies or to the theater. They cannot go anywhere alone. Their mothers decide what they wear. When they come home from work, they have to do housework and take care of the children. They have absolutely no rights, and if they oppose, they will be hit," in *Ausländische Mädchen*, 7.

81 Umut Erel, "The Politics of Identity and Community: Migrant Women from Turkey in Germany," in *Gender and Insecurity: Migrant Women in Europe*, ed. Jane Freedman (Burlington, VT: Ashgate, 2003), 153–71, emphasis added.

82 "Elif," Berlin, 2003.

83 Nermin Abadan-Unat and Neşe Kemiksiz write, "Turkish women living abroad have a certain independence, which they have developed through their participation in financial decisions, over which their control has grown ... this 'pseudo-independence, [however] does not always mean that they begin new lifestyles [or] become a new, real self-confidence," in *Türkische Migration 1960–1984: Annotierte Bibliographie*, ed. Nermin Abadan-Unat and Neşe Kemiksiz, trans. Kirkor Osyan and Claudia Schöning-Kalender (Zentrum für Türkeistudien, Essen, Frankfurt am Main: Dağyeli Verlag, 1992); see also, Nermin Abadan-Unat, "Dış Göç Akımının Türk Kadınının Özgürleşme ve Sözde Özgürleşme Sürecine Etkisi" [The Effects of Immigration on Turkish Women and the Emancipation Process], *Amme İdaresi Dergisi* [*Journal of Public Adminstration*] 10 no.1 (1977): 107–32; G. Aslantepe, *Federal Almanya'da Yaşayan Türk Kadınlarının Soruları, Birinci Nesil-İkinci Nesil* [Concerns of First and Second Generation Turkish Women Living in the Federal Republic of Germany] (Düsseldorf Çalışma Ataşeliği [Dusseldorf Labor Attache], March 1982), 7; Seval Gürel and Ayşe Kudat, "Türk Kadınının Avrupa'ya Göçünün Kişilik, Aile eve Topluma Yansıyan Sonuçları," [Study of Turkish Migrant Women to Germany in Terms of Self-Hood, Family and Community] *Ankara Üniversitesi Siyasal Bilgiler Fakültesi Dergisi*, [Ankara University Faculty of Political Science Journal] 33 no. 93/4 (September–December 1978): 109–34.

84 Ibid.

85 Ibid.

86 "Elif," Berlin, 2003.
87 Jenny B. White, email, 12 September 2005.
88 It is unclear how many female guest workers chose to come to West Germany on their own versus at the prodding of family members. West German companies aggressively recruited female workers for certain industries, even contacting employed married men to inquire if their wives could apply, BAVAV Türkei, Istanbul an BAVAV Nürnberg, 24 Juli 1964, BArch B 119/ 4035.
89 DOMiD Interview 18–19, "Almanya'ya yalnız gelen bir Anne ve kızın gelen bir Anne ve kızı" 1995.
90 Jamin, "Fremde Heimat: Zur Geschichte der Arbeitsmigration aus der Türkei," in *50 Jahre*, ed. Motte et al., 158.
91 Metin Uyaner and Sami Özkara, "Arbeiterwohnheime für die Migranten," 18.
92 Nermin Abadan-Unat, *Batı Almanya'daki Türk Işçileri* [Turkish workers in West Germany], 103–4.
93 *Hallo Mustafa!*, 34.
94 Ibid.
95 Ibid.
96 Ibid.
97 Maria Höhn, *GIs and Fräuleins*; Petra Goedde, *GIs and Germans: Culture, Gender and Foreign Relations, 1945–1949* (New Haven, CT: Yale University Press, 2003).
98 *Hallo Mustafa!*, 35.
99 "Adil," DOMiD Interview 28, Essen, 22 June 1995.
100 Ibid.
101 Y. Diricks and Ayşe Kudat, "Instability of Migrant Workers' Housing" Preprint-International Institute of Comparative Social Studies (Berlin: Wissenschaftszentrum Berlin, 1975). Compare with Ger Mik and Mia Verkoren-Hemelaar, "Segregation in the Netherlands and Turkish Migration" in *Turkish Workers in Europe, 1960–1975: A Socio-Economic Reappraisal*, ed. Abadan-Unat, 253–86; Günther Glebe, "Housing and Segregation of Turks in Germany" in *Turks in European Cities: Housing and Urban Segregation*, ed. Sule Öüekren and Ronald van Kempern, (Utrecht: Ercomer, 1997), 122–57; Herbert, *A History of Foreign Labor*, 238.

4. Contested Borders

1 "Cahit," DOMiD Interview 15, Berlin, 30 August 1995.
2 Ibid.

3 Gary Bruce has noted that political and economic histories, especially
  those focusing on East German state power have dominated the
  scholarship from 1990–2009, with the trend only recently adding more
  social and cultural history, see "Participatory Repression? Reflections on
  Popular Involvement with the *Stasi*" in "The Stasi at Home and Abroad:
  Domestic Order and Foreign Intelligence," ed. Uwe Spiekermann,
  supplement, *Bulletin of the German Historical Institute* S9 (2014): 47–58.

4 The historiography of the GDR has focused on a notion of *"Eigensinn,"*
  an increasingly hard to define term that now stands for a broad model
  of comprehending everyday life in the GDR dictatorship. See Esther
  von Richthofen, *Bringing Culture to the Masses: Control, Compromise and
  Participation in the GDR* (New York: Berghahn, 2009), 11.

5 Alf Lüdtke, "Geschichte und Eigensinn," in *Alltagskultur, Subjektivität
  und Geschichte: Zur Theorie und Praxis von Alltagsgeschichte*, ed. Berliner
  Geschichtswerkstatt (Münster: Westfälisches Dampfboot, 1994);
  Thomas Lindenberger, ed., *Herrschaft und Eigen-Sinn in der Diktatur:
  Studien zur Gesellschaftsgeschichte der DDR* (Köln, Weimar, Wien:
  Böhlau, 1999).

6 Johannes Huinink, "Individuum und Gesellschaft in der DDR – Theoretische
  Ausgangspunkte einer Rekonstruktion der DDR-Gesellschaft in den
  Lebensläufen ihrer Bürgers," in *Kollektiv und Eigensinn: Lebensläufe in der
  DDR und Danach*, ed. Johannes Huinink, Karl Ulrich Meyer, Martin Diewald,
  and Heike Solga (Berlin: Akademie Verlag, 1995), 25–44, here 38, quoted in
  Esther von Richthofen, *Bringing Culture to the Masses,*15.

7 Hans-Hermann Hertle, *The Berlin Wall Story: Biography of a Monument*
  (Berlin: Ch. Links Verlag, 2011), 30.

8 Steffen Alisch, "Berlin-Berlin: Die Verhandlungen zwischen Beauftragten
  des Berliner Senats und Vertretern der DDR-Regierung zu Reise- und
  humanitären Fragen: 1961–1972" (FU Berlin: Arbeitspapiere des
  Forschungsverbundes SED-Staat), 3 (2000): 34.

9 Astrid M. Eckert, "Zaun-Gäste: Die innerdeutsche Grenze
  als Touristenattraktion" in *Grenzziehungen, Grenzerfahrungen,
  Grenzüberschreitungen: Die Innerdeutsche Grenze, 1945–1990*, Catalog of the
  Exhibition of the Hannover Historical Museum, ed. Thomas Schwark,
  Detlef Schmeichen-Ackermann, and Carl-Hans Hauptmeyer (Darmstadt:
  Wissenschaftliche Buchgesellschaft, 2001), 243–51, here 245–6.

10 Frederick Taylor, writes that the Berlin Wall resulted in the guest worker
   agreement between Turkey and West Germany: "Robbed of the previous
   supply of new labour for its booming industries by the sealing off of the
   East, in October 1961 West Germany took the radical and far-reaching

step of signing a treaty with Muslim Turkey, allowing for Turkish 'guest workers' to fill vacant jobs," in *The Berlin Wall: A World Divided, 1961–1989* (New York: Harper Collins, 2006), 345.

11　Faruk Şen notes that in 1964 West Berlin recruited more Turkish women than men, see Faruk Şen, "Berlin's Turkish Community" in *The Spirit of the Berlin Republic*, ed. Dieter Dettke (New York: Berghahn, 2003), 130–44, here 133.

12　Nadja Milewski, *Fertility of Immigrants: A Two-Generational Approach in Germany* (Heidelberg: Springer, 2010), 8.

13　Mike Dennis and Norman LaPorte, *State and Minorities in Communist East Germany* (New York: Berghahn, 2011), 90.

14　Milewski, *Fertility*, 8.

15　Dennis and LaPorte, *State and Minorities*, 89.

16　Herman Kurthen, Werner Bergmann, and Rainer Erb eds., *Antisemitism and Xenophobia in Germany after Unification* (Oxford and New York: Oxford University Press, 1997), 144–5.

17　Kurthen et al., *Antisemitism*, 144.

18　Nadja Milewski, *Fertility*, 8.

19　Kurthen et al., *Antisemitism*, 145.

20　"Wirtschaftliche und soziale Aspekte der Wanderarbeit" *Neues Deutschland*, 2 August 1975, BSTU MfS ZAIG, Nr. 11129.

21　Hertle, *Berlin Wall Story*, 124.

22　Jens Gieseke, *The GDR State Security: Shield and Sword of the Party*, trans. Mary Carlene Forszt (Berlin: The Federal Commissioner for the Records of the State Security Service of the former German Democratic Republic, 2006), 108–17

23　Hertle, *Berlin Wall*, 100.

24　Gieseke, *GDR State Security*, 108–17.

25　Remark from CPSU General Secretary Leonid Brezhnev to Erich Honecker, 28 July 1970, quoted in Hertle, *Berlin Wall*, 135.

26　Hertle, *Berlin Wall*, 134.

27　Communist countries had large debts to the World Bank, IMF, and private bankers for hard currency with which to purchase consumer goods they needed and that their citizens would buy. Historian Tony Judt noted that by its last years the GDR admitted to spending over 60 per cent of its annual income on interest on western loans, see *Postwar*, 582.

28　Jonathan Zatlin, "Consuming Ideology: The Intershops, Genex, and Retail Trade under Honecker" in *The Currency of Socialism: Money and Political Culture in East Germany* (Cambridge: Cambridge University Press and GHI, 2007), 243–85.

29 Hertle, *Berlin Wall*, 136.
30 Alisch, "Berlin-Berlin: Die Verhandlungen," 34.
31 Wolfgang Henrich ed., *Wehrdienstgesetz und Grenzgesetz der DDR: Dokumentation und Analyse* (Bonn: Urheber, 1983), 237–39; Henrich outlines the border crossing stations for pedestrians, autos, plains, trains, and light rail travel (*S-Bahn*).
32 Friedrich Christian Delius and Peter Jochim Lapp, *Transit Westberlin: Erlebnisse im Zwischenraum* (Berlin: Ch. Links Verlag, 1999), 177.
33 Important early work empathetically exposed guest workers' miserable conditions, though such depictions have also effaced complex human experiences: see, among others, John Berger and Jenn Mohr, A *Seventh Man: Migrant Workers in Europe* (New York: Viking, 1975); Inga Steinen, *Leben zwischen zwei Welten*; Gunter Wallraff, *Ganz Unten* (Köln: Kiepenheuer & Witsch, 1985); Rainer Werner Fassbinder, *Angst essen Seele auf* (Tango-Film, Munich, 1974); Feo Aladağ, *Die Fremde* (ARTE, Independent Artists Filmproduktion, RBB, WDR, 2010). For important studies on xenophobia in East Germany see Jonathan Zatlin, "Scarcity and Resentment: Economic Sources of Xenophobia in the GDR, 1971–1989," *Central European History* 40 (2007): 683–720.
34 Hertle, *Berlin Wall*, 136.
35 Ibid.
36 Ibid.
37 Gary Bruce, "Participatory Repression?" 48.
38 Josie McLellan "'Even Under Socialism, We Don't Want to Do Without Love': East German Erotica," in "East German Material Culture and the Power of Memory," ed. Uta A. Balbier, Cristina Cuevas-Wolf, and Joes Segal, supplement 7, *Bulletin of the German Historical Institute* (2011), 49–65, here 51; in the post-war period, abortion was illegal in both Germanys, but arguably stricter in West Germany because the Federal Republic offered fewer exceptions. In 1976 West Germany legalized abortion for reasons of medical necessity; broad reform came in 1992 after reunication. Susanne Dieper, "The Legal Framework of Abortions in Germany,"American Institute for Contemporary German Studies, Johns Hopkins University, 23 February 2012, accessed 4 March 2016, http://www.aicgs.org/issue/the-legal-framework-of-abortions-in-germany/.
39 McLellan "'Even Under Socialism, We Don't Want to Do Without Love,'"51.
40 BStU MfS - HA II Nr. 22858, 13 June 1981.
41 Ibid.
42 Ibid.

43 BStU, MfS - HA II, Nr. 27442 Berlin, 7 August 1979.
44 BStU MfS – HA II Nr. 27962 Berlin 7 May 1985.
45 BStU MfS HA II 27836 Berlin 4 August 1980.
46 Ibid.
47 BStU MfS HA II 27836 Berlin 4 August 1980.
48 BStU MfS HA II 28084 Berlin 26 May 1977.
49 Da der Türke fast täglich aus Berkub (West) einreiste, kann man davon ausgehen, daß es sich um ein dauerhaftes Verhältnis handelt." BStU MfS ZKG Nr. 286, Ministerium des Innern, Leiter, Berlin 21 November 1980, Schwarze Oberstleutnant, d. VP.
50 BstU BfS ZKG Nr 286; Berlin 15 May 1980, Präsidium der Volkspolizei, Arbeiter Abt. Paß – und Meldewesen, Genn. Oberstleutnant der der VP Stertz.
51 I have chosen these two pseudonyms to ease reading this couple's narrative. In the files their names are completely redacted.
52 BSTU MfS HA XX Nr. 18529, Berlin, 1967.
53 BSTU MfS – HA XX Nr. 18529, An den Herrn Vorsitzenden des Staatsrates der DDR, Saarbrücken den 32 January 1963.
54 Ibid.
55 Ibid.
56 Ibid.
57 Ibid.
58 BSTU MfS – HA XX Nr. 18529, Würzburg, An den Herrn Vorsitzenden des Staatsrates der DDR, undated.
59 Ibid.
60 Ibid.
61 BSTU MfS HA XX Nr. 18529, Der Leiter des Bundesnotaufnahmeverfahrens in Berlin, 3 May 1967.
62 BSTU MfS HA XX Nr. 18529, Familienzusammenführung und Kinderdienst, Arbeitsgemeinschaft der Spitzenverbände der Freien Wohlfahrtspflege, Hamburg-Osdorf, undated.
63 BSTU MfS HA XX Nr. 18529, Würzburg, 18 December 1963.
64 BSTU MfS HA XX Nr. 18529, Berlin, 1967.
65 BSTU MfS HA XX Nr. 18529, Berlin, 13 October 1967.
66 Ibid.
67 Ibid.
68 Mfs HA II 27.002.
69 Mfs HA II 27.002 Berlin, 5 April 1989.
70 MfS HA II 27081. Starting in the mid-1980s, East German citizens exploited a part of the 1975 Helsinki accords that guaranteed the freedom of movement.

71 MfS HA II 27081.

72 Ibid.

73 "Cahit," DOMID Interview 15, Berlin, 30 August 1995.

74 Ibid.

75 Ibid.

76 BstU MfS HA II Nr. 27962 Berlin 24 August 1984.

77 BStU Archive der Zentralstelle, MfS-HA11, Nr. 29668, Berlin, 6 November 1979.

78 Ibid.

79 Ibid.

80 Ibid.

81 Ina Merkel, "Sex and Gender in the Divided Germany: Approaches to History from a Cultural Point of View" in *The Divided Past: Rewriting Post-war German History*, ed. Christoph Klessmann (New York: Oxford University Press, 2001), 91–105.

82 "Cahit," DOMiD Interview 15, Berlin, 30 August 1995.

83 Ibid.

84 "Diskothek - Gelsenkirche 1974 – Gelsenkirchen'de bir diskotek, 1974" [Discotheque in Gelsenkirchen 1974] photo by Manfred Vollmer, Essen in Aytaç Eryılmaz and Mathilde Jamin eds. *Fremd Heimat – Yaban, Sılan olur: Eine Geschichte die Einwanderung aus der Türkei – Türkiye'den Almanya'ya Göçün Tarihi* (Essen: Klartext Verlag, 1998), 310.

85 Stephen Castles and Mark Miller, *The Age of Migration: International Population Movements in the Modern World*, 3rd ed. (New York: Guilford Press, 2003), 215.

86 BStU MfS – HA II Nr.28079 Berlin, 6 March 1977; BStU MfS- HAII Nr. 27962 12 December 1982; BStU MfS HA II Nr. 27962 5 March 1983.

87 BStU MfS HA II Nr. 27962, 14 Feburary 1983; BStU MfS HA II Nr. 27962 Berlin 22 March 1983. It is worth noting that scholars disagree on whether or not East German citizens became unofficial collaborates out of willingness or coercion, and in each case to what degree. Starting in 1979, *Stasi* officers were first to access a candidate's suitability so as to avoid resorting to coercion. Mary Fulbrook writes that the majority of *Stasi* informants did not have to be coerced in what she terms a "participator dictatorship," but Gary Bruce casts doubt on this interpretation. See Mary Fulbrook, *The People's State: East German Society from Honecker to Hitler* (New Haven, CT: Yale University Press, 2005) and Gary Bruce, "Participatory Repression? 51–2.

88 Jens Gieseke, *Mielke-Konzern: Die Geschichte der Stasi* (Stuttgart: Deutsche Verlages-Anstalt, 2001), 113.

89 BStU MfS – HAII Nr. 27962 Berlin, 24 January 1983.
90 Ibid.
91 Ibid.
92 BStU MfS HA II Nr. 27962, Berlin, 5 March 1983.
93 Ibid.; 5 May 1983, Peter Falk.
94 BstU MfS - HA II, No. 29778.
95 BStU MfS – HA II nr. 28209, Berlin, 23 May 1983, "Vieles sei hier anders, u.a., sei ihr hier die ausgeprägte Ausländerfeindlichkeit, die in WB herrsche, noch nicht begegnet."
96 Ibid.
97 BStU HA – VI, Passkontrolleinheit, Friedrich/Zimmerstr, Berlin, 11 March 1986.
98 Ibid.
99 Ibid.
100 Ibid.
101 BStU MfS – HA VIII, Nr.3506.
102 BStU MfS – HAVIII, Nr. 3506, 18 December 1985.
103 Ibid.
104 Ibid.
105 BStU MfS – HAVIII, Nr. 3506, 22 November 1985.
106 BStU MfS – HAVIII, Nr. 3506, 18 December 1985.
107 Ibid.
108 Ibid.
109 Ibid.
110 BStU MfS HA VIII, Nr. 3506, 15 January 1986.
111 Yade Kara, *Selam Berlin* (Zürich: Diogenes, 2003).
112 Petra Fachinger, "Yadé Kara's *Selam Berlin*," in *The Novel in German since 1990*, ed. Stuart Taberner (Cambridge: Cambridge University Press, 2011), 241.
113 Fachinger, "Yadé Kara's *Selam Berlin*," 242–5.
114 DOMiD Interview 15, "Cahit," Berlin, 12 October 1995.
115 Paula Bren and Mary Neuburger eds., *Communism Unwrapped: Consumption in Cold War Eastern Europe* (Oxford: Oxford University Press, 2012).
116 See Jennifer V. Evans, "The Moral State: Men, Mining, and Masculinity in the Early GDR," *German History* 23, no. 3 (2005): 355–70; Jennifer V. Evans, "*Bahnhof* Boys: Policing Male Prostitution in Post-Nazi Berlin," *Journal of the History of Sexuality* 12, no. 4 (2003): 605–36; Uta G. Poiger, *Jazz, Rock, and Rebels: Cold War Politics and American Culture in a Divided Germany* (Berkeley: University of California Press, 2000); Deborah A. Field, *Private Life and Communist Morality in Khrushchev's Russia* (New York: Peter Lang, 2007).

117 Jennifer Evans, "Decriminalization, Seduction, and 'Unnatural Desire' in East Germany," *Feminist Studies* 36, no. 3 (2010): 553–77, here 554.
118 MfS HA II Nr. 27962 (1982–5), Berlin, 13 February 1983.
119 BStU MfS HA II Nr. 27962, 13 February 1983.
120 Josie McLellan, "'Even Under Socialism, We Don't Want to Do Without Love.'" 49–65.
121 Ibid.
122 BStU MfS HA I, Nr. 15176, Berlin, 6 April 1979.
123 BStU Gh 73/78 Hauptabteilung Passkontrolle und Fahndung der Leiter, Berlin, 14 August 1967.
124 BStU Zentralarchiv MfS- HA VI Nr. 441, Ministerium für Staatssicherheit Hauptabteilung VI, Anlagekarte zur verhinderten Personenschleusung an der GÜST Friedrich/Zimmerst 21 December 1973.
125 BStU MfS HA I, Nr. 15176, Berlin, 6 April 1979.
126 BStU Zentralarchiv MfS – HA VI, Nr. 919, Fotodokumentation Verhinderte Personenschleusung eines türkischen Bürgers aus der BRD unter Missbrauch des Transitverkehrs nach WB an der GüST Drewitz am 06.07.1987 gegen 16.50 Uhr.
127 Gary Bruce, "Access to Secret Police Files, Justice, and Vetting in East Germany since 1989," *German Politics and Society* 26, no.1 (Spring 2008): 82–111, here 93–4.
128 Ibid.
129 BStU MfS HA II 24068, Berlin 30.01.1981; MfS HA II Nr. 24068 Berlin, 19 February 1981.
130 Jens Gieseke, "German Democratic Republic" in *A Handbook of the Communist Security Apparatus in East Central Europe, 1944–1989*, ed. Krysztof Persak and Lukasz Kaminski (Warsaw: Institute of National Remembrance, 2005), 198–202. Using data for convictions in 1972, 1980, and 1989 Jens Gieseke reported on the total number offenses and by category, citing archival evidence and work by Schröder and Wilke (1999).
131 Ibid.
132 See Mary Fulbrook, *The People's State*.
133 Ibid., 203.
134 Though coercion to become an informant was not officially allowed, as it was suspected that it would led to subpar information, many recruitments occurred after compromising situations or materials were found. Gary Bruce, "Participatory Repression," 52.
135 BStU MfS HA II 28872, 21 August 1980 Peter Falk.
136 BStU MfS HA II 28084, Berlin, 09 April 1977 Möller.

137 BStU MfS – HA II nr. 28079, 6 June 1977.
138 BStU MfS AIM 8196/78 I/1, Verwaltung Grossberlin, Abteilung VII/2, Berlin den. 30 November 1971; in 1974 he transitioned from an IMV (*Inoffizieller Mitarbeiter, der unmittelbar an der Bearbeitung und Entlarvung im Verdacht der Feindtätigkeit stehender Personen mitarbeitet*) to IMF (*Inoffizieller Mitarbeiter der inneren Abwehr mit Feindverbindungen zum Operationsgebiet*) BStU MfS AIM 8196/78, Berlin den 27 November 1974. For a complete lexicon of *Stasi* informants, see Roger Engelmann, Bernd Florath, and Walter Süß, eds., *Das MfS-Lexikon – Begriffe, Personen und Strukturen der Staatssicherheit der DDR* (Berlin: Links, 2011).
139 BStU MfS AIM 8196/78 Verwaltung Grossberlin, Abteilung VII/2, 26 November 1971; Berlin; BStU MFs AIM 8196/78 I/1 Berlin, 30 November 1971.
140 BStU MfS AIM 8196/78 Verwaltung Grossberlin, Abteilung VII/2, 26 November 1971.
141 BStU MfS AIM 8196/78 I/1 Berlin den 30 November 1971.
142 BStU MfS AIM 8196/78 I/1, Verwaltung Grossberlin, Abteilung VII/2, Berlin, 30 November 1971.
143 Ibid.
144 Ibid.
145 BStU MfS HA II, AG Ausländer, Berlin, 11 March 1982: Bericht der KP "Georg."
146 Ibid.
147 Ibid.
148 BstU MfS H Nr. 27838 Berlin, 8 April 1982 and 23 April 1982.

5. Imperfect Solidarities

Part of this chapter was originally published in *International Labor and Working-Class History* 84 (2013): 226–47 and is reprinted here with permission.

   1 "Streik bei Mannesmann, Duisburg-Huckingen," in *Spontane Streiks 1973, Krise der Gewerkschaftspolitik* (Offenbach: Verlag 2000 GmbH, Januar 1974), 64. This is a published source complied by the collective Zeitung für sozialistische Betriebs- und Gewerkschaftsarbeit, in which the editors collected strike materials and interviewed participants of the strikes during the year 1973. Other scholars drawing on *Spontane Streiks* include Eckart Hildebrandt and Werner Olle, *Ihr Kampf ist unser Kampf. Ursachen, Verlauf und Perspektiven der Ausländerstreiks 1973 in der BRD. Teil I* (Offenbach, 1975) and the excellent study by Manuela Bojadzijev,

Die windige Internationale: Rassismus und Kämpfe der Migration (Munster: Westfälsches Dampfboot, 2008).

2 "Streik bei Mannesmann, Duisburg-Huckingen," 64.

3 Ibid., 63.

4 "Elif," Berlin, 2003.

5 Scholars have argued that multiple identities (e.g. female, foreign) "intersect" to create unique forms of discrimination. For more on "intersectionality" see Kimberle Crenshaw, "Mapping the Margins: Intersectionality, Identity Politics, and Violence against Women of Color" *Stanford Law Review* 43, no. 6 (July 1991): 1241–99; Philomena Essed, *Everyday Racism: Reports from Women in Two Cultures* (Claremont, CA: Hunter House, 1990); Philomena Essed, *Diversity: Gender, Color, and Culture* (Amherst: University of Massachusetts Press, 1996); Patricia Hill Collins, *Black Feminist Thought: Knowledge, Consciousness and the Politics of Empowerment* (New York: Routledge, 2000); Chandra Mohanty, "Under Western Eyes: Feminist Scholarship and Colonial Discourses" *Feminist Review* 30 (1988): 61–88; Gloria Anzaldua, *Borderlands/ La Frontera: The New Mestiza* (San Francisco: Aunt Lute Books, 1987); Irene Browne and Joya Misra, "The Intersection of Gender and Race in the Labor Market," *Annual Review of Sociology* 29 (August 2003): 487–513.

6 John J. Kulczycki, *The Foreign Worker and the German Labor Movement: Xenophobia and Solidarity in the Coal Fields of the Ruhr, 1871–1914* (Providence: Berg, 1994); Kulczycki argues against the idea that ethnic Poles chose between class interests and national consciousness, which Christoph Klessman terms, "double loyalty" in Klessman, "Zjednoczenie Zawodowe Polskie (ZZP-Polnische Berufsvereinigung) und Alter Verband im Ruhrgebiet," *Internationale Wissenschaftliche Korrespondenz zur Geschichte der deutschen Arbeiterbewegung* 15 (1979): 68; Erhard Lucas, *Zwei Formen von Radikalismus in der deutschen Arbeiterbewegung* (Frankfurt am Main: Roter Stern, 1976); Erhard Lucas, *Der bewaffnete Arbeiteraufstand im Ruhrgebiet in seiner inneren Struktur und in seinem Verhältnis zu den Klassenkämpfen in den verschiedenen Regionen des Reiches* (Frankfurt am Main: Roter Stern, 1973).

7 David F. Crew, *Town in the Ruhr: A Social History of Bochum* (New York: Columbia University Press, 1986), 181.

8 Karin Hunn, *Nächstes Jahr*; Gottfried E. Voelker, "More Foreign Workers – Germany's Labour Problem No. 1?" in *Turkish Workers in Europe, 1960–1975*, 331–45, here 336; Ulrich Herbert, *A History of Foreign Labor in Germany*. Herbert points out that in 90 per cent of foreign males were

blue-collar workers compared with only 49 per cent of the German male work force, p. 216.

9 Ulrich Herbert, *A History of Foreign Labor*, 230.

10 Ibid.

11 Ibid.

12 Oliver Trede, "Misstrauen, Regulation und Integration: Gewerkschaften und 'Gastarbeiter' in der Bundesrepublik in den 1950er bis 1970er Jahren" in *Das "Gastarbeiter" System: Arbeitsmigration und ihre Folgen in der Bundesrepublik Deutschland und Westeuropa*, ed. Jochen Oltmer, Axel Kreienbrink, and Carlos Sanz Diaz (Munich: Oldenbourg, 2012), 183–97.

13 Ibid., 186.

14 Ibid., 188; Hunn, "Die türkischen Arbeitsmigranten und ihre Arbeitgeber," in *Nächest Jahr*, 101–36.

15 Bojadzijev, Manuela, *Die windige Internationale*, 151.

16 Der Bundesminister für Arbeit und Sozialordnung, Bonn, an BAVAV Nürnberg, 2 May 1962, BArch B119/ 3071 II.

17 Ibid.

18 Ibid.

19 *Hallo Mustafa!*, 22.

20 Ibid.

21 "Mindeststundenlöhne," BAVAV Türkei, an BAVAV Nürnberg, 7 December 1965 BArch B119/3073.

22 Hunn, *Nächest Jahr*, 117.

23 Herbert, *A History of Foreign Labor*, 241.

24 Ali Gitmez, *Göçmen İşçilerin Dönüşü* [*Immigrant Workers Return*]: *Return Migration of Turkish Workers to Three Selected Regions* (Ankara: Orta Doğu Teknik Üniversitesi, idari Ilimler Fakültesi, 1977), 81.

25 Ibid.

26 Bundesverband der Deutschen Süßwarenindustrie, Vereinigung der Schokolade- und Süßwarenfabrikanten, E.V. an BAVAV Nürnberg, 8 December 1965, BArch B 119/ 3073.

27 Ibid. A memo from the "Fine Ceramic Industry" in Bavaria lists foreign women's wages, for those over twenty-one years as DM2.33 and for those twenty years old, as just DM2.26. In contrast, unskilled men who were over twenty-one years old would earn DM2.85 and twenty years old DM2.79, "Lohntarifvertrag vom 2.6.1965 für die gewerblichen Arbeitnehmer der feinkeramischen Industrie, BArch B119/ 3073.

28 Bundesverband der Deutschen Süßwarenindustrie Vereinigung der Schokolade und Süßwarenfabrikanten, e.v., an BAVAV 4 February 1966.

29 Ibid.

30 It is noteworthy that this was not an issue necessarily targeted
   at guest workers, but more reflective of West Germany's overall
   aversion to minimum wage policies, which was first approved in
   2014, implemented in 2015, and will be renewed on an annual bases
   starting in 2016. Unlike the United States, West Germany has relied
   on collective bargaining among sectors rather than at the state level.
   "Germany Approves First-Ever National Minimum Wage," *BBC News*,
   3 July 2014, accessed 1 March 2016, http://www.bbc.com/news/
   business-28140594.
31 Edith Schmidt and David Wittenberg, *Pierburg: Ihr Kampf ist unser Kampf*
   (West Germany, 1974/75) motion picture. 49 min.
32 Ibid.
33 *Augsburger Allgemeine*, 22 August 1973.
34 "Akort nedir?" [What is Accord?] in *Eilermark'a Hoş geldiniz: Türk İşçi
   Arkadaşlarımız için Kılavuz*, [Welcome to Eilermark: A Guide for Our
   Turkish Worker Friends] Eilermark AG, Spinnerei u. Zwirnerei, Gronau,
   (2 May 1973, National Library, 5262, DM 4671–73), 17–19.
35 Ibid., 17–18.
36 "Elif," Berlin 2003.
37 Mathilde Jamin reports that Turkish workers worked faster than their
   West German co-workers, who complained that they were "spoiling the
   Akkord," "Migrationserfahrungen," in *Fremde Heimat*, ed. Aytaç Eryılmaz
   and Mathilde Jamin, 216.
38 "Elif," Berlin 2003.
39 Ibid.
40 Jamin says that many of her interview partners described the relationship
   between Germans and Turks as having changed over time: "In the
   beginning it was no problem and the relations were good (in the 1960s),
   difficulties came later, (1970s) and racist discrimination was a later
   development (1980s)" "Migrationserfahrungen," *Fremde Heimat*, 224.
41 Herbert, *A History of Foreign Labor*, 241.
42 BAVAV Nürnberg an den Herrn Bundesminister für Arbeit und
   Sozialordnung Bonn, "Beschäftigung türkischer Bergarbeiter im
   deutschen Steinkohlenbergbau," 2 May 1962, BArch B119/ 3071 II; ten
   workers were fired and given train tickets back to Istanbul. Apparently
   these ten did not give up easily; they got off the train in Bonn to look for
   work there but were denied work permits from the Bonn Employment
   Office. See also, "10 Türken wegen Aufwiegelung ausgewiesen: Rabiate
   'Gäste' verprügelten besonnen Kollegen, Große Tumulte in Wohnlager,"
   Solinger Tageblatt 17 March 1962, BArch B119/ 3071 II.

43 Richard L. Carson, *Comparative Economic Systems, Part III Capitalist Alternatives* (New York: M.E. Sharpe, 1990), 618.

44 Hunn, "Die Rezession von 1966/67: Auswirkungen und Reaktionen" in *Nächstes Jahr*, 188–202.

45 Ibid.

46 Carson, *Comparative*, 618.

47 "The CDU and the 'Social Market Economy': Düsseldorf Guidelines for Economy Policy, Agricultural Policy, Social Policy, and Housing," in German History in Documents and Images, taken from Düsseldorfer Leitsätze über Wirtschaftspolitik, Landwirtschaftspolitik, Sozialpolitik,Wohnungsbau [Düsseldorf Guidelines for Economic Policy, Agricultural Policy, Social Policy, and Housing], trans. Adam Blauhut (15 July 1949; repr. in Ossip Kurt Flechtheim, *Die Parteien der Bundesrepublik Deutschland* [The Parties of the Federal Republic of Germany] Hamburg, 1973, 162–3), accessed 1 March 2016, http://germanhistorydocs.ghi-dc.org/pdf/eng/Parties%20WZ%206_Eng.pdf.

48 "Schwerpunkte, Aufmaß und Verlauf der Streikbewegung" in Reihe Betrieb und Gewerkschaften: Redaktionskollektiv 'express,' in *Spontane Streiks*, 22.

49 *Spontane Streiks*, 18.

50 *Spontane Streiks*, 127.

51 Hans Schuster, "Wilde Streiks als Warnsignal," *Süddeutsche Zeitung*, 13 September 1969; "Streikbewegung greift auf den Bergbau über: Tarifgespräche schon in dieser Woche," *General-Anzeiger für Bonn und Umgebungen*, 8 September 1969; Wilhem Throm, "Wilde Streiks treffen die Gewerkschaften," *Frankfurter Allgemeine Zeitung*, 8 September 1969; "Eine große Lohnwelle kündigt sich an: Die Stahlarbeiter fordern 14 Prozent mehr," *Frankfurter Allgemeine*, 8 September 1969; "Lohnverhandlung am Donnerstag," *Solinger Tageblatt*, 8 September 1969; "Auch im Bergbau" *Butzbacher Zeitung*, 8 September 1969; "Jetzt Streiks um Bergbau: Neue Lohnforderungen im Rheinland," *Hannoversche Rundschau*, 9 September 1969; "Wilde Streikwelle nun auch im Saar-Bergbau: Tarifpartner bemühen sich um schnelle Entspannung," *Ludwigsburger Kreiszeitung*, 9 September 1969.

52 Ibid.

53 "Streik bei Hella, Lippstadt," in *Spontane Streiks*, 75.

54 Ibid.

55 Ibid., "Du schon machen gut!" [*sic*].

56 Ibid.

57 "Die Türken probten den Aufstand" *Die Zeit*, 7 September 1973.

58 Strikes about vacation time for foreign workers were common across West Germany, such as when 1,600 Portuguese workers at the Karmann factory and 250 Spanish workers in Wiesloch went on strike to argue for the right to use their vacation days contiguously. "Zur Rolle der Ausländischen Arbeiter," in *Spontane Streiks*, 30.

59 Zur Rolle der Ausländischen Arbeiter," *Spontane Streiks*, 30.

60 "Einwanderung und Selbstbewusstsein: Der Fordstreik 1973," in *Geschichte und Gedächtnis in der Einwanderungsgesellschaft: Migration zwischen historischer Rekonstruktion und Erinnerungspolitik*, ed. Jan Motte and Rainer Ohliger (Essen: Klartext, 2004); *Der Spiegel*, 3 September 1973; Karin Hunn, "Der 'Türkenstreik' bei Ford von August 1973: Verlauf und Analyse" and "Die zeitgenössischen Deutungen des Fordstreiks und dessen Konsequenzen für die türkischen Arbeitnehmer," in *Nächstes Jahr*, 243–61; Manuela Bojadzijev, *Die windige Internationale*, 157–62.

61 "Die Türken probten den Aufstand," *Die Zeit*, September 7, 1973.

62 "Beispiele für Maßregelungen," in *Spontane Streiks*, 46; Hans-Günter Kleff, "Täuschung, Selbsttäuschung, Enttäuschung und Lernen: Anmerkungen zum Fordstreik im Jahre 1973" in *Geschichte und Gedächtnis in der Einwanderungsgesellschaft*, 251–9.

63 "Die Türken probten den Aufstand," *Die Zeit*, 7 September 1973.

64 "Rebellion am Fließband: Erfahrungen aus Frauenstreiks," Barbara Schleich, WDR II 13 December 1973, 15 min.

65 Ibid.

66 "Dossiers: Die Chronik der neuen Frauenbewegung: 1973," Frauen Media Turm, Das Archiv und Dokumentationszentrum, accessed 3 February 2013, http://www.frauenmediaturm.de/themen-portraets/chronik-der -neuen-frauenbewegung/1973/.

67 Mattes, *Gastarbeiterinnen*.

68 Ibid.

69 Miller and Çetin, *Migrant Workers*; Mattes, *Gastarbeiterinnen*, 39.

70 "Frauen im Beruf: Arbeiten und kuschen," *Stern*, no. 44 (1973).

71 Ute Frevert, *Women in German History: From Bourgeois Emancipation to Sexual Liberation*, trans. Stuart McKinnon-Even, Terry Bond and Barbara Norden (New York: Berg, 1989), 279.

72 Harry Schaffer, *Women in the Two Germanies: A comparative Study of A Socialist and Non-Socialist Society* (New York: Pergamon, 1981); the female labour union executive mentioned was Liesel Winkelraeter, who wrote, "Entlohnung weiblicher Arbeitsnehmer – Standortanalyse," *Probleme der Frauen – Problem der Gesellschaft, Arbeitschancen, Lohngleichheit, Vorurteile*, Protokoll des Arbeitstagung

des DGB (a symposium) November 6–7, 1975 (Cologne: Europäische Verlagsanstalt, 1976); see also, Ute Frevert "Family or Career? Women's Dilemma in the Land of the Economic Miracle" in *Women in German History: From Bourgeois Emancipation to Sexual Liberation*, trans. Stuart McKinnon-Evans (New York: Berg, 1989), 265–86; Gertraude Krell, "Gesellschaftliche Arbeitsteilung und Frauenlöhne," in *Frauen als bezahlte und unbezahlte Arbeitskräften: Beiträge zur Berliner Sommeruniversität für Frauen* (Berlin: Selbsverl., 1978), 58–68.

73 Harry Shaffer, *Women in the Two Germanies*, 100.

74 Walter Rohmert and Josef Rutenfranz, *Arbeitswissenschaftliche Beurteilung der Belastung und Beanspruchung an unterschiedlichen industriellen Arbeitsplätzen* (Berlin: Federal Ministry for Labor and Social Order, 1 July 1975).

75 "Lohntarifvertrag vom 2.6.1965 für die gewerblichen Arbeitnehmer der feinkeramischen Industrie" Bayern, quoted in, BAVAV Türkei an BAVAV Nürnberg 7 December 1965, BArch B 119/ 3073.

76 "Es geht nicht ohne Italiener," *Industriekurier*, 4 October 1955, quoted in Herbert, *A History of Foreign Labor*, 206.

77 For a reference to recruiters' demands specifically for female foreign workers, see, "Wochenbericht der deutschen Verbindungsstelle in der Türkei": 26 November 1969, BArch B 119/4031; Berlin Aa 10 November 1965, "Informationsbesuch bei der Firma Sarotti AG" Landesarchiv Berlin, B Rep 301 Nr 297 Acc 2879 "Arbeitsmarktpolitik."

78 *Pierburg-Neuss: Deutsche und Ausländische Arbeiter – Ein Gegner- Ein Kampf/ Alman ve Meslektaslar Tek Rakıp tek Mücadele / Streikverlauf, Vorgeschichte, Analyse, Dokumentation, Nach dem Streik* (Internationale Sozialistische Publikationen, 1974) DOMiD Archive, Sig. No. 1177, 6.

79 Ibid., 167.

80 These numbers vary slightly based on publication. Bojadzijev bases her numbers on information provided by the union, in Bojadzjiev, *Die windige Internationale: Rassismus und Kämpfe der Migration* (Münster: Westfälisches Dampfboot, 2008), 163.

81 "Interview mit einem Betriebsratmitglied über die Arbeitskonflikte Ausländischer Arbeiter bei Pierburg Neuss im Februar 1975," in Hildebrandt and Olle, *Ihr Kampf*, 39.

82 Godula Kosack, "Migrant Women: The Move to Western Europe – A Step towards Emancipation?" *Race and Class* 70, no. 4 (1976): 374–5.

83 "Interview mit einem Betriebsratmitglied über die Arbeitskonflikte Ausländischer Arbeiter bei Pierburg Neuss im Februar 1975," in *Ihr Kampf*, ed. Hildebrandt and Olle, 155; the source, *Pierburg-Neuss: Deutsche*

und Ausländische Arbeiter, cites the number as four hundred Yugoslavian women, 6.

84 Hildebrandt and Olle, *Ihr Kampf*, 155.
85 Hildebrandt and Olle, *Ihr Kampf*, 37.
86 *Deutsche Volkszeitung*, 29 May 1970.
87 Ibid.
88 Hildebrandt and Olle, *Ihr Kampf*, 37.
89 *Deutsche Volkszeitung*, 29 May 1970.
90 "Forderungen der Beschäftigten der Versammlung der Belegschaftsmitglieder der Firma Pierburg," DOMiD Archive Pierburg File.
91 Multi-lingual Flier, referring to the 7–8 June 1973 strike. DOMiD Archive, Pierburg File.
92 Ibid.
93 Kosack, "Migrant Women," 375.
94 "Telefonnotiz," 14 June 1973 in "Telefongespräch mit Herrn Prof. Pierburg am 14. Juni 1973 nach 16 Uhr," Neuss, 15 June 1973, DOMiD Pierburg File.
95 Hildebrandt and Olle, *Ihr Kampf*, 38.
96 "IG Metall: Gastarbeiter nicht Diskriminiert: Der Streik bei Pierburg in Neuss ist illegal," *Handelsblatt*, 17–18 August 1983.
97 Micheal Geuenich, Industriegewerkschaft Metall, F. D Bundesrepublik Deutschland, Verwaltungsstelle Neuss-Grevenbroich 15 August 1973 in "Flugblatt-Dokumentation" in *Pierburg-Neuss: Deutsche und Ausländische Arbeiter – Ein Gegner- Ein Kampf*, 27; DOMiD Archive, Pierburg file.
98 Ibid.
99 Pierburg," *Spontane Streiks.*
100 "Ibid., 79.
101 Ibid.
102 Hildebrandt and Olle, *Ihr Kampf*, 40.
103 Ibid.
104 "Frauen im Beruf: Arbeiter und kuschen," *Stern*, 25 October 1973, no. 44, 84.
105 Hildebrandt and Olle, *Ihr Kampf*, 40.
106 "Pierburg," *Spontane Streiks 1973*, 80.
107 Ibid.
108 Hildebrandt and Olle, *Ihr Kampf*, 40.
109 Ibid.
110 Godula Kosack, "Migrant Women," 375; The DOMiD Archive, Pierburg file contains a dried rose from the strike.
111 Ibid.

112 Ibid.; Hildebrandt and Olle, *Ihr Kampf*, 40.
113 "Streik Bei Pierbrug Neuss," *Spontane Streiks*, 80.
114 Ibid., 81.
115 Ibid.
116 Ibid.
117 Ibid.
118 "Keine Ruhe nach dem Streik: Wieder kurze Arbeitsniederlegung, wieder Polizei vor dem Werkstor," *Kölner Stadtanzeiger* 22 August 1973; "Unternehmensleitung in Neuss glaubt an politische Motive: 'Streik war von außen gesteuert'," *Frankfurter Rundschau*, 22 August 1973.
119 Hildebrandt and Olle, *Ihr Kampf*, 41.
120 Quoted in Kosack, "Migrant Women," 376; see also, "Anna, geh du voran: Anna Satolias – die Geschichte einer griechischen Gastarbeiterin, die die Sprecherin der Frauen in einem deutschen Betrieb wurde," *Jasmin* 20 (1973); Barbara Schleich, "Streik am laufenden Band: In der Vergaserfirma Pierburg streikten vor allem ausländische Arbeiterinnen," *Vorwärts*, 25 August 1973.
121 Kosack, "Migrant Women," 376.
122 Ibid.
123 "Anna, geh du voran," *Jasmin* 20 (1973).
124 Kosack, "Migrant Women," 376
125 Ibid., 369.
126 Ibid.
127 Wiebke Buchholz-Will, "Wann wird aus diesem Traum Wirklichkeit? Die gewerkschaftliche Frauenarbeit in der Bundesrepublik Deutschland" in *Geschichte Der Deutschen Frauen Bewegung*, ed. Florence Herve (Cologne: PapyRossa Verlag, 1995), 185–208.
128 *Augsburger Allgemeine*, 22 August 1973.
129 Harry G. Shaffer, *Women in the Two Germanies: A Comparative Study of a Socialist and Non-Socialist Society* (New York: Pergamon Press, 1981).
130 Ibid., 101–2.
131 Ibid.
132 "*Das ist kein Streik mehr, das ist eine Bewegung,*" quoted in Martin Rapp and Marion von Osten "Ihr Kampf ist unser Kampf," *Bildpunkt: Zeitschrift der IG Bildende Kunst* (Spring 2006): 23.
133 Ibid.
134 Ibid.
135 Martin Slater, "Migrant Employment, Recessions, and Return Migration: Some Consequences for Migration Policy and Development," *Studies in Comparative International Development* (Fall–Winter 1979): 4, emphasis added.

136　Karen Schönwälder, "The Difficult Task of Managing Migration: The 1973 Recruitment Stop," in *German History from the Margins,* ed. Mark Roseman, Neil Gregor, and Nils Roemer (Bloomington: Indiana University Press 2006), 252–67.

137　Ursula Mehrländer, "The Second Generation of Migrant Workers in Germany: The Transition from School to Work," in *Education and the Integration of Ethnic Minorities,* ed. D. Rothermund and J. Simon (London: Pinter, 1986), 12–24.

138　David F. Crew "Foundations of Worker Protest" in *Town in the Ruhr* (New York: Columbia University Press, 1979), 159–94.

Conclusion

1　"Secret Thatcher Notes: Kohl Wanted Half of Turks Out of Germany" Claus Hecking, *Spiegel Online International,* 1 August 2013, accessed 17 December 2014, http://www.spiegel.de/international/germany/secret -minutes-chancellor-kohl-wanted-half-of-turks-out-of-germany-a-914376 .html.

2　"Recruitment of Guest Workers Stopped" in *Germany in Transit,* ed. Göktürk et al., 44–5.

3　Ibid.

4　Philip L. Martin, "Working Paper Comparative Immigration and Integration Program-1, "Germany: Managing Migration in the 21st Century," 1 May 2002, accessed 9 January 2015, http://ies.berkeley.edu/ pubs/workingpapers/CIIP-1-PLM_Germany.pdf, 12.

5　Ibid.

6　Göktürk, et al., *German in Transit,* 44.

7　Duncan Miler and İhsan Çetin, *Migrant Workers, Wages, and Labor Markets: Emigrant Turkish Workers in the Federal Republic of Germany* (Istanbul: Elektronik, 1974), 63.

8　"Europe's Imported Labor Force Begins to Cost More," *Business Week,* 31 March 1973, 94, quoted in Miller and Çetin, eds. *Migrant Workers, Wagers, and Labor Markets,* 63.

9　Ibid.

10　Ibid., 64.

11　Herbert and Hunn, "Guest Workers and Policy on Guest Workers in the Federal Republic: From the Beginning of Recruitment in 1955 until its Halt in 1973," in *The Miracle Years,* ed. Schissler, 211; Eryılmaz and Jamin eds., *Fremde Heimat,* 225.

12　Ibid.

13 TES statistics, quoted in Gitmez, "Göçmen işçilerin Dönüşü [Migrant Workers Return], 2.
14 Judt, *Postwar*, 333.
15 Ibid.
16 Castles and Miller, *The Age of Migration*, 94.
17 Cathryn Cluver, "French Immigration Policy: History Repeated?" *Foreign Policy Association Network, Foreign Policy* (blog), 11 April 2007, accessed 9 January 2015, www.google.com/url?sa=t&rct=j&q=&esrc=s&source=web&cd=4&ved=0CDoQFjAD&url=http%3A%2F%2Fforeignpolicyblogs .com%2F2007%2F04%2F11%2Ffrench-immigration-policy-history -repeated%2F&ei=dFKTVO7_La61sQT69oLgBA&usg=AFQjCNEjBY -Jp2hUObPVa7vTjK9f-7kHbg&bvm=bv.82001339,d.cWc.
18 James Hollifield, Phillip Martin, and Pia Orrenius, *Controlling Immigration: A Global Perspective*, 3rd ed. (Stanford: Stanford University Press, 2014), 230.
19 Chin, *Guest Worker Question*,150–1.
20 Ibid., 151.
21 Herbert and Hunn, "Guest Workers," in *Miracle Years*, 205.
22 Ibid., 207.
23 Deutsche Bundestag 7. Sitzung vom 18.1.1973," 11, quoted in Herbert and Hunn, 209–10.
24 Philip L. Martin, "Germany: Managing Migration in the 21st Century," Working Paper Comparative Immigration and Integration Program, Institue of European Studies, University of California Berkeley, 1 May 2002, accessed 3 May 2017, http://escholarship.org/uc/item/1gb6j203.
25 Philip L. Martin, *The Unfinished Story: Turkish Labour Migration to Western Europe: With special reference to the Federal Republic of Germany* (Geneva: International Labour Organisation, 1991), 83; Klaus Bade, ed., *Das Manifest der 60: Deutschland und die Einwanderung* (Munich: C.H. Beck Verlag, 1984).
26 Kristen McCabe, Serena Yi-Ying Lin, Hiroyuki Tanaka, and Piotr Plewa, "Pay to Go: Countries Offer Cash to Immigrants Willing to Pack Their Bags," *The Online Journal of the Migration Policy Institute*, 5 November 2009, accessed 18 December 2014, http://www.migrationpolicy.org/article/ pay-go-countries-offer-cash-immigrants-willing-pack-their-bags.
27 Göktürk et al., *Germany in Transit*, 502.
28 Triandafyllidou, ed., *Muslims in 21st Century Europe*, 63.
29 "Surprisingly, the majority [of guest workers] refused to leave ... [In] spite of exploitation, many of the supposedly temporary 'guest' ultimately decided to stay," Konrad H. Jarausch and Michael Geyer, in *Shattered Past:*

Reconstructing German Histories (Princeton, NJ: Princeton University Press, 2003), 212.

30 "Elif," Berlin 2003.

31 Touraj Atabaki and Gavin D. Brockett, "Introduction," in "Ottoman and Republican Turkish Labor History," ed. Touraj Atabaki and Gavin D. Brockett, supplement, *International Review of Social History* (*IRSH*), Internationaal Instituut voor Sociale Geschiedenis, 54 no. S17 (2009): 1–17, here 2.

32 Donald Quataert, "Epilogue" in "Ottoman and Republican," supplement *International Review of Social History* 54 no. S17 (2009): 189–93, here 189.

33 Ali S. Gitmez, *Göçmen İşçilerin Dönüşü* [*Migrant Workers Return*], 6. Gitmez's valuable study offers one of the few studies from the 1970s that includes interviews with return migrants to Turkey.

34 Ibid., 6.

35 Miller and Çetin, *Migrant Workers*, 10–11.

36 Ibid.

37 Gitmez, *Göçmen İşçilerin*, 5.

38 Ibid.

39 Ibid.

40 Ibid.

41 Ibid., 71–2.

42 Ibid.,73.

43 Ibid.

44 Ibid., 75.

45 "Murat," interviewed by author, Istanbul, 2004.

46 Ibid.

47 "Ahmet," DOMiD Interview, Berlin, 30 August 1995.

48 Ibid.

49 "15 bin kadar Müslüman iffet ve namusu için yürüdü: Bonn-Bad Godesberg, ilk defa bu kadar çok Müslüman'ı bir arada gördü" ["Almost 15,000 Muslims Marched for Their Honor: The Largest Concentration of Muslims Ever Seen in Bonn-Bad Godesberg"] *Hicret*, 15 February 1982, 10–11.

50 Ibid.

51 "Köln Radyosu Türkçe Yayınlar Servisine protesto mektubu" ["Protest Letter to Cologne Radio Turkish Broadcast Services"] *Hicret*, 15 February 1982, 13.

52 James Helicke writes, "To some extent, Muslim identity is constructed in response to the dominant and exclusive German, and Christian, culture. Turks understand themselves to be Muslim specifically as a way to locate

themselves in relation and in contrast to Christian Germans," in "Turks in Germany: Muslim Identity: 'Between' States'" in *Muslim Minorities in the West: Visible and Invisible,* ed. Yvonne Yazbeck Haddad and Jane I. Smith (New York: Altamira, 2002), 183.

53 Ibid.

54 "Prime Minister and Chancellor Merkel statement on Paris terrorist attack," *Prime Minister's Office,* 7 January 2015, accessed 27 February 2015, https://www.gov.uk/government/news/prime-minister-and-chancellor -merkel-statement-on-paris-terrorist-attack.

55 Kate Connolly, "Pegida: What does the German far-right movement actually stand for?" *The Guardian,* 6 January 2015, accessed 27 February 2015, http://www.theguardian.com/world/shortcuts/2015/jan/06/ pegida-what-does-german-far-right-movement-actually-stand-for.

56 "Germany Protests: Dresden Marches against Anti-Islamists Pegida," *BBC News,* 10 January 2015, accessed 27 February 2015, http://www.bbc.com/ news/world-europe-30765674.

57 David Lepeska, "The ticking time bomb of Syrian refugees," *Al Jazeera,* 10, May 2015, accessed 17 January 2016, http://www.aljazeera.com/indepth/ opinion/2015/05/ticking-time-bomb-syrian-refugees-150509062906684 .html.

58 "Cologne Carnival: Police Record 22 Sexual Assaults," *BBC News,* 5 February 2016, accessed 4 March 2016, http://www.bbc.com/news/ world-europe-35502223.

59 Melissa Eddy, "Angela Merkel Calls for European Unity to Address the Migrant Influx," *New York Times,* 31 August 2015, accessed 4 March 2016, http://www.nytimes.com/2015/09/01/world/europe/germany -migrants-merkel.html.

60 In August and September 2015 media covered news reports of corpses found in a smuggler's truck in Austria, of a drowned three-year-old boy, and of violent skirmishes as migrants tried to illegally move into other European countries. Luke Harding, "Hungarian police Arrest Driver of Lorry That Had 71 Dead Migrants Inside," *The Guardian,* 28 August 2015, accessed 4 March 2016, http://www.theguardian.com/ world/2015/aug/28/more-than-70-dead-austria-migrant-truck-tragedy; Joe Parkinson and David George-Cosh, "Image of Drowned Syrian Boy Echoes Around World, *The Wall Street Journal,* 3 September 2015, accessed 4 March 2016, http://www.wsj.com/articles/image-of-syrian -boy-washed-up-on-beach-hits-hard-1441282847; Kirsten Grieshaber, "6 Syrian Refugees Injured in Attacks across Germany," *Associated Press,* 1 November 2015, accessed 4 March 2016, http://bigstory.ap.org/article/

c33a0f30f8c54dc19ddd0e358694a67a/6-syrian-refugees-injured-attacks
-across-germany.

61 Michelle Martin, "Merkel Says Germany Must Learn from Its 'Guest
    Worker' Mistakes from Refugee Crisis," *Reuters*, 9 September 2015,
    accessed 3 March 2016, http://www.reuters.com/article/us-europe
    -migrants-germany-merkel-idUSKCN0R90S520150909.

62 Michael Kimmelman, Andrew Higgins, and Alison Smale, "The Refugee
    Crisis: What it Means for Europe" *New York Times*, 7 October 2015,
    accessed 4 March 2016, http://www.nytimes.com/2015/10/08/world/
    europe/refugee-migrant-crisis-asylum-seekers-germany.html.

63 Rick Lyman and Alison Smale, "Paris Attacks Shift Europe's Migrant
    Focus to Security," *New York Times*, 15 November 2016, accessed 4 March
    2016, http://www.nytimes.com/2015/11/16/world/europe/paris
    -attacks-shift-europes-migrant-focus-to-security.html?_r=0.

64 "Cologne Sex Attacks: Women Describe 'Terrible' Assaults'," *BBC News*,
    7 January 2016, accessed 5 February 2016, http://www.bbc.com/news/
    world-europe-35502223.

65 "Cologne Carnival: Police Record 22 Sexual Assaults," *BBC News*,
    5 February 2016, accessed 4 March 2016, http://www.bbc.com/news/
    world-europe-35502223.

66 Rick Noack, "Why Germany's Merkel Will Continue to Welcome Refugees,
    despite Calling Multiculturalism a Sham," *The Washington Post*, 16 December
    2015, accessed 4 March 2016, https://www.washingtonpost.com/news/
    worldviews/wp/2015/12/16/why-germanys-merkel-will-continue-to
    -welcome-refugees-despite-calling-multiculturalism-a-sham/.

Bibliography

PRIMARY SOURCES

Archiv der sozialen Demokratie – Friedrich-Ebert Stiftung (AdsD)

Ausländische Arbeitnehmer: 5/IGMA 26001–260026

Archiv für Soziale Bewegung (AfsB) Bochum, Germany

AGE A (org) 18: Abteilung Organisation IGBE, BR, Ausländerpolitik/
    Ausländerrecht
Files: 19092–19096
1069B
1069A
19100

Bundesarchiv (BArch) Koblenz, Germany

B 119: Bundesanstalt für Arbeitsvermittlung und Arbeitslosenversicherung
    (BAVAV) ab 1969 Bundesanstalt für Arbeit (BA)
B 119 Files:
    3070: Anwerbung und Vermittlung türkischer Arbeitskräfte –
    Verschiedenes, Bd 1: 1953–61; Bd 2, 1961–3
    3072: Anwerbung und Vermittlung türkischer Arbeitskräfte
    Verschiedenes, Bd 3 1961–4
    3073: Anwerbung und Vermittlung türkischer Arbeitskräfte
    Verschiedenes, Bd 4 1964–6
    3074: Anwerbung und Vermittlung türkischer Arbeitskräfte

Verschiedenes, Bd 5 1965–8
3945: Verfahrungsabsprachen mit der Partnerverwaltung Türkei im
Bereich der Arbeitsvermittlung Verschiedenes, Bd 1, 1969–73
3946: Verfahrungsabsprachen mit der Partnerverwaltung Türkei im
Bericht der Arbeitsvermittlung Verschiedenes; Bd 2, 1971–3
3952: 1966–73 Enthält u.a. Reiseverpflegung türkischer Arbeitnehmer
4029: Ärztliche Versorgung von Kinder ausländischer Arbeitnehmer bei
Ankunft der Enthält u.a.: Sammelreisezüge in den Weiterleitungsstellen
1972; Bd 1 1956–73
4030: Kopie des Flugzeug-bereitstellungs- und
Überlassungsrahmenvertrag zwischen der Bundesanstalt für Arbeit und der
Condor Flugdienst GmBH Frankfurt am Main 1973
4035: Sammelreisenangelegenheiten Türkei, 1961–5
4036: Vermittlung ausländischer Arbeitnehmer durch die Bundesanstalt
im Ausland, Allgemeines, Bd 2, 1966–70
5192: Zusammenarbeit mit den ARD Hörfunkredaktionen für
Ausländerprogram

Die Behörde des Bundesbeauftragten für die Stasi-Unterlagen – (BStU)

*Unterlagen des Staatssicherheitsdienstes der ehemaligen
Deutschen Demokratischen Republik*

Archive der Zentralstelle,
MfS AS 9/73
MfS HA 1: 15176
MfS HA II: 22858; 24068; 27002; 27081; 27084; 27442; 27575; 27836; 27837; 27838;
27962; 28079; 28084; 28209; 28872; 29717; 29668; 29778; 40416
MfS HA VI: 441; 919
MfS HA VIII: 3506
MfS HA XX: 10221; 18529
MfS AIM: 8196/78 1/1
MfS AIM: 8196/78 1/2
MfS AIM: 8196/78 1/3
MfS GH: 73/78
MfS ZAIG: 11129
BfS ZKG: 286
MfS ZKG 11540
MfS Sekr. Neiber: 225
MfS Sekr. Mittig: 63

*Dokumentationszentrum und Museum über die Migration
in Deutschland e. V. (DOMiD) Cologne, Germany*

File Collections:
DC Wohnsituation
SD 99–114, 122–61
SD 306–317, 320–25, 327, 329–33, 367, 370–1
SD 432–41, 445–72
SD BT 623
Pierburg: Bestandt K 6, 3, Pierburg Streik,
   Peter Leipziger, Pierburg Streik, E 887, 16
   Peter Leipziger, E 887, 5–16
   *Pierburg-Neuss: Deutsche und Ausländische Arbeiter – Ein Gegner- Ein Kampf/
   Alman ve Meslektaslar Tek Rakıp tek Mücadele / Streikverlauf, Vorgeschichte,
   Analyse, Dokumentation, Nach dem Streik.* Internationale Sozialistische
   Publikationen, 1974. Sig. No. 1177
Rapportbuch, Bergmannsheim, Westfalen I, 1971–3
Interview Collection
Newspaper Collection
   Kurtuluş: İşçiler Birleşin, Avrupa'da Türkiyeli İşçilerin Gazetesi 1971–4
   Gerçek 1975
   Halkçı
Edith Schmidt and David Wittenberg. *"Pierburg: Ihr Kampf ist Unser Kampf."*
(West Germany 1974/75), 49' motion picture.

Landesarchiv Berlin

B Rep 301 Nr 297 "Arbeitsmarktpolitik"
Nr 298 "Frauenerwerbsarbeit – Allgemeines – Januar 1965 bis Dezember 1965
Nr 299 "Frauenerwerbsarbeit – Allgemeines – Januar 1966–
   Nr 302 "Frauenerwerbsarbeit – Allgemeines" Januar 1969–Dezember 1969"
   Nr 304 "Arbeitsvermittlung für Wirtschaftszweige, Berufe, und Arbeitssuchende,
   August 1952–68

*International Institute of Social History (IISG)
Amsterdam, The Netherlands*

Periodical Collection:
   İşbaşı: Haftalık İş ve İşçi Haberler
   Hicret

Tarih Vakfı, [History Institute] Istanbul, Turkey

"Göçmen"
Ali Gitmez, "Göçmen Dönüşü: Return Migration of Türkish Workers to Three Selected Regions." Ankara: Orta Doğu Teknik Üniversitesi idari ilimler Fakültesi, 1977.

Milli Kütüphanesi [National Library], Ankara, Turkey

"Almanya": [Germany]:
İşçi Olarak Almanya'ya Nasıl Gidiler? [How Does One Go to Germany to Work?] İş ve İşçi Bulma Kurumu Genel Müdürlüğü Yayınları, no. 28. Ankara: Mars Matbaası, 1963.
Egeli, Münir Hayri. *Almanya'ya Gidiyorum.* [I'm Going to Germany] İstanbul, İnkılâp ve Aka, 1962. Hamle Matbaası, 1963.
Eilermark'a Hoş Geldiniz! Türk işçi Arkadaşlarımız için Kılavuz [Welcome to Eilermark! A Guide for Our Turkish Worker Friends], *Eilermark AG, Spinnerei und Zwirnerei.* İstanbul: Fidan Matbaası, 1973.
Avrupa Memleketlerinde Türk İşçileri ve Problemleri [Turkish Workers and Their Problems in European Countries]. F. Almanya, Hollanda, Belçika, İsviçre ve Avusturya'da Yapılan bir inceleme Gezisinin Notları, 14 Nisan 1966–14 Mayıs 1966. İş ve İşçi Bulma Kurumu Yayını, no 32, 1967. Milli Kütüphanesi, AD 591.

Published Primary Sources

"15 bin kadar Müslüman iffet ve namusu için yürüdü: Bonn-Bad Godesberg, ilk defa bu kadar çok Müslüman'ı bir arada gördü" ["Almost 15,000 Muslims Marched for their Honor: The largest concentration of Muslims ever seen in Bonn-Bad Godesberg"]. *Hicret*, 15 February 1982, 10–11.
"1964 yılının 10 bininci işçisi Almanya'ya gitti" [1964's Ten Thousandth Worker Arrives in Germany]. *Cumhuriyet*, 17 March 1964.
"76 Günde 10,400 İşçi Gitti" [76 in a Day, 10,400 Workers Arrived]. *Milliyet*, 17 March 1964.
"Almanya'ya on bininci işçi gitti" [Ten Thousandth Worker Arrives in Germany]. *Dünya*, 17 March 1964.
"Angela Merkel Calls for European Unity to Address the Migrant Influx." *New York Times*, 31 August 2015. Accessed 4 March 2016. http://www.nytimes.com/2015/09/01/world/europe/germany-migrants-merkel.html.
"Anna, geh du voran: Anna Satolias–die Geschichte einer griechischen

Gastarbeiterin, die die Sprecherin der Frauen in einem deutschen Betrieb wurde." *Jasmin* 20 (1973).

"Auch im Bergbau" *Butzbacher Zeitung*, 8 September 1969.

Augsberger Allgemeine Zeitung, 22 August 1973.

Becke, Klaus, Heiner Halberstadt, Walter Hanesche, Adalbert Hepp, Otto Jacobi, Reiner Kessler, HG Lang, Heide Langguth, Willi Michel, Walther Müller-Jentsch, Eberhard Schmidt, Klaus Vack, and Edgar Weick, who comprise the Redaktionskollektiv "express." *Spontane Streiks 1973: Krise Der Gewerkschaftspolitik*. Offenbach: Verlag 2000, 1974.

Broder, Henryk M. "Integrationsdebatte: Die Parallelgesellschaft, sie lebe hoch!" *Spiegel Online*, 21 October 2010. Accessed 25 February 2016. http://www.spiegel.de/kultur/gesellschaft/integrationsdebatte-die -parallelgesellschaft-sie-lebe-hoch-a-723895.html.

"Cologne Sex Attacks: Women Describe 'Terrible' Assaults'." *BBC News*, 7 January 2016. Accessed 5 February 2016. http://www.bbc.com/news/world-europe-35502223.

"Cologne Carnival: Police Record 22 Sexual Assaults," *BBC News*, 5 February 2016. Accessed 4 March 2016. http://www.bbc.com/news/world-europe -35502223

"The CDU and the 'Social Market Economy': Düsseldorf Guidelines for Economy Policy, Agricultural Policy, Social Policy, and Housing." Translated by Adam Blauhut, German History in Documents and Images, taken from Düsseldorfer Leitsätze über Wirtschaftspolitik, Landwirtschaftspolitik, Sozialpolitik, Wohnungsbau [Düsseldorf Guidelines for Economic Policy, Agricultural Policy, Social Policy, and Housing]. 15 July 1949; reprinted in Ossip Kurt Flechtheim, Die Parteien der Bundesrepublik Deutschland [The Parties of the Federal Republic of Germany] Hamburg, 1973, 162–3. Accessed 1 March 2016. http://germanhistorydocs.ghi-dc.org/pdf/eng/ Parties%20WZ%206_Eng.pdf.

Der Spiegel. 3 September 1973.

Deutsche Volkszeitung. 29 May 1970.

"Die Türken probten den Aufstand." *Die Zeit*, 7 September 1973.

"Dossiers: Die Chronik der neuen Frauenbewegung: 1973." Frauen Media Turm, Das Archiv und Dokumentationszentrum. Accessed 3 February 2013. http://www.frauenmediaturm.de/themen-portraets/chronik-der-neuen -frauenbewegung/1973/.

"Eine große Lohnwelle kündigt sich an: Die Stahlarbeiter fordern 14 Prozent mehr." *Frankfurter Allgemeine*, 8 September 1969.

"Erdoğan Urges Turks Not to Assimilate: 'You Are Part of Germany, but Also Part of Our Great Turkey." *Spiegel Online International*, 28 February 2011.

Accessed 20 February 2015. http://www.spiegel.de/international/europe/
    erdogan-urges-turks-not-to-assimilate-you-are-part-of-germany-but-also
    -part-of-our-great-turkey-a-748070.html.
"Erste Sendung der ARD für, Gastarbeiter' startet." 21 October 2011. Accessed
    2 March 2016. http://www1.wdr.de/stichtag6058.html.
"Frauen im Beruf: Arbeiten und kuschen." *Stern*, no. 44, 25 October 1973.
"Germany Approves First-Ever National Minimum Wage." *BBC News*, 3 July
    2014. Accessed 1 March 2016. http://www.bbc.com/news/business-28140594.
"Germany Protests: Dresden Marches against Anti-Islamists Pegida." *BBC
    News*, 10 January 2015. Accessed 27 February 2015. http://www.bbc.com/
    news/world-europe-30765674.
Grieshaber, Kirsten. "6 Syrian Refugees Injured in Attacks across Germany,"
    Associated Press, 1 November 2015. Accessed 4 March 2016. http://bigstory
    .ap.org/article/c33a0f30f8c54dc19ddd0e358694a67a/6-syrian-refugees
    -injured-attacks-across-germany.
Harding, Luke. "Hungarian Police Arrest Driver of Lorry That Had 71 Dead
    Migrants Inside," *The Guardian*, 28 August 2015. Accessed 4 March 2016.
    http://www.theguardian.com/world/2015/aug/28/more-than-70-dead
    -austria-migrant-truck-tragedy.
Hildebrandt, Eckart and Werner Olle, eds. *Ihr Kampf ist unser Kampf: Ursachen,
    Verlauf und Perspektiven der Ausländerstreiks 1973 in der BRD* (Teil I). Offenbach:
    Sozialistisches Büro, Verlag 2000 GMBH, 1975.
Hills, Denis. *My Travels in Turkey.* London: George Allen & Unwin, 1964.
"IG Metall: Gastarbeiter nicht Diskriminiert: Der Streik bei Pierburg in Neuss
    ist illegal." *Handelsblatt*, 17–18 August 1983.
"The International Press on Turkey's European Union Membership Bid,
    Comment and Analysis from London, Dubai, Beirut, Frankfurt, and Istanbul."
    World Press, 8 October 2004. Accessed 3 March 2016. http://www.worldpress
    .org/Europe/1951.cfm.
"Keine Ruhe nach dem Streik: Wieder kurze Arbeitsniederlegung, wieder
    Polizei vor dem Werkstor." *Kölner Stadtanzeiger*, 22 August 1973.
Krell, Gertraude. "Gesellschaftliche Arbeitsteilung und Frauenlöhne."
    In *Frauen als bezahlte und unbezahlte Arbeitskräften: Beitrage zur Berliner
    Sommeruniversität für Frauen*. Berlin: Self Published, 1978. Archiv der
    deutschen Frauenbewegung, Kassel, Germany.
Kolars, John. *Tradition, Season, and Change in a Turkish Village.* NAS-NRC
    Foreign Field Research Program Report no. 15. Chicago: University of
    Chicago Press, 1963.
"Köln Radyosu Türkçe Yayınlar Servisine protesto mektubu" ["Protest Letter
    to Cologne Radio Turkish Broadcast Services"]. *Hicret*, 15 February 1982, 13.

"Jetzt Streiks um Bergbau: Neue Lohnforderungen im Rheinland." *Hannoversche Rundschau*, 9 September 1969.

"Lohnverhandlung am Donnerstag." *Solinger Tageblatt*, 8 September 1968.

Lyman, Rick and Alison Smale. "Paris Attacks Shift Europe's Migrant Focus to Security." *New York Times*, 15 November 2016. Accessed 4 March 2016. http://www.nytimes.com/2015/11/16/world/europe/paris-attacks-shift -europes-migrant-focus-to-security.html?_r=0.

Maturi, Giacomo. *Arbeitsplatz Deutschland: Wie Man Südlandische Gastarbeiter verstehen lernt*. [Workplace Germany: How one learns to understand Guest Workers from Mediterranean Regions]. Mainz: Krausskopf Verlag, 1964.

– "Die zweite Phase der Ausländerbeschäftigung in der Bundesrepublik" (Heidelberg: Heidelberger Verlagsanstalt und Druckerei GmbH, undated) DOMiD Archive 424 SD.

Maturi, Giacomo, Willi Baumgartner, Stefan Bobolis, Konstantin Kustas, Vittorio Bedolli, Guillermo Arrillage, and Sümer Göksuyer, eds. Illustrations by Richard Haschberger. *Hallo Mustafa! Günther Türk arkadaşı ile konuşuyor* [Hello Mustafa! Günther speaks with his Turkish friend]. Heidelberg: Dr Curt Haefner Verlag, 1966.

"Merkel Says German Multicultural Society Has Failed." *BBC News*, 17 October 2010. Accessed 5 March 2016. http://www.bbc.com/news/ world-europe-11559451.

"Merkel Says Germany Must Learn from Its 'Guest Worker' Mistakes from Refugee Crisis." *Reuters*, 9 September 2015. Accessed 3 March 2016. http://www.reuters.com/article/us-europe-migrants-germany-merkel -idUSKCN0R90S520150909.

Noack, Rick. "Why Germany's Merkel Will Continue to Welcome Refugees, despite Calling Multiculturalism a Sham." *The Washington Post*, 16 December 2015. Accessed 4 March 2016. https://www.washingtonpost .com/news/worldviews/wp/2015/12/16/why-germanys-merkel-will -continue-to-welcome-refugees-despite-calling-multiculturalism-a-sham/.

Organisation for Economic Co-Operation and Development, *Turkey 1965–66*, Economic Surveys by the OECD, Economic Development Review Committee, 1966.

Parkinson, Joe. and David George-Cosh. "Image of Drowned Syrian Boy Echoes around World." *The Wall Street Journal*, 3 September 2015. Accessed 4 March 2016. http://www.wsj.com/articles/image-of-syrian-boy-washed -up-on-beach-hits-hard-1441282847.

"Police under Fire in German Unrest." *The New York Times*, 27 December 1992. Accessed 20 February 2015. http://www.nytimes.com/1992/12/27/world/ police-under-fire-in-german-unrest.html.

"Pegida: What Does the German Far-Right Movement Actually Stand For?" *The Guardian*, 6 January 2015. Accessed 27 February 2015. http://www .theguardian.com/world/shortcuts/2015/jan/06/pegida-what-does -german-far-right-movement-actually-stand-for.

"Prime Minister and Chancellor Merkel Statement on Paris Terrorist Attack," Prime Minister's Office, 7 January 2015. Accessed 27 February 2015. https://www.gov.uk/government/news/prime-minister-and-chancellor -merkel-statement-on-paris-terrorist-attack.

"Rebellion am Fließband: Erfahrungen aus Frauenstreiks," Barbara Schleich, WDR II 13 December 1973, 15 min.

"The Refugee Crisis: What It Means for Europe." *New York Times*, 7 October 2015. Accessed 4 March 2016. http://www.nytimes.com/2015/10/08/ world/europe/refugee-migrant-crisis-asylum-seekers-germany.html.

Reihe Betrieb und Gewerkschaften: Redaktionskollektiv 'express,' eds., *Spontane Streiks 1973 Krise der Gewerkschaftspolitik.* Verlag 2000 GmbH, January 1974.

Rohmert, Walter, and Josef Rutenfranz. *Arbeitswissenschaftliche Beurteilung der Belastung und Beanspruchung an unterschiedlichen industriellen Arbeitsplätzen.* Berlin: Federal Ministry for Labor and Social Order, 1 July 1975.

Schleich, Barbara. "Streik am laufenden Band: In der Vergaserfirma Pierburg streikten vor allem ausländische Arbeiterinnen." *Vorwärts*, 25 August 1973.

Schuster, Hans. "Wilde Streiks als Warnsignal." *Süddeutsche Zeitung*, 13 September 1969.

Solinger Tagebatt, 17 March 1962.

"Streikbewegung greift auf den Bergbau über: Tarifgespräche schon in dieser Woche." *General-Anzeiger für Bonn und Umgebungen*, 8 September 1969.

"The ticking time bomb of Syrian refugees," 10 May 2015. Accessed 17 Jan 2016. http://www.aljazeera.com/indepth/opinion/2015/05/ticking-time -bomb-syrian-refugees-150509062906684.html

Throm, Wilhem. "Wilde Streiks treffen die Gewerkschaften." *Frankfurter Allgemeine Zeitung*, 8 September 1969.

"Unternehmensleitung in Neuss glaubt an politische Motive: 'Streik war von außen gesteuert'." *Frankfurter Rundschau*, 22 August 1973.

"Wilde Streikwelle nun auch im Saar-Bergbau: Tarifpartner bemühen sich um schnelle Entspannung." *Ludwigsburger Kreiszeitung*, 9 September 1969.

Motion Pictures

Almanya, Willkommen in Deutschland. Directed by Yasemin Şamdereli. Roxy: Infa, Concord, 2011. DVD.

Angst essen Seele auf. Directed by Rainer Werner Fassbinder. Tango-Film, Munich, 1974.
Die Fremde. Directed by Feo Aladağ. ARTE, Independent Artists Filmproduktion, RBB, WDR, 2010.
Shirins Hochzeit. Directed by Helma Sanders-Brahms. Cologne, West Germany: Westdeutscher Rundfunk, Arbeitsgemeinschaft Kino, 1975. 35mm.
Pierburg: Ihr Kampf ist unser Kampf. Directed by Edith Schmidt and David Wittenberg. Western Germany, 1974/75. Motion picture, 49 min.

Author Interviews

Interview with "Elif." Berlin, Germany, May 2003.
Interview with "Murat." Istanbul, August 2004.

Secondary Literature

Abadan, Nermin. *Batı Almanya'daki Türk İşçiler ve Sorunları.* Ankara: T.C. Başbakanlık Devlet Plânlama Teşkilâtı, 1964.
Abadan-Unat, Nermin. *Turkish Workers in Europe, 1960–1975: A Socio-Economic Reappraisal.* Leiden: E. J Brill, 1975.
– "Dış Göç Akımının Türk Kadınının Özgürleşme ve Sözde Özgürleşme Sürecine Etkisi." [The Effects of Immigration on Turkish Women and the Emancipation Process.] *Amme İdaresi Dergisi. [Journal of Public Administration]* 10, no.1 (1977): 107–32.
– "Turkey: Late Entrant into Europe's Work Force." In *The Politics of Migration Polices: Settlement and Integration, the First World into the 1990s,* edited by Daniel Kubat, 307–36. New York: Center for Migration Studies, 1993.
– *Turks in Europe: From Guest Worker to Transnational Citizen.* New York: Berghahn Books, 2011.
– and Neşe Kemiksiz, eds. *Türkische Migration 1960–1984: Annotierte Bibliographie.* Zentrum für Türkeistudien. Translated by Kirkor Osyan and Claudia Schöning-Kalender. Frankfurt am Main: Dağyeli Verlag, 1992.
Abelshauser, Werner. *Deutsche Wirtschaftsgeschichte seit 1945.* Munich: Beck, 2004.
– "The First Post-Liberal Nation: Stages in Development of Modern Corporatism in Germany." *European History Quarterly* 14 (1984): 285–317.
Abrams, Lynn. *Worker's Culture in Imperial Germany: Leisure and Recreation in the Rhineland and Westphalia.* New York: Routledge, 1992.
Adelson, Leslie. *The Turkish Turn in Contemporary German Literature: Toward a New Critical Grammar of Migration.* New York: Palgrave Macmillan, 2005.

Aker, Ahmet. *A Study of Turkish Labour Migration to Germany*. Institute of Foreign Policy Research: The Johns Hopkins University Bologna Center School of Advanced International Studies, 1974.

Akgündüz, Ahmet. "Guest Worker Migration in Post-war Europe (1946–1974): An Analytical Appraisal." In *An Introduction to International Migration Studies*, edited by Marco Martiniello and Jan Rath, 181–210. Chicago: University of Chicago Press, 2012.

– *Labour Migration from Turkey to Western Europe, 1960–1974*. Burlington: Ashgate, 2008.

Alisch, Steffen. "Berlin–Berlin: Die Verhandlungen zwischen Beauftragten des Berliner Senats und Vertretern der DDR-Regierung zu Reise- und humanitären Fragen: 1961-1972." FU Berlin: Arbeitspapiere des Forschungsverbundes SED-Staat 3 (2000): 34.

Amiraux, Valerie. "Restructuring Political Islam: Transnational Belonging and Muslims in France and Germany." In *Transnational Political Islam: Religion, Ideology, and Power*, edited by Azza Kara, 28–57. Sterling, VA: Pluto, 2004.

Anzaldua, Gloria. *Borderlands/ La Frontera: The New Mestiza*. San Francisco: Aunt Lute Books, 1987.

Artz, Helmut. *Almanya'yı Tanımak istermisiniz?* [Would you like to get to know Germany?] Wiesbaden: Wiesbadener Graphischer Betriebe, 1965.

Aslantepe, G. *Federal Almanya'da Yaşayan Türk Kadınlarının Soruları, Birinci Nesil-İkinci Nesil* [Concerns of First and Second Generation Turkish Women Living in the Federal Republic of Germany]. Düsseldorf: Düsseldorf Çalışma Ataşeliği [Dusseldorf Labor Attache], March 1982.

Atabaki, Touraj, and Gavin D. Brockett. "Introduction." In "Ottoman and Republican Turkish Labor History," edited by Touraj Atabaki and Gavin D. Brockett, supplement, *International Review of Social History (IRSH)*. Internationaal Instituut voor Sociale Geschiedenis [International Institute for Social History] 54, no. S17 (2009): 1–17.

Bade, Klaus J., *Auswanderer, Wanderarbeiter, Gastarbeiter: Bevölkerung, Arbeitsmarkt und Wanderung in Deutschland seit der Mitte des 19. Jahrhunderts*. 2 vols. Referate und Diskussionsbeiträge des Internationalen Wissenschaftlichen Symposiums "Vom Auswanderungsland zum Einwanderungsland?" an der Akademie für Politische Bildung Tutzing 1982. Ostfilder: Scripta Mercaturae, 1984.

– *Das Manifest der 60: Deutschland und die Einwanderung*. Munich: C.H. Beck Verlag, 1984.

– *Population, Labour, and Migration in Nineteenth- and Twentieth-Century Germany*. New York: Berg, 1987.

– *Ausländer, Aussiedler, Asyl in der Bundesrepublik Deutschland.* Bonn:
Bundeszentrale für politische Bildung, 1992.
– *Deutsche im Ausland – Fremde in Deutschland: Migration in Geschichte und
Gegenwart.* München: Beck, 1993.
– *Migration Past, Migration Future: Germany and the United States.* New York:
Berghahn Books, 1997.
– *Migration in European History.* Translated by Allison Brown. Malden, MA:
Blackwell, 2003.
Bade, Klaus J., and Jochen Oltmer, eds. *Normalfall Migration: Texte zur
Einwandererbevölkerung und neue Zuwanderung im vereinigten Deutschland seit
1990.* Bonn: Bundeszentrale für politische Bildung, 2004.
– *Zuwanderung und Integration in Niedersachsen Zeit dem Zweiten Weltkrieg.*
Osnabrück: Universitätsverlag Rasch, 2002.
Baumgartner-Karabak, Andrea, and Gisela Landesberger. *Die verkauften
Bräute: Türkische Frauen zwischen Kreuzberg und Anatolien.* Reinbek bei
Hamburg: Rowohlt Taschenbuch, 1978.
Berger, John, and Jenn Mohr. *A Seventh Man: Migrant Workers in Europe.* New
York: Verso, 1975.
Berghahn, Volker, and Paul J. Friedrich. *Otto A. Friedrich, Ein politischer
Unternehmer: Sein Leben und seine Zeit, 1902–1975.* Frankfurt: Campus, 1993.
Bloemraad, Irene. "Who Claims Dual Citizenship? The Limits of
Postnationalism, the Possibilities of Transnationalism, and the Persistence of
Traditional Citizenship" *International Migration Review* 38 (2004): 389–426.
Bloemraad, Irene, Anna Korteweg, and Gökçe Yurdakul. "Citizenship and
Immigration: Multiculturalism, Assimilation, and Challenges to the Nation-
State." *Annual Review of Sociology* 34 (2008): 153–179.
Boehling, Rebecca. "Gender Roles in Ruins: German Women and Local
Politics under American Occupation, 1945–1955." In *Gender and the Long
Postwar: The United States and the Two Germanys, 1945–1989*, edited by Karen
Hagemann and Sonya Michel, 51–72. Baltimore: John Hopkins University
Press, 2014.
Bojadzijev, Manuela. *Die windige Internationale: Rassismus und Kämpfe der
Migration.* Munster: Westfälsches Dampfboot, 2008.
Bren, Paula, and Mary Neuburger, eds. *Communism Unwrapped: Consumption
in Cold War Eastern Europe.* Oxford: Oxford University Press, 2012.
Brody, David. *In Labor's Cause: Main Themes on the History of the American
Worker.* New York: Oxford University Press, 1993.
Browne, Irene, and Joya Misra. "The Intersection of Gender and Race in the
Labor Market." *Annual Review of Sociology* 29 (August 2003): 487–513.
Bruce, Gary. "Access to Secret Police Files, Justice, and Vetting in East

Germany since 1989." *German Politics and Society* 26, no.1 (Spring 2008): 82–111.

- "Participatory Repression? Reflections on Popular Involvement with the *Stasi*." In "The Stasi at Home and Abroad: Domestic Order and Foreign Intelligence," edited by Uwe Spiekermann, supplement, *Bulletin of the German Historical Institute* S9 (2014): 47–58.

- "The Old Labor History and the New: In Search of the American Working Class." *Labor History* 20 (1979): 111–26.

Bucerius, Sandra M. *Unwanted: Muslim Immigrants, Dignity, and Drug Dealing.* Oxford: Oxford University Press, 2014.

Buchholz-Will, Wiebke. "Wann wird aus diesem Traum Wirklichkeit? Die gewerkschaftliche Frauenarbeit in der Bundesrepublik Deutschland." In *Geschichte Der Deutschen Frauen Bewegung*, edited by Florence Herve, 185–208. Cologne: PapyRossa Verlag, 1995.

Buruma, Ian. *Murder in Amsterdam: Liberal Europe, Islam, and the Limits of Tolerance.* New York: Penguin Press, 2006.

Campt, Tina, and Michelle Maria Wright, eds. "Reading the Black German Experience." Special issue, *Callaloo* 26 (2003).

Carson, Richard L. *Comparative Economic Systems, Part III Capitalist Alternatives.* New York: M.E. Sharpe, 1990.

Castles, Stephen, and Mark Miller. *The Age of Migration: International Population Movements in the Modern World.* 3rd ed. New York: Guilford Press, 2003.

Castles, Stephen, and Godula Kosack. *Immigrant Workers and Class Structure in Western Europe.* London: Oxford University Press, 1973.

Ceylan, Rauf. *Die Turkensiedlung.* Leipzig: Engelsdorfer, 2015.

Chin, Rita. *The Guest Worker Question in Postwar Germany.* New York: Cambridge University Press, 2007.

- "The Politics of Sexual Democracy in the New Europe." Paper presented at the "Mobilizing Difference: Gender, Islam and the Production of Contemporary Europeanness" Conference, The University of Illinois at Urbana-Champaign. September 2013.

Chin, Rita, Heide Fehrenbach, Geoff Eley, and Atina Grossmann, eds. *After the Nazi Racial State: Difference and Democracy in Germany and Europe.* Ann Arbor: University of Michigan Press, 2009.

Clarkson, Alexander. *Fragmented Fatherland: Immigration and Cold War Conflict in the Federal Republic of Germany 1945–1980.* New York: Berghahn, 2013.

Cluver, Cathryn. "French Immigration Policy: History Repeated?" Foreign Policy Association Network, Foreign Policy Blog. 11 April 2007. Accessed 9 January 2015. www.google.com/url?sa=t&rct=j&q=&esrc=s&source=web&cd=4&ved=0CDoQFjAD&url=http%3A%2F%2Fforeignpolicyblogs

.com%2F2007%2F04%2F11%2Ffrench-immigration-policy-history-repeated%
2F&ei=dFKTVO7_La61sQT69oLgBA&usg=AFQjCNEjBY-Jp2hUObPVa7vTjK9f
-7kHbg&bvm=bv.82001339,d.cWc.

Collins, Patricia Hill. *Black Feminist Thought: Knowledge, Consciousness and the Politics of Empowerment*. New York: Routledge, 2000.

Cowie, Jefferson. *Capital Moves: RCA"s Seventy-Year Quest for Cheap Labor*. Ithaca: Cornell University Press, 1999.

Crenshaw, Kimberle. "Mapping the Margins: Intersectionality, Identity Politics, and Violence against Women of Color." *Stanford Law Review* 43, no. 6 (July 1991): 1241–99.

Crew, David F. *Town in the Ruhr: A Social History of Bochum*. New York: Columbia University Press, 1986.

"Decolonization and Immigration in Britain and France." In *Europe since 1945: A Concise History*, edited by J. Robert Wegs and Robert Ladrech, 98–9. New York: Palgrave MacMillan, 1996, 2006.

Delius, Friedrich Christian, and Peter Jochim Lapp. *Transit Westberlin: Erlebnisse im Zwischenraum*. Berlin: Ch. Links Verlag, 1999.

Dennis, Mike, and Norman LaPorte. *State and Minorities in Communist East Germany*. New York: Berghahn, 2011.

Diefendorf, Jeffry M. *In the Wake of the War: The Reconstruction of German Cities after World War II*. New York: Oxford University Press, 1993.

Dieper, Susanne. "The Legal Framework of Abortions in Germany." American Institute for Contemporary German Studies, Johns Hopkins University. 23 February 2012. Accessed 4 March 2016. http://www.aicgs.org/issue/the-legal-framework-of-abortions-in-germany/.

Diricks, Yvo., and Ayşe Kudat. Instability of Migrant Workers' Housing. Berlin: International Institute for Comparative Social Studies of the Science Centre Berlin, 1975.

Doomernik, Jeroen. "The Institutionalization of Turkish Islam in Germany and the Netherlands: A Comparison." *Ethnic and Racial Studies* 18 (1995): 46–63.

Eckert, Astrid M. "Zaun-Gäste: Die innerdeutsche Grenze als Touristenattraktion." In *Grenzziehungen, Grenzerfahrungen, Grenzüberschreitungen: Die Innerdeutsche Grenze, 1945–1990*. Catalog of the Exhibition of the Hannover Historical Museum, edited by Thomas Schwark, Detlef Schmeichen-Ackermann, and Carl-Hans Hauptmeyer, 243–51. Darmstadt: Wissenschaftliche Buchgesellschaft, 2001.

Engelmann, Roger, Bernd Florath, and Walter Süß, eds., *Das MfS-Lexikon— Begriffe, Personen und Strukturen der Staatssicherheit der DDR*. Berlin: Links, 2011.

Eren, Nuri. *Turkey Today and Tomorrow: An Experiment in Westernization*. New York: Frederick Praeger, 1963.

Eryılmaz, Aytaç, and Mathilde Jamin, eds. *Fremde Heimat: Eine Geschichte der Einwanderung aus der Türkei / Yaban, Sılan olur: Türiye'den Almanya'ya Göçün Tarihi*. Cologne: Klartext, 1998.

Eryılmaz, Aytaç. "Das Leben im Wohnheim." In *Fremde Heimat: Eine Geschichte der Einwanderung aus der Türkei / Yaban, Sılan olur: Türiye'den Almanya'ya Göçün Tarihi*, edited by Aytaç Eryılmaz and Mathilde Jamin, 171–91. Cologne: Klartext, 1998.

Essad, Philomena. *Everyday Racism: Reports from Women in Two Cultures*. Claremont, CA: Hunter House, 1990.

– *Diversity: Gender, Color, and Culture*. Amherst: University of Massachusetts Press, 1996.

Evans, Jennifer V. "*Bahnhof* Boys: Policing Male Prostitution in Post-Nazi Berlin." *Journal of the History of Sexuality* 12, no. 4 (2003): 605–36.

– "The Moral State: Men, Mining, and Masculinity in the Early GDR." *German History* 23, no. 3 (2005): 355–70.

– "Decriminalization, Seduction, and 'Unnatural Desire' in East Germany." *Feminist Studies* 36, no. 3 (2010): 553–77.

Fachinger, Petra. "Yadé Kara's *Selam Berlin*." In *The Novel in German since 1990*, edited by Stuart Taberner, 241–54. Cambridge: Cambridge University Press, 2011.

Fehrenbach, Heide. *Race after Hitler: Black Occupation Children in Postwar Germany and America*. Princeton: Princeton University Press, 2005.

Field, Deborah A. *Private Life and Communist Morality in Khrushchev's Russia*. New York: Peter Lang, 2007.

Franger, Gaby. *Wir Haben Es Uns Anders Vorgestellt: Türkische Frauen in der Bundesrepublik*. Frankfurt am Main: Fischer, 1984.

Frevert, Ute. *Women in German History: From Bourgeois Emancipation to Sexual Liberation*. Translated by Stuart McKinnon-Even, Terry Bond, and Barbara Norden. New York: Berg, 1989.

Fulbrook, Mary. *The People's State: East German Society from Honecker to Hitler*. New Haven, CT: Yale University Press, 2005.

Füruzan. *Frau ohne Schleier: Türkische Erzählungen*. Vienna: Europa Verlag, 1976.

Gieseke, Jens. *Mielke-Konzern: Die Geschichte der Stasi*. Stuttgart: Deutsche Verlages-Anstalt, 2001.

– "German Democratic Republic." In *A Handbook of the Communist Security Apparatus in East Central Europe, 1944–1989*, edited by Krysztof Persak and Lukasz Kaminski, 198–202. Warsaw: Institute of National Remembrance, 2005.

– *The GDR State Security: Shield and Sword of the Party*. Translated by Mary Carlene Forszt. Berlin: The Federal Commissioner for the Records of the State Security Service of the former German Democratic Republic, 2006.

Gigliotti, Simone. *The Train Journey*. New York: Berghahn Books, 2009.

Gitmez, Ali. *Göçmen İşçilerin Dönüşü [Immigrant Workers Return]: Return Migration of Turkish Workers to Three Selected Regions*. Ankara: Orta Doğu Teknik Üniversitesi [Middle East Technical University], 1977.

– *Dışgöç Öyküsü: araştırma-deneme* [Immigration Story: A Research Report]. Ankara: Maya Matbaacılık, 1979.

Glebe, Günter. "Housing and segregation of Turks in Germany." In *Turks in European Cities: Housing and Urban Segregation*, edited by Sule Öüekren and Ronald van Kempern, 122–57. Utrecht: Ercomer, 1997.

Göçek, Fatma Müge. "Why is there Still a 'Sèvres Syndrome'? An Analysis of Turkey's Uneasy Association with the West." In *The Transformation of Turkey: Redefining State and Society from the Ottoman Empire to the Modern Era*, 98–184. New York: I.B. Tauris, 2011.

Godula, Kosack. "Migrant Women: The Move to Western Europe – a Step towards Emancipation?" *Race and Class* 70, no. 4 (1976): 374–5.

Goedde, Petra. "From Villains to Victims: Fraternization and the Feminization of Germany, 1945–1947." *Diplomatic History* 23 (1999): 1–20.

– *GIs and Germans: Culture, Gender and Foreign Relations, 1945–1949*. New Haven: Yale University Press, 2003.

Gokay, Bulent. *Soviet Eastern Policy and Turkey, 1920–1991: Soviet Foreign Policy, Turkey and Communism*. New York: Routledge, 2006.

Göktürk, Deniz. "Mobilität and Stillstand im Weltkino digital." In *Kultur als Ereignis: Fatih Akın's Film* Auf der Anderen Seite *als transkulturelle Narration*, edited by Özkan Ezli, 15–45. Bielefeld: Transcript Press, 2010.

Göktürk, Deniz, David Gramling, and Anton Keas, eds. *Germany in Transit: Nation and Migration, 1955–2005*. Berkeley: University of California Press, 2007.

Goldberg, Andreas. "Status and Problems of the Turkish Community in Germany." Essen: Zentrum für Türkeistudien und Integrationsforschung, 1996.

Goldberg, Andreas, and Faruk Sen. *Türken als Unternehmer: Eine Gesamtdarstellung und Ergebnisse neuere Untersuchungen*. Opladen: Leske and Budrich, 1996.

Gramling, David. "On the Other Side of Monolingualism: Fatih Akın's Linguistic Turn." *The German Quarterly* 83 (2010): 353–72.

Grossmann, Atina. *Jews, Germans, and Allies: Close Encounters in Occupied Germany*. Princeton: Princeton University Press, 2007.

Gueneli, Berna. "Challenging European Borders: Fatih Akın's Filmic Visions of Europe" (PhD diss., University of Texas at Austin, 2011).

Gürel, Seval, and Ayşe Kudat. "Türk Kadınının Avrupa'ya Göçünün Kişilik, Aile eve Topluma Yansıyan Sonuçları." [Study of Turkish migrant women to Germany in Terms of Self-hood, Family and Community.] *Ankara Üniversitesi Siyasal Bilgiler Fakültesi Dergisi* [Ankara University Faculty of Political Science Journal] 33 no. 93/4 (September–December 1978): 109–34.

Hagemann Karen, and Sonya Michel, eds. *Gender and the Long Postwar: The United States and the Two Germanys, 1945–1989*. Baltimore: Johns Hopkins University Press, 2014.

Harsh, Donna. "Women, Family, and 'Postwar': The Gendering of the GDR's Welfare Dictatorship." In *Gender and the Long Postwar*, edited by Karen Hagemann and Sonya Michel, 253–73. Baltimore: John Hopkins University Press: 2014.

Hecking, Claus. "Secret Thatcher Notes: Kohl Wanted Half of Turks Out of Germany." *Spiegel Online International*. 1 August 2013. Accessed 17 December 2014. http://www.spiegel.de/international/germany/secret-minutes-chancellor-kohl-wanted-half-of-turks-out-of-germany-a-914376.html.

Heineman, Elizabeth. "The Hour of the Woman: Memories of Germany's 'Crisis Years' and West German National Identity." *American Historical Review* 101 (1996): 354–95.

Helicke, James. "Turks in Germany: Muslim Identity: 'Between' States." In *Muslim Minorities in the West: Visible and Invisible*, edited by Yvonne Yazbeck Haddad and Jane I. Smith, 175–92. New York: Altamira, 2002.

– *What Difference Does a Husband Make? Women and Marital Status in Nazi and Postwar Germany*. Berkeley: California University Press, 1999.

Henrich, Wolfgang, ed. *Wehrdienstgesetz und Grenzgesetz der DDR: Dokumentation und Analyse*. Bonn: Urheber, 1983.

Herbert, Ulrich, and Karin Hunn, "Guest Workers and Policy on Guest Workers in the Federal Republic: From the Beginning of Recruitment in 1955 until its Halt in 1973." In *The Miracles Years: A Cultural History of West Germany, 1949–1968*, edited by Hanna Schissler, 187–218. Princeton: Princeton University Press, 2001.

Hertle, Hans-Hermann. *The Berlin Wall Story: Biography of a Monument*. Berlin: Ch. Links Verlag, 2011.

Hildebrandt, Eckart, and Werner Olle. *Ihr Kampf ist unser Kampf. Ursachen, Verlauf und Perspektiven der Ausländerstreiks 1973 in der BRD*. Teil I, Offenbach, 1975.

Höhn, Maria. "Frau im Haus, Girl im Spiegel: Discourse on Women in the Interregnum Period of 1945–1949 and the Question of German Identity." *Central European History* 26 (1993): 57–90.

– *GIs and Fräuleins: German-American Encounter in 1950s West Germany*. Chapel Hill: University of North Carolina Press, 2002.

Huth-Hildebrant, Christine, and Jürgen Micksch, *Ausländische Frauen: Interviews, Analysen und Anregungen für die Praxis*. Frankfurt am Main: Otto Lembeck Verlag, 1982.

Herbert, Ulrich. *A History of Foreign Labor in Germany: Seasonal Workers, Forced Laborers, Guest Workers*. Translated by William Templer. Ann Arbor: Michigan University Press, 1993.

Hoerder, Dirk. *Cultures in Contact: World Migrations in the Second Millennium*. Durham: Duke University Press, 2002.

Hollifield, James, Phillip Martin, and Pia Orrenius. *Controlling Immigration: A Global Perspective*. 3rd ed. Stanford: Stanford University Press, 2014.

Huinink, Johannes. "Individuum und Gesellschaft in der DDR – Theoretische Ausgangspunkte einer Rekonstruktion der DDR-Gesellschaft in den Lebensläufen ihrer Bürgers." In *Kollektiv und Eigensinn: Lebensläufe in der DDR und Danach*, edited by Johannes Huinink, Karl Ulrich Meyer, Martin Diewald, and Heike Solga, 25–44. Berlin: Akademie Verlag, 1995.

Hunn, Karin. *Nächstes Jahr kehren wir zurück ...' Die Geschichte der türkischen ‚Gastarbeiter' in der Bundesrepublik*. Gottingen: Wallstein, 2005.

Jamin, Mathilde. "Die deutsch-türkischen Anwerbevereinbarung von 1961 und 1964." In *Fremde Heimat, Eine Geschichte der Einwanderung aus der Türkei/ Yaban, Sılan olur. Türkiye'den Almanya'ya Göçün Tarihi*, edited by idem and Aytaç Eryılmaz, 69–82. Essen: Klartext, 1998.

– "Fremde Heimat: Zur Geschichte der Arbeitsmigration aus der Türkei." In *50 Jahre Bundesrepublik 50 Jahre Einwanderung: Nachkriegsgeschichte als Migrationsgeschichte*, edited by Jan Motte, Rainer Ohliger, and Anne von Oswald, 145–64. Frankfurt: Campus, 1999.

Jarausch, Konrad H., and Michael Geyer. *Shattered Past: Reconstructing German Histories*. Princeton: Princeton University Press, 2003.

Judt, Tony. *Postwar: A History of Europe since 1945*. London and New York: Penguin, 2005.

Kara, Yade. *Selam Berlin*. Zürich: Diogenes, 2003.

Karakayli, Serhat. *Gespenster der Migration: Zur Genealogie illegaler Einwanderung in der Bundesrepublik Deutschland*. Bielefeld: Transcript, 2008.

Karakayali, Serhat, and Enrica Rigo. "Mapping the European Space of Circulation." In *The Deportation Regime: Sovereignty, Space, and the Freedom of Movement*, edited by Nicholas de Genova and Nathalie Peutz, 123–46. Durham: Duke University Press, 2010.

Kern, Steven. *The Culture of Time and Space, 1880–1918*. Cambridge: Harvard University Press, 1986.

Keser, Ulvi. "Bloody Christmas of 1963 in Cyprus in the Light of American Documents." *Journal of Modern Turkish History Studies* 13 (2013): 249–71.

Kleff, Hans-Günter. "Täuschung, Selbsttäuschung, Enttäuschung und Lernen: Anmerkungen zum Fordstreik im Jahre 1973." In *Geschichte und Gedächtnis in der Einwanderungsgesellschaft: Migration zwischen historischer Rekonstruktion und Erinnerungspolitik*, edited by Jan Motte and Rainer Ohliger, 251–9. Essen: Klartext, 2004.

Kleßmann, Christoph. "Zjednoczenie Zawodowe Polskie (ZZP-Polnische Berufsvereinigung) und Alter Verband im Ruhrgebiet." *Internationale Wissenschaftliche Korrespondenz zur Geschichte der deutschen Arbeiterbewegung* 15 (1979): 68–71.

Kocka, Jürgen. "Wo liegst du, Europe." *Die Zeit*. 28 November 2002. Accessed 6 December 2016. http://www.zeit.de/2002/49/Wo_liegst_du_Europa_.

Koopmans, Ruud, and Paul Statham. "Challenging the Liberal Nation-State? Postnationalism, Multiculturalism, and the Collective Claims Making of Migrants and Ethnic Minorities in Britain and Germany." *American Journal of Sociology* 105 (1999): 652–96.

Kudat, Ayşe, and Ali Gitmez. *Emigration Effects on the Turkish Countryside: A Representative Study of Settlement Units*. Berlin: International Institute for Comparative Social Studies of the Science Center Berlin, May 1975.

Kuhlmann, Michael, and Alwin Meyer. *Ayşe und Devrim: Wo gehören wir hin?* Göttingen: Lamu Taschenbuch, 1983.

Kulczycki, John J. *The Foreign Worker and the German Labor Movement: Xenophobia and Solidarity in the Coal Fields of the Ruhr, 1871–1914*. Providence: Berg, 1994.

Kurthen, Herman, Werner Bergmann, and Rainer Erb, eds., *Antisemitism and Xenophobia in Germany after Unification*. Oxford, New York: Oxford University Press, 1997.

Lehman, Brittany. "Education and Immigration: Federal Debates and Policies in West Germany, 1963–1989." Master's thesis. University of North Carolina, 2010.

Levinson, Amanda. "Why Countries Continue to Consider Regularization." *The Online Journal of the Migration Policy Institute*, 1 September 2005. Accessed 15 January 2015. http://www.migrationpolicy.org/article/why-countries-continue-consider-regularization.

Lewis, Bernard. *The Emergence of Modern Turkey*. London: New Oxford University Press, 1961.

Lindenberger, Thomas, ed. *Herrschaft und Eigen-Sinn in der Diktatur: Studien zur Gesellschaftsgeschichte der DDR*. Cologne, Weimar, Vienna: Böhlau, 1999.

Lucas, Erhard. *Zwei Formen von Radikalismus in der deutschen Arbeiterbewegung*. Frankfurt am Main: Roter Stern, 1976.

- *Der bewaffnete Arbeiteraufstand im Ruhrgebiet in seiner inneren Struktur und in seinem Verhältnis zu den Klassenkämpfen in den verschiedenen Regionen des Reiches*. Frankfurt am Main: Roter Stern, 1973.
Lüdtke, Alf. "Geschichte und Eigensinn." In *Alltagskultur, Subjektivität und Geschichte: Zur Theorie und Praxis von Alltagsgeschichte*, edited by Berliner Geschichtswerkstatt, 139–56. Münster: Westfälisches Dampfboot, 1994.
Mandel, Ruth. *Cosmopolitan Anxieties: Turkish Challenges to Citizenship and Belonging in Germany*. Durham: Duke University Press, 2008.
- "'Fortress Europe' and the Foreigners Within: Germany's Turks." In *The Anthropology of Europe: Identity and Boundaries in Conflict*, edited by Victoria A. Goddard, Joseph R. Llobera, and Cris Shore, 113–25. Oxford: Berg, 1994.
Mani, B. Venkat. *Cosmopolitical Claims: Turkish-German Literatures from Nadolny to Pamuk*. Iowa City: University of Iowa Press, 2007.
Martin, Philip L. *The Unfinished Story: Turkish Labour Migration to Western Europe: With Special Reference to the Federal Republic of Germany*. Geneva: International Labour Organisation, 1991.
- "Germany: Managing Migration in the 21st Century." Working paper, Comparative Immigration and Integration Program, Berkeley University, 1 May 2002. Accessed 9 January 2015. http://ies.berkeley.edu/pubs/workingpapers/CIIP-1-PLM_Germany.pdf.
Mattes, Monika. "Zum Verhältnis von Migration und Geschlecht: Anwerbung und Beschäftigung von 'Gastarbeiterinnen' in der Bundesrepublik 1960–1973." In *50 Jahre Bundesrepublik 50 Jahre Einwanderung: Nachkriegsgeschichte als Migrationsgeschichte*. Edited by Jan Motte, Rainer Ohliger, and Anne von Oswald, 285–309. Frankfurt: Campus, 1999.
Mattes, Monika. *'Gastarbeiterinnen' in der Bundesrepublik: Anwerbepolitik, Migration und Geschlecht in den 50er bis 70er Jahren*. Frankfurt am Main: Campus, 2005.
McCabe, Kristen, Serena Yi-Ying Lin, Hiroyuki Tanaka, and Piotr Plewa. "Pay to Go: Countries Offer Cash to Immigrants Willing to Pack Their Bags." Migration Policy Institute, *The Online Journal of the Migration Policy Institute*. 5 November 2009. Accessed 18 December 2014. http://www.migrationpolicy.org/article/pay-go-countries-offer-cash-immigrants-willing-pack-their-bags.
McLellan, Josie. "'Even under Socialism, We Don't Want to Do without Love': East German Erotica." In "East German Material Culture and the Power of Memory," edited by Uta A. Balbier, Cristina Cuevas-Wolf, and Joes Segal, supplement, *Bulletin of the German Historical Institute* S7 (2011): 49–65.
Mehrländer, Ursula. "The Second Generation of Migrant Workers in Germany: The Transition from School to Work," in *Education and the Integration of*

Ethnic Minorities, edited by D. Rothermund and J. Simon, 12–24. London: Pinter, 1986.

Meng, Michael. *Shattered Spaces: Encountering Jewish Ruins in Postwar Germany and Poland.* Cambridge: Harvard University Press, 2011.

Merkel, Ina. "Sex and Gender in the Divided Germany: Approaches to History from a Cultural Point of View." In *The Divided Past: Rewriting Post-war German History*, edited by Christoph Kleßmann, 91–105. New York: Oxford University Press, 2001.

Meske, Sigrid. *Situations Analyse türkische Frauen in der BRD.* Fulda: Express ed, 1983.

Meyer, Sibylle, and Eva Schultz. *Wie wir das alles geschafft haben: Alleinstehende Frauen berichten über ihr Leben nach 1945.* Munich: Beck, 1985.

Mik, Ger, and Mia Verkoren-Hemelaar. "Segregation in the Netherlands and Turkish Migration." In *Turkish Workers in Europe, 1960–1975: A Socio-economic Reappraisal*, edited by Nermin Abadan-Unat, 253–86. Leiden: E.J. Brill, 1976.

Milewski, Nadja. *Fertility of Immigrants: A Two-Generational Approach in Germany.* Heidelberg: Springer, 2010.

Miller, Brian J.K. "Reshaping the Turkish Nation-State: Migrant Communities in Western Europe and Return Migration, 1960–1985." PhD diss., University of Iowa, 2015.

Miller, Duncan, and İshan Çetin. *Migrant Workers, Wages, and Labor Markets: Emigrant Turkish Workers in the Federal Republic.* Istanbul: Istanbul University Faculty of Economics, Institute of Economic Development, 1974.

Moeller, Robert G. *Protecting Motherhood: Women and the Family in the Politics of Postwar West Germany.* Berkeley: University of California Press, 1993.

Mohanty, Chandra. "Under Western Eyes: Feminist Scholarship and Colonial Discourses." *Feminist Review* 30 (1988): 61–88.

Molnar, Christopher A. "Imagining Yugoslavs: Migration and the Cold War in Postwar West Germany." *Central European History* 47 (2014): 138–69.

Motte, Jan, and Rainer Ohliger, eds. *Geschichte und Gedächtnis in der Einwanderungsgesellschaft: Migration zwischen historischer Rekonstruktion under Erinnerungspolitik.* Essen: Klartext, 2004.

Mushaben, Joyce. *The Changing Faces of Citizenship: Integration and Mobilization among Ethnic Minorities in Germany.* New York: Berghahn Books, 2008.

Nökel, Sigrid. *Die Töchter der Gastarbeiter und der Islam: zur Soziologie alltagsweltlicher Anerkennungspolitiken. Ein Fallstudie.* Bielefeld: Transcript, 2002.

Oezcan, Veysal. "Germany: Immigration in Transition." Migration Policy Institute, 1 July 2004. Accessed 23 February 2016. http://www.migrationpolicy .org/article/germany-immigration-transition.

Opitz, May, Katharina Oguntoye, and Dagmar Schultz, eds. *Showing Our Colors: Afro-German Women Speak Out.* Translated by Anne V. Adams. Amherst, MA: University of Massachusetts Press, 1986.

Özdamar, Emine Sevgi. *Die Brücke vom Goldenen Horn.* Cologne: Kiepenheuer and Witsch, 2000.

Özdoğan, Mehmet Mıhrı. "Zum EU-Beitritt der Türkei: Grenze der Erweiterung oder Grenze der Vernunft?" *Werkstattgeschichte* 37 (2004): 93–9.

Panayi, Panikos. *Ethnic Minorities in Nineteenth and Twentieth Century Germany.* New York: Longman, 2000.

– "Exploitation, Criminality, Resistance: The Everyday Life of Foreign Workers and Prisoners of War in the German Town of Osnabrück, 1939–49." *Journal of Contemporary History* 40 (2005): 483–502.

Partridge, Damani J. *Hypersexuality and Headscarves: Race, Sex and Citizenship in the New Germany.* Bloomington: Indiana University Press, 2012.

Pierce, Joe. *Life in a Turkish Village.* New York: Holt, Rinehart, Winston, 1964.

Poiger, Uta G. *Jazz, Rock, and Rebels: Cold War Politics and American Culture in a Divided Germany.* Berkeley: University of California Press, 2000.

"Postimperial Europe, 1947–1980." In *Europe in the Contemporary World: 1900 to the Present,* edited by Bonnie G. Smith, 498–553. New York: Bedford St Martin's, 2007.

"Post-war European Society: A Consumer Society and Welfare State." In *Europe since 1945: A Concise History,* edited by J. Robert Wegs and Robert Ladrech, 139–72. New York: Palgrave MacMillan, 1996, 2006.

Pratt Ewig, Katherine. "Legislating Religious Freedom: Muslim Challenges to the Relationship between 'Church' and 'State' in Germany and France." *Daedalus: Journal of the American Academy of Arts and Sciences* 129 (2000): 31–54.

– *Stolen Honor: Stigmatizing Muslim Men in Berlin.* Stanford: Stanford University Press, 2008.

Presner, Todd Samuel. *Mobile Modernity: Germans, Jews, Trains.* New York: Columbia University Press, 2007.

Quataert, Donald. "Epilogue," supplement, *International Review of Social History.* 54, no. S17 (2009): 189–93.

Rapp, Martin, and Marion von Osten. "Ihr Kampf ist unser Kampf." *Bildpunkt: Zeitschrift der IG Bildende Kunst* (Spring 2006): 22–5.

Ritsch, Woffgang. *Die Rolle des Islams für die Koranschulerziehung in der Bundesrepublik Deutschland.* Cologne: Rahl-Rugenstein, 1987.

Roediger, David R. *The Wages of Whiteness: Race and the Making of the American Working Class.* New York: Verso, 1999.

Rosen, Rita. "Ausländische Frauen: Ignoriert, im Stich gelassen, Unterdrückt." *Informationsdienst zur Ausländerarbeit* 4 (1980): 20–7.

– *Muss Kommen, aber nix von Herzen: Zur Lebensituation von Migratinnen unter besonderer Berücksichtigung der Biographien türkischer Frauen.* Opladen: Leske and Budrick, 1986.
– "On the situation of Foreign Women Living in the Federal Republic of Germany: An Outline of the Problem." *International Migration* 19 (1981) 108–13.
– *Sie müssen bestimmen, wo sie lang gehen wollen. Zur Sozialpädagogischen Arbeit mit ausländischen Frauen und Mädchen.* Frankfurt am Main: ISS Materialien, 1984.
Rosen, Rita, and Gerd Stüwe. *Ausländische Mädchen in der Bundesrepublik.* Opladen: Leske, 1985.
Sarrazin, Thilo. *Deutschland Schafft Sich Ab: Wie wir unser Land aufs Spiel setzen.* Munich: Deutsche Verlags-Anstalt, Random House, 2010.
Schaffer, Harry G. *Women in the Two Germanies: A Comparative Study of a Socialist and Non-Socialist Society.* New York: Pergamon, 1981.
Schiffauer, Werner. *Die Gottesmänner: Türkische Islamisten in Deutschland.* Frankfurt am Main: Suhrkamp, 2000.
– *Die Migranten aus Subay: Türken in Deutschland: Eine Ethnographie.* Stuttgart: Ernst Klett Verlag für Wissen und Bildung, 1991.
– *Parallelgesellschaften: Wie viel Wertekonsens braucht unsere Gesellschaft? Für eine kluge Politik der Differenz.* Bielefeld: Transcript, 2008.
Schlisser, Hanna. "'Normalization' as Project: Some Thoughts on Gender Relations in West Germany during the 1950s." In *Miracle Years: A Cultural History of West Germany, 1949–1968*, edited by Hanna Schissler, 359–75. Princeton: Princeton University Press, 2001.
Schönwälder, Karen. *Einwanderung und ethnische Pluralität. Politische Entscheidungen und öffentliche Debatten in Großbritannien und der Bundesrepublik von den 1950er bis zu den 1970er Jahren.* Essen: Klartext, 2001.
– "West German Society and Foreigners in the 1960s." In *Coping with the Nazi Past: West German Debates on Nazism and Generational Conflict, 1955–1975*, edited by Philipp Gassert and Alan Steinweis, 113–27. New York: Berghahn, 2006.
– "The Difficult Task of Managing Migration: The 1973 Recruitment Stop." In *German History from the Margins*, edited by Mark Roseman, Neil Gregor, and Nils Roemer, 252–67. Bloomington: Indiana University Press, 2006.
Schumann, Dirk. "Is the EU Complete Without Turkey? Opportunities and Challenges for Europe's Identity and the Foreign and Security Policy of the European Union and the United States." *GHI Bulletin* 34 (2004): 190–2.
Şen, Faruk. "Berlin's Turkish Community." In *The Spirit of the Berlin Republic*, edited by Dieter Dettke, 130–44. New York: Berghahn, 2003.

Slater, Martin. "Migrant Employment, Recessions, and Return Migration: Some Consequences for Migration Policy and Development." *Studies in Comparative International Development* 14, no. 3 (1979): 3–22.

Sökefeld, Martin. *Struggling for Recognition: The Alevi Movement in Germany and in Transnational Space.* New York: Berghahn Books, 2008.

Sonnenberger, Barbara. "Verwaltete Arbeitskraft: die Anwerbung von 'Gastarbeiter' in den 1950er und 1960er Jahren." In *Migration Steuern und Verwalten*, edited by Jochen Oltmer, 145–76, IMIS (Das Insitut für Migrationsforschung und Interkulturelle Studien [Institute for Migration Research and Intercultural Studies]) Schriften 12. Göttingen: Hubert & Co, 2003.

Soysal, Yasemin Nuhoğlu. *Limits of Citizenship: Migrants and Postnational Membership in Europe.* Chicago: University of Chicago Press, 1995.

Spicka, Mark E. *Selling the Economic Miracle: Economic Reconstruction and Politics in West Germany, 1949–1957.* New York and Oxford: Berghahn Books, 2007.

Steinen, Inga. *Leben zwischen zwei Welten: Türkische Frauen in Deutschland.* Berlin: Quadriga, 1994.

Stirling, Paul. *Turkish Village.* London: Weidenfeld and Nicolson, 1965.

Taylor, Frederick. *The Berlin Wall: A World Divided, 1961–1989.* New York: Harper Collins, 2006.

Thomä-Veske, Hanns. *Islam und Integration: Zur Bedeutung des Islam im Prozeß der Integration türkischer Arbeiterfamilien in die Gesellschaft der Bundesrepublik.* Hamburg: Rissen, 1981.

Thompson, E.P. *The Making of the English Working Class.* New York: Vintage, 1963.

Trede, Oliver. "Misstrauen, Regulation und Integration: Gewerkschaften und 'Gastarbeiter' in der Bundesrepublik in den 1950er bis 1970er Jahren." In *Das "Gastarbeiter" System: Arbeitsmigration und ihre Folgen in der Bundesrepublik Deutschland und Westeuropa*, edited by Jochen Oltmer, Axel Kreienbrink, and Carlos Sanz Diaz, 183–97. Munich: Oldenbourg, 2012.

Triadafilopolous, Triadafilos and Karen Schönwälder. "How the Federal Republic Became an Immigration Country: Norms Politics and the Failure of West Germany's Guest Worker System." *German Politics and Society* 24 (2006): 1–19.

Triandafyllidou, Anna, ed. *Muslims in 21st Century Europe: Structural and Cultural Perspectives.* New York: Routledge, 2010.

Umut, Erel. "The Politics of Identity and Community: Migrant Women from Turkey in Germany." In *Gender and Insecurity: Migrant Women in Europe*, edited by Jane Freedman, 153–71. Burlington, VT: Ashgate, 2003.

Uyaner, Metin, and Sami Özkara. "Arbeiterwohnheime für die Migranten im Ruhrgebiet: Eine historische Darstellung der 60er und 70er Jahre." Untersuchung 2. Essen: DOMiT, 1996.

Voelker, Gottfried E. "More Foreign Workers – Germany's Labour Problem No. 1?" In *Turkish Workers in Europe, 1960–1975*, edited by Nermin Abadan-Unat, 331–45. Leiden: E. J. Brill, 1976.

Von Richthofen, Esther. *Bringing Culture to the Masses: Control, Compromise and Participation in the GDR*. New York: Berghahn, 2009.

Wallraff, Günter. *Ganz Unten*. Köln: Kiepenheuer & Witsch, 1985.

Ward, Robert E., and Dankwart A. Rustow, eds. *Political Modernization in Japan and Turkey*. Princeton: Princeton University Press, 1964.

Wehler, Hans-Ulrich. "Das Türkenproblem." *Die Zeit*. 12 September 2002.

Weiker, Walter F. *The Turkish Revolution 1960–1961: Aspects of Military Politics*. Washington, DC: Brookings Institution, 1963.

Weil, Frederick D. "Ethnic Intolerance, Extremism, and Democratic Attitudes in Germany since Unification." In *Antisemitism and Xenophobia in Germany after Unification*, edited by Hermann Kurthen and Rainer Erb. Oxford: Oxford University Press, 1997.

Weische-Alexa, Pia. "Sozial-Kulturelle Probleme junger Türkinnen in der Bundesrepublik Deutschland mit einer Studie zum Freizeitverhalten türkischer Mädchen in Köln." Unpublished manuscript, Pia Weische-Alexa, Manderscheider Str. 29, 5000 Köln 41. DOMiD Archive.

Welke, Barbara Young. *Recasting American Liberty: Gender, Race, Law, and the Railroad Revolution, 1865–1920*. New York: Cambridge University Press, 2001.

"West Germany." In *Muslims in Western Europe*, edited by Jorgen S. Nielsen, 23–38. Edinburgh: Edinburgh University Press, 1992.

White, Jenny B. "Belonging to a Place: Turks in Unified Berlin." *City and Society: Annual Review of the Society of Urban Anthropology*. American Anthropological Association (1996): 15–28.

– "Turks in the New Germany." *American Anthropologist* 99 (1997): 754–69.

Winkler, Heinrich August. "Grenzen der Erweiterung: Die Türkei ist kein Teil des 'Projekt Europe.'" *Internationale Politik* 2 (2002): 59–66.

– "Europa am Scheideweg." *Frankfurter Allgemeine Zeitung*. 12 November 2003.

Woollacott, Angela. "'All This Is the Empire, I told Myself': Australian Women's Voyages 'Home' and the Articulation of Colonial Whiteness." *American Historical Review* 102 (1997): 1003–29.

Yurdakul, Gökçe. *From Guest Workers into Muslims: The Transformation of Turkish Immigrant Associations in Germany*. Newcastle upon Tyne: Cambridge Scholars, 2009.

Zatlin, Jonathan. "Consuming Ideology: The Intershops, Genex, and Retail Trade under Honecker." In *The Currency of Socialism: Money and Political Culture in East Germany*, 243–85. Cambridge: Cambridge University Press and GHI, 2007.

– "Scarcity and Resentment: Economic Sources of Xenophobia in the GDR, 1971–1989." *Central European History* 40 (2007): 683–720.

Zieris, Ernst. *Betriebsunterkünfte für Ausländische Arbeitnehmer und ihre Familien.* Opladen: North Rhein Westphalia Labor Ministry for Labor, Health, and Social Welfare, 1973.

Zürcher, Erik-Jan. "How Europeans Adopted Anatolia and Created Turkey." *European Review* 13 (2005): 379–94.

Index

References referring to illustrations, photographs, and tables appear in italics.

9/11. *See* September 11 attacks

Abadan-Unat, Nermin, 16, 99, 147
abortion, 220n38
Adil (guest worker), 44, 46, 102–3
Ahmet (guest worker), 172
Aker, Ahmet, 72–3
Akkordarbeit (piecework system),
   141, 142
amnesty. *See* regularization
Ankara, 39
anti-Pegida protest marches, 176.
   See also Pegida
Arab Spring (2011), 176
Ms Arikan (tourist without
   work visa), 49
Association of Chocolate and
   Sweets, 140
Atabaki, Touraj, 169
Atatürk, 41, 135, 172, 187n60
Atsu, Mete, 87–90
Ausländer (foreigners), 18, 188n71.
   See also guest workers; Turks
ausländische Mitarbeiter (foreign
   co-worker). *See* guest workers

BA. See *Bundesanstalt für Arbeit*
Bade, Klaus, 22
Basic Treaty (December 1972), 113
Berlin, 4, 11, 26. *See also* Berlin Wall;
   border crossings
Berlin Wall, 6, 10, 26, 110–11, 184n31,
   218n10. *See also* border crossings
Bloody Christmas (1963), 3
border crossings, 112–14.
   See also Berlin Wall
bribery, 43–5
Brockett, Gavin, 169
Bruce, Gary, 130
Bundesanstalt für Arbeit (BA)
   (Federal Employment Office):
   liaison offices, 33, 39, 43, 55, 64–5;
   transportation of guest workers, 9,
   59–61, 61–8

Cafe Moskau, 120, 123, 124, 126
Cahit (guest worker), 70, 74, 85, 107,
   115, 121–2, 123, 127
Castles, Stephen, 165
Çetin, İhsan, 163, 170
Charlie Hebdo shooting, 175–6

Çiçek, Hidir (guest worker, IM), 131–2
Cologne attacks (2016), 177–8
colonization, 9–10
Corinna (East German woman),
    118–20
Cyprus, 3
Czechoslovakia, 10

Das Magazin, 128
decolonization, 10–11
deportation, 138, 144, 151, 152, 165
Die Brücke vom Goldenen Horn
    (novel), 83, 90–1
discos, 96, 97–8, 103, 120, 123, 126
dormitories. *See also* housing: as
    dominant form of housing for
    guest workers, 78–9, 81–5, 86–104,
    150, 212n4; female visitors to
    (men's dormitories), 89, 97, 100,
    101–2, 215n76; heating, 92, 93–4;
    kitchen and dining facilities,
    88, 90–1, 93, 97; management
    and maintenance, 87–96, 100–2;
    policing of female residents, 150;
    toilets and sanitation, 83, 84, 88,
    92–3, 95–6
Duinger Steinzeugwerk Mühle &
    Co., 9

Eastern Europe, 10
East German State Security Police.
    See *Stasi*
East Germany, 110–15, 219n27.
    See also Berlin; Berlin Wall; *Stasi*
Elif (guest worker's pseudonym):
    on becoming a guest worker, 3–4,
    50–1, 64, 82–3; on life in (West)
    Germany, 27, 82–3, 97–100, 141–2,
    168, 172–3, 215n77
Erdoğan, Recep Tayyip, 18

Erel, Umut, 98
Erol (guest worker): on becoming a
    guest worker, 45, 48, 55, 70, 74–5;
    on life in West Germany, 70, 86–7,
    96, 97–8
Europe: boundaries, 6, 8, 22–3; use of
    foreign labour, 9–11, 12, 15. *See also*
    guest workers
European Economic Community
    (EEC), 12–13
Evans, Jennifer, 128
Evren, Kenan, 167

Federal Employment Office.
    See *Bundesanstalt für Arbeit*
Federal Republic of Germany.
    See West Germany
Fehrenbach, Heide, 82
Five-Year Development Plan
    (Turkey), 16–17, 169
food, 59–61, 64, 65, 203n24, 207n69
foreigners (in Germany), 8, 18–19,
    21–2, 85–6. *See also* guest workers;
    Turks
France, 165
Frevert, Ute, 147–8
Frisch, Max, 80

Ganz Unten (*On the Bottom*,
    1985), 20
Gastarbeiter (guest workers).
    See guest workers
Gastarbeiterliteratur (guest worker
    literature), 20–1. *See also* guest
    workers
gender and gender roles, 6–7,
    149–50, 183n17, 183n20. *See also*
    men; women
Georg (KP), 132
German (language), 27, 53–4

German Commission for
  Employment in Italy, 83
German Democratic Republic
  (GDR). *See* East Germany
German Rail, 60–1, 62, 67–8, 69
German Trade Union Federation,
  87–90
German-Turkish agreement
  (30 October 1961), 40–1
Germany, 18–23. *See also* East
  Germany; West Germany
Gieseke, Jens, 130
Gitmez, Ali, 170–1
guest workers: activism, 26–7, 94–6,
  135–61. *See also* labour activism;
  strikes; application process, 38–41,
  43–52, *53*, 56, 198n60; context, 8,
  9–18. *See also* labour agreements;
  contracts, 53–4; deportation, 151;
  desire to stay in West Germany,
  164, 166–9, 171–3; eligibility
  for social benefits, 15, 186n57;
  employers, 8–9, 47–9, 198n58.
  See also specific companies;
  employment statistics, 138,
  142–3, 144, 147, *148*, 150, 226n8;
  end of guest worker program,
  162–4, 164–7; guidebooks and
  instructional materials. See *Hallo
  Mustafa!*; instructional materials;
  housing, 78–104, 140–1, 212n4.
  See also dormitories; individual
  perspectives. *See* Adil; Ahmet;
  Cahit; Çiçek, Hidir; Elif; Erol;
  Hasan; M; Mehmet; Mesut;
  Murat; Remzi; Yalcın; Italian,
  11; language competencies, 27,
  53–4; legal status, 15, 113–14,
  151, 186n57; length of stay, 40–1;
  medical examination, 44, 45,
49–52, *53*; motivations, 38, 73;
  numbers, 33, 39, 71–2; overview
  of experiences and actions,
  17–18, 24, 25–7; perceptions of,
  32–3, 111–12, 123, 162–3, 174–8.
  See also xenophobia; recruiting
  and marketing, 31, 32–4. See also
  Hallo Mustafa!; relationships with
  East Germans, 107–9, 115–34;
  relationships with West Germans,
  82, 135–7, 141–2, 143–6, 155,
  159–61. *See also* labour activism;
  strikes; religious identities, 21,
  174–6. *See also* Muslims; return to
  home countries, 166–7, 169–71;
  social lives, 96–104; as source of
  remitted wages for home country,
  170, 187n65; as *Stasi* informants,
  128, 130–3. See also *Inoffizieller
  Mitarbeiter*; *Kontaktpersonen*;
  surveillance and control, 88–91,
  93–4, 96–7, 100–2. See also *Stasi*;
  terminology used to refer to, 19,
  70–1, 91–2, 188n71; transportation,
  9, 54, 57–71, 74–5, 200n7, 203n18,
  207n65, 207n69, 208n76, 208n83.
  See also train travel; Turkish, 11–12,
  32–8, 39, 51, 61, 70. *See also* Turks;
  unofficial entry, 196n23; visits
  to East Germany, 107–9, 113–14,
  115–34; wage rates, 47, 137, 138–40,
  142–56, *145*, 158, 227n27; women.
  See guest workers, women;
  writing and studies about, 20–1
guest workers, women: constraints,
  98, 99–100, 150; demographics,
  36–7, 71–2, 100, 147, *148*, 215n79;
  dormitory life, 82–3, 88, 90–1,
  97–100, 150; exploitation, 20,
  149–50, 157; foreign life as

liberating, 98–9, 216n83; labour
activism, 146–59; medical
examination, 50–1; recruitment,
32–3, 217n88; relationships with
former *Trümmenfrauen*, 5–7,
141–2; stories and studies about,
20; wages, 147–9, 150–9, 227n27.
See also wages; women

Mr Halil (Turkish smuggler), 128
Hallo Mustafa! (1966): analysis and
description, 34–6; depiction of
dormitory life, 86–7, *87*; depiction
of male sexuality, 101–2; depiction
of medical examination, 52, *53*;
depiction of punctuality, *30*,
31; depiction of Turkish guest
workers, *30, 31*, 34–6, *35*, 85–6;
on employment deductions,
139; on finding housing, 80; on
permanency of stay, 40–1. *See also*
instructional materials
Hasan (guest worker), 44
Havemann, Robert, 133
headscarves, 21, 174, 191n91
Hellas-Istanbul Express. *See* train
travel
Helsinki Accords (1975), 113, 221n70
Herbert, Ulrich, 22, 81
housing, 78–104. *See also*
dormitories
*How Does One Go to Germany to
Work?*, 41, *42*. *See also* instructional
materials
Huinink, Johannes, 108
Hungary, 10

IM. See *Inoffizieller Mitarbeiter*
immigrants, illegal. *See* regularization
Ina (*Stasi* IM), 120–1

informants. See *Inoffizieller
Mitarbeiter*; *Kontaktpersonen*
Inoffizieller Mitarbeiter ("Unofficial
Informer[s]" or IM), 120, 123–4,
128, 130, 131–2, 222n87, 224n134.
See also *Stasi*
Institute for the World Economy
(IWE), 11–12
instructional materials: confusing
messages, 40; depiction of
Germany, 41–3, 197n34; depiction
of medical examination, 52, *53*;
depiction of Turks and Turkey,
30, 31, 34–6, *35*, 41, 43–4; failure
to read, 202n17; sexual cautions,
101–2; travel instructions, 60.
See also *Hallo Mustafa!*
Islam, 21, 174–6, 191n91
Istanbul, 3–4, 39
Italy, 11, 13, 83, 84–5
IWE. *See* Institute for the World
Economy

Jamin, Mathilde, 50
Judt, Tony, 6, 164

Kindergeld (child benefit payments),
138–9
Kobes, Werner, 57–8
Kohl, Helmut, 19, 162, 165
Kontaktpersonen ("contact persons"
or KP), 130. See also *Stasi*
"Korean Crisis/Boom," 12, 185n41
Kosack, Godula, 150, 157
KP. See *Kontaktpersonen*
Krupp Company, 81

labour, forced, 70–1, 81
labour activism, 26–7, 135–61.
See also strikes

labour agreements, 12–16, 16–17, 24–5, 32, 40–1
labour unions, 138, 144, 152–3, 154
Law of Housing Regulation (1934, updated 1959), 83–5
legalization (of illegal immigrants). *See* regularization
Lindencorso (disco), 120, 123, 126. *See also* discos
long post-war, 6

M (guest worker), 75
Marmela, Elefteria, 153–4
marriage and "marriage-like relationships," 107, 115–20, 121–2, 128–30, 132–3
Mattes, Monika, 147
Maturi, Giacomo, 34. See also *Hallo Mustafa!*
Mehmet (guest worker), 44
Mehmet (*Stasi* IM), 132–3
Mehrländer, Ursula, 78
men, guest workers, 51–2, *53*, 86–7, *87*, 89–97, 100–2, 107–9, 114–34, *117*; West German, 7. *See also* gender and gender roles; women
Mesut (guest worker), 118–20
Metal Workers Union, 144, 152–3, 154
migration post-war, 34, 185n32
Miller, Mark, 165, 170
Mitterand, François, 165
Molnar, Christopher, 22
MSP. *See* National Salvation Party
Murat (guest worker), 38, 171
Murat (*Stasi* IM), 120
Mushaben, Joyce, 23
Muslims, 21, 22–3, 84

National Salvation Party (*Millî Selâmet Partisi*, or MSP), 174

Nazi state, 10, 21–2, 41–2, 70–1
normalization (of illegal immigrants). *See* regularization

"the Object" (Turkish man under *Stasi* surveillance), 125–6
OPEC oil embargo (1973), 143. *See also* strikes
orientation materials. *See* instructional materials
Özdamar, Emine Sevgi, 83, 90–1

Parallelgesellschaft ("parallel society"), 18
Paris terrorist attacks (13 November 2015), 177
Pawlowski, Tatjana, 158
Pegida (Patriotic Europeans Against the Islamization of the West *Patriotische Europäer gegen die Islamisierung des Abendlandes*), 176
Pierburg Auto Parts Factory strikes, 137, 140–1, 146–59. *See also* strikes
Poland, 10
pornography, 128

race, 21–2
rail administrations, 61–3, 65–7, 204n33
Rapp, Martin, 159
recession (1966–7), 142–3
recession (1982–3), 165–6
refugees, 3, 10–11, 19, 119, 176–8, 188n71
regularization, 164–5
relationships, 26, 107–9, 114–34, *117*. *See also* marriage and "marriage-like relationships"; sexual relations
Remzi (guest worker), 54, 173

Sabel, Anton, 32–3
Sammelreiseliste (group-trip list), 71
sanitation, 65–6, 67–8, 92–4, 95–6
Satolias, Anna, 156–7
Satolias, Nikiforus, 156–7
Schönwälder, Karen, 81, 86
Selam Berlin (2003), 126–7
September 11 attacks, 22–3
sexual relations, 101–2, 107, 108–9,
    115–22, *117*, 122–7, 128, 134. *See also*
    marriage and "marriage-like
    relationships"; relationships
Shaffer, Harry, 148
Shirins Hochzeit (film, 1975), 20, 190n82
Slater, Martin, 159–60
smuggling, 122, 127–30, *129*, 131–3
Soviet Union, 10, 11, 110, 112, 116,
    185n32, 186n51
Spicka, Mark, 7
Stasi (East German State Security
    Police), 107–9, 114–21, 122–7, 127–34.
    See also *Inoffizieller Mitarbeiter*;
    Kontaktpersonen
strikes: Cologne Ford factory
    "Turkish Strike," 144–5, 146, 159;
    Duisburg-Huckingen steel mill
    strike, 135; Hella Automobile
    Producer strike, 143–4; Hellawerk
    Factory strike, 146; Opel factory
    strike, 146; Pierburg Auto Parts
    Factory strikes, 137, 140–1, 146–59.
    See also labour activism
sucuk (Turkish spiced sausage), 60–1,
    203n24
Syrian refugee crisis, 176–7

Taylor, Frederick, 111
train stations, 3–4, 55, 69–70
train travel, 57–71, 74–6, 76–7, 200n6
Transportlisten (transport list), 71

Treaty of Friendship and
    Cooperation, 111
Trümmerfrauen ("rubble women"),
    5–7, 182n14. *See also* women
"Tunte," 126
Türken. See Turks
Turkey: agreements signed with
    European countries, 11, 14–16,
    24–5. *See also* specific countries;
    desire to be seen as modern,
    "Western," 14, 15–17, 22–3, 24,
    169, 186n51, 187n60; economic
    troubles, 167; effects of the guest
    worker program on, 169–71,
    187n65; Five-Year Development
    Plan, 16–17, 169; frustrations
    with German counterparts
    regarding guest worker process,
    55; membership in international
    organizations, 16; regional
    differences, 51, 61, 70; as source
    of workers, 14, 15, 72–3, 169–70;
    unrest, 167
Turkish (language), 53
Turkish Employment Service, 140
Turkish Ministry of Foreign
    Affairs, 12
Turkish Rail, 62. *See also* rail
    administrations
Turkish Republic. *See* Turkey
Turkish Revolution (1960–1), 187n60
"Turkish Strike," 144–5, 146, 159.
    See also strikes
Turks: attacks on, 18–19; as foreign
    workers, 15, 37–8, 39, 71–2, 166,
    196n23. *See also* guest workers;
    as generic label for foreigners,
    8, 18–19, 188n71; as inherently
    not "European," 23, 193n103;
    as members of German society,

19–20, 27, 188n72; as Muslims, 21,
22–3, 174–6, 236n52; radicalism
in Germany, 174–5; as refugees
and asylum seekers, 37; regional
differences, 51, 61, 70; *Stasi*
surveillance and suspicion of,
115–16, *117*, 122–7, 127–34, *129*;
stereotypes about, *30*, 31, 34–6, *35*,
85–6, 95–6, 101–2, 121, 216n80. See
also *Hallo Mustafa!*; as "Western"
to East Germans, 114, 121–2, 127;
women. *See* women; xenophobia
towards, 111–12, 123, 125

vacation time, 144–5, 230n58
Vertriebene (ethnic German
expellees), 81–2
Volkswagen Company, 84–5
von Oswald, Anne, 145, *145*

wages, 47, 137, 138–40, 142–59, *145*,
227n27. *See also* labour activism;
strikes
Wallraff, Günter, 20
West German Employers
Association, 56
West Germany: attitudes
towards foreigners and ethnic
minorities, 18–19. *See also*
xenophobia; economy, 11, 12,
185n40, 186n57; effects of the
guest worker program, 173–8,
186n57; employers, 8–9, 83–5.
See also specific companies;
foreign population, 166; housing
shortages, 79, 80–2; international
image, 57–8, 69–71, 76–7, 80–1,
201n10; labour pools, 15, 163–4;
minimum wage policies, 228n30;
relationship with East Germany,

110–15; relationship with Turkey,
11, 14–15, 24–5; relationships with
other nations, 10, 11, 14–15, 24–5;
remaking in the postwar period,
6–8, 12, 24, 182n10
Wirtschaftswunder ("economic
miracle"), 12
Wohnkultur (culture of the home),
85–6
women: abortion, 220n38; East
German, 26, 107–9, 114–34,
117; guest workers (*see* guest
workers, women); relationships
(*see* marriage and "marriage-like
relationships"; relationships;
sexual relations); religious
practices, 191n91 (*see also*
headscarves); Turkish, 20, 32–3,
36–7, 51, 147, *148*, 216n80 (*see also*
guest workers, women; Turks);
as visitors to men's dormitories,
89, 97, 100, 101–2; West German,
5–7, 32–3, 70, 74, 101–2, 149–50,
157–8, 182n10, 182n14. See also
Trümmerfrauen
Wonaym (mispronunciation of
dormitory in German), 83
*Would You Like to Get to Know
Germany?*, 41–3. *See also*
instructional materials

xenophobia, 111–12, 189n76, 196n19

Yalcın (guest worker), 64
Yugoslav Rail, 62–3, 65–7

"Zero Hour" (start of rebuilding
post-war Germany), 5–6, 182n10
Zieris, Ernst, 79
Zürcher, Erik-Jan, 16

GERMAN AND EUROPEAN STUDIES

General Editor: Jennifer J. Jenkins

1 Emanuel Adler, Beverly Crawford, Federica Bicchi, and Rafaella Del Sarto, *The Convergence of Civilizations: Constructing a Mediterranean Region*
2 James Retallack, *The German Right, 1860–1920: Political Limits of the Authoritarian Imagination*
3 Silvija Jestrovic, *Theatre of Estrangement: Theory, Practice, Ideology*
4 Susan Gross Solomon, ed., *Doing Medicine Together: Germany and Russia between the Wars*
5 Laurence McFalls, ed., *Max Weber's 'Objectivity' Revisited*
6 Robin Ostow, ed., *(Re)Visualizing National History: Museums and National Identities in Europe in the New Millennium*
7 David Blackbourn and James Retallack, eds., *Localism, Landscape, and the Ambiguities of Place: German-Speaking Central Europe, 1860–1930*
8 John Zilcosky, ed., *Writing Travel: The Poetics and Politics of the Modern Journey*
9 Angelica Fenner, *Race under Reconstruction in German Cinema: Robert Stemmle's Toxi*
10 Martina Kessel and Patrick Merziger, eds., *The Politics of Humour in the Twentieth Century: Inclusion, Exclusion, and Communities of Laughter*
11 Jeffrey K. Wilson, *The German Forest: Nature, Identity, and the Contestation of a National Symbol, 1871–1914*
12 David G. John, *Bennewitz, Goethe,* Faust: *German and Intercultural Stagings*
13 Jennifer Ruth Hosek, *Sun, Sex, and Socialism: Cuba in the German Imaginary*
14 Steven M. Schroeder, *To Forget It All and Begin Again: Reconciliation in Occupied Germany, 1944–1954*
15 Kenneth S. Calhoon, *Affecting Grace: Theatre, Subject, and the Shakespearean Paradox in German Literature from Lessing to Kleist*

16 Martina Kolb, *Nietzsche, Freud, Benn, and the Azure Spell of Liguria*
17 Hoi-eun Kim, *Doctors of Empire: Medical and Cultural Encounters between Imperial Germany and Meiji Japan*
18 J. Laurence Hare, *Excavating Nations: Archaeology, Museums, and the German-Danish Borderlands*
19 Jacques Kornberg, *Pope Pius XII's Dilemma: Facing Atrocities and Genocide in World War II*
20 Patrick O'Neill, *Transforming Kafka: Translation Effects*
21 John K. Noyes, *Herder: Aesthetics against Imperialism*
22 James Retallack, *Germany's Second Reich: Portraits and Pathways*
23 Laurie Marhoefer, *Sex and the Weimar Republic: German Homosexual Emancipation and the Rise of the Nazis*
24 Bettina Brandt and Daniel Purdy, eds., *China and the German Enlightenment*
25 Michael Hau, *Performance Anxiety: Sport and Work in Germany from the Empire to Nazism*
26 Celia Applegate, *The Necessity of Music: Variations on a German Theme*
27 Richard J. Golsan and Sarah M. Misemer, *The Trial Never Ends: Hannah Arendt's* Eichmann in Jerusalem *in Retrospect*
28 Lynne Taylor, *In the Children's Best Interests: Unaccompanied Children in American-Occupied Germany, 1945–1952*
29 Jennifer A. Miller, *Turkish Guest Workers in Germany: Hidden Lives and Contested Borders, 1960s–1980s*